Racism and the Underclass

Racism and the Underclass

State Policy and Discrimination Against Minorities

Edited by
George W. Shepherd, Jr. and
David Penna

E
184
.A1
R327
1991
West

STUDIES IN HUMAN RIGHTS, NUMBER 13

GREENWOOD PRESS
New York • Westport, Connecticut • London

Library of Congress Cataloging-in-Publication Data

Racism and the underclass : state policy and discrimination against
  minorities / edited by George W. Shepherd, Jr. and David Penna.
      p.   cm.—(Studies in human rights, ISSN 0146–3586 ; no.
  13)
    Includes bibliographical references and index.
    ISBN 0–313–27863–6 (alk. paper)
    1. Race discrimination—Government policy—United States.
  2. Socially handicapped—Government policy—United States.
  3. United States—Race relations—Government policy.
  4. Discrimination—Government policy—United States.   5. Minorities—
  Government policy—United States.   I. Shepherd, George W.
  II. Penna, David.   III. Series.
  E184.A1R327   1991
  323.1′73—dc20   91–9547

British Library Cataloguing in Publication Data is available.

Library of Congress Catalog Card Number: 91–9547
ISBN: 0–313–27863–6
ISSN: 0146–3586

First published in 1991

Greenwood Press, 88 Post Road West, Westport, CT 06881
An imprint of Greenwood Publishing Group, Inc.

Printed in the United States of America

The paper used in this book complies with the
Permanent Paper Standard issued by the National
Information Standards Organization (Z39.48–1984).

10 9 8 7 6 5 4 3 2 1

Copyright Acknowledgment

   A previous version of Chapter 2, ''The Human Rights of the Underclass,'' by Peter Weiss originally
appeared in *Global Justice* 1, no. 1 (June/July 1990), published by the Center on Rights Development,
Graduate School of International Studies, University of Denver.

This book is dedicated to
the United Nations Campaign Against Racial Discrimination

Contents

Illustrations

TABLES

FIGURES

Preface

This volume presents the findings of a study undertaken over two years by the Center of Rights Development (CORD) at the University of Denver. The original impetus was a routine request from the United Nations for a report on efforts to eradicate racial discrimination in the United States. The initial result was a 1989 report on race relations in the United States, which focused upon issues such as immigration, race and the media, recent Supreme Court cases affecting remedies for discrimination, as well as other aspects of the problem.

In 1989–1990 CORD undertook an extensive research project culminating in a lecture series at the Graduate School of International Studies (GSIS) at the University of Denver. Each lecture was in the form of a panel with a main paper, a moderator, and several discussants. There was substantial participation from an audience of students, faculty, businesspeople, professionals, governmental representatives, activists, and the general public. The series provided a forum for the raising of otherwise ignored issues and for the exchange of viewpoints.

In the light of the exchanges, the chapters were substantially revised and edited for this volume. Therefore, an intellectual debt is owed to all those who partic-ipated in the lecture series. Since participants and audience numbered several hundred, it would be difficult to acknowledge all by name. It is appropriate, however, to acknowledge the role of the panelists in provoking discussion. Panelists included Saul Rosenthal, Gary Gerhardt, Dean William Beany, Ved Nanda, Dana Wilbanks, Paula Rhodes, Patrick Lyness, Audrey Alvarado, Arlen Rhoads, Lynda Popejoy, Colorado State Representative Barbara Phillips, Rita Montero, Richard Onizuka, and Peggy Lore. Professor Stephen Pepper and Kevin Flynn also participated in presentations outside of the lecture series that provoked thoughtful comments. Dean Thomas Rowe of GSIS also provided insight, enthusiasm, and encouragement for this endeavor. Joy Sobrepeña and Debra Kreisberg Voss provided organizational assistance for the lecture series. Anita Alexander and Mark Brady provided invaluable and timely assistance in the preparation of the manuscript.

Finally, the project, as most of the work of CORD, would have been improbable without the generous assistance of the Ford Foundation.

Despite these enormous debts—intellectual, organizational, and financial—the work in this volume remains the responsibility of the contributors since there is hardly agreement among the panelists and presenters on the many controversial points presented in this study. Still, we hope that, despite the controversy, this work will provide a useful starting point for discussion on state policy toward the underclass. The solutions we present are few and tentative, though we hope the dialogue we present will be sustained. In any case, it is clear, unfortunately, that the problems we confront are persistent.

_____ *PART I*

Introduction _____

Backlash in the American Dream: Resurgence of Racism and the Rise of the Underclass _____

GEORGE W. SHEPHERD, JR.

There was a resurgence of racism and disadvantage during the Reagan years, not only in the United States but throughout the world. A major revision of policy toward the American underclass is urgently needed. The reasons are not simply the failures of the Reagan-Bush policies or even the rise in consciousness of neoconservative ideas and violent racist groups. The explanation lies in our failure to understand the underlying social and economic changes in the United States and the world. Moreover, the policies of liberal reform of the 1960s are in many respects antiquated by these changes.

New opportunities such as the ending of the Cold War provide both a framework and resources for new policies. The "American dream" of real equal opportunity for all, free from discrimination, exploitation, and repression, is alive and can be revived. To reverse the trend, however, will require a much wider public consciousness of the relevance of freedom from want for everyone and a reconstructed system of global justice.

BACKLASH

There are several major points that emerge from the preliminary study by the University of Denver Center on Rights Development (CORD). The most important is that the progress made in the 1960s in the United States and in the southwest region is now being reversed. Opportunity for employment and housing for minorities has diminished, and there has been a reaction against affirmative action procedures that were introduced by the federal government and courts in the 1960s and 1970s. In addition to this attack on poverty and antidiscrimination measures is the growth of racial violence in the community and in a paramilitary form. Some of the policies against discriminatory conditions, such as the employment of Native Americans and the policy on asylum of nonwhite immigrants, have not shown any substantial progress.

New issues have emerged, such as harassment on college campuses and the subtle use of quotas against Asian students to maintain the racial balance of the student body. The positive attitude of support in the media for minorities in employment, welfare, and education has been replaced with a rejection and ridicule of affirmative action. The predominant public mood has become a nationalistic jingoism that justifies institutionalization of discrimination and rejects moral obligation to the poor and refugees from U.S.-supported dictatorships abroad.

In 1989, *City of Richmond v. J. A. Croson Company*, in which the Supreme Court struck down city legislation providing for a percentage of contracts for minority contracting firms, exemplified the reversal trend. Thurgood Marshall, in discussing the recent Supreme Court decisions on civil rights, declared, "We are back where we started."[1] He believes the Court has gone beyond legal questions to incorporate broad political opinion into the decisions on race and affirmative action. In a study titled "White Racial Nationalism in the United States," Ronald Walters notes that the center of the problem is a middle- and lower-class reaction, primarily among whites, to what they conceive to be a threat to their job prospects and their living environments.[2] Today this takes the form of a strong national racism sometimes caught up in political formulations of the far right who attack government welfare programs as unwarranted subsidies of minorities. Government intervention on behalf of poverty groups, which appeared to be accepted practice a decade ago, has fallen under fierce attack made legitimate by eight years of the Reagan administration.

ENGLISH ONLY

One of the largest backlash groups is the "English only" coalition, which is attempting to make English the only "official U.S. language."[3] It is a reaction against immigrants and illegal aliens who the lower middle class sees as a threat to its own employment, education, and promotion opportunities. The deterioration of inner-city schools, the high dropout rate especially of Hispanics, and the atmosphere of violence in the schools and communities associated with crime and drug trafficking have also accelerated this paranoia. While there are grounds for fear among middle-class whites in urban centers, and while abuses of affirmative action have happened, the general attribution of the deterioration of education to the minorities is wrongly placed.

S. I. Hayakawa and other opponents of bilingual education expect Spanish-speaking immigrants to make the same progress other minorities, such as Polish and Japanese, have made in assimilating and learning English.[4] According to David Lopez, a professor at the University of California–Los Angeles (UCLA), in a Rand Corporation study, nearly half the permanent Mexican immigrants living in California speak English well, and only about 25 percent speak Spanish exclusively. Their children are bilingual, and over half of their grandchildren speak only English.[5]

However, in the inner cities, where most Hispanics live today, the rise of the underclass phenomenon has cut many of them off from the employment and assimilation pressures of the early twentieth century. Their progress cannot be maintained unless special programs are provided.

Allegations about the failure of bilingual education by President Reagan's former Secretary of Education, William Bennett, led to extensive cuts in federal funding. Whites in urban areas have been quick to attribute the deterioration of standards to the introduction of multicultural curricula and affirmative action hiring. This new racial nationalism has been exploited by the U.S. English organization that advocates a constitutional amendment to make English the only official language.

PREJUDICE IN POLITICS

The National Association for the Advancement of White People (NAAWP) has also played on these national racial emotions. The NAAWP has a growing national membership and is especially strong in the south. Its leader, David Duke, was elected a representative to the state legislature of Louisiana in 1989. The extent of this phenomenon as a force in American politics should not be underestimated, as the famous case of Willie Horton in the 1988 presidential elections showed. Many white people are not aware that they have feelings of fear and rejection of minorities. But when George Bush linked the crimes of Horton to his parole issued by Michael Dukakis through clever television advertisements, although frequently disowned by the Republican Party National Campaign, the effect was to sway many middle-class and blue collar voters. The precedent this has set became deeply etched into American political consciousness.

Another form of this prejudice against African-Americans in U.S. politics is the role it played against Jesse Jackson as a possible Democratic presidential nominee in 1988. The minority who will make up their minds on the basis of race is clearly a part of the electorate, but how numerous are they? This was studied in the gubernatorial preliminaries in Georgia, where another black American, Andrew Young, tested the waters. The Joint Center for Political Studies poll in 1986 showed that 17 percent of the white respondents would not support a qualified black candidate nominated by their party for governor.[6]

The other side of the racial factor is black support for Democratic candidates who are black. However, these statistics do not weigh the differences in the quality of the candidates. Thus, although race is a deterrent to the election of a black as a candidate for high office in many states and most directly in the presidential races, this appears to be changing. The election in 1989 of the first black governor, L. Douglas Wilder, in Virginia shows that racial campaign issues and the demagogue may be the losers.

RACIAL VIOLENCE

Another important aspect of the rise of racism in the United States is the spread of violence cults. These range from the youthful skinheads, who are now a national phenomenon, to the Aryan Nations or Silent Order, the Covenant, the Sword, and the Arm of the Lord. These are clearly neo-Fascist in character, and members of the Silent Order were convicted for the murder of the liberal radio broadcaster Alan Berg.[7] Though under surveillance pressure from police authorities, these groups manage to grow.

Another manifestation of this hate category is the rise of the number of racist incidents reported by such organizations as the Anti-Defamation League and the National Urban League. The anti-Semitism of these groups is a major revival of racism in the United States and is manifested through the desecration of synagogues and attacks on African students (an African teacher, Hope Klagba, was driven out of a small town, Cheyenne Wells, Colorado; another student was killed in Washington state).

Individuals who are apprehended for acts of violence are prosecuted under U.S. law. While there has been a shift away from lynch-mob-type white violence in the south, there have been growing numbers of gang violence incidents and racially motivated killings in communities such as Howard Beach and Bensonhurst in New York City. This violence appears to be spreading, as evidenced by the alleged racial bombings of judges and NAACP members in late 1989.

THE TWO NATIONS ARE NOW THREE

In 1969, the Kerner Commission published its report on the dangerous trend toward two Americas, "one white and the other black."[8] The report received much attention at the time, and it contributed to the legislation and interracial activity of the United States for the next decade. The trend has now been reversed, and the danger is once again rising.

The spread of poverty and crime are the two essential ingredients of this change. For minorities, the figures are striking over the 1970s to 1980s. The figures for crime and unemployment among blacks in comparison with the general population in the city of Denver are illustrative of the national problem. Reverend James D. Peters, Jr. of the New Hope Baptist Church in Denver reported: "Unemployment among black adults in northeast Dever is 20%; the citywide adult rate is 5.9%. For black teens in northeast Denver, the unemployment rate is 40%; the citywide rate for teens is 15.3%. About 40% of black families live below the poverty line." Also, while blacks make up 12 percent of Denver's population, they are arrested for 42.3 percent of the city's violent crimes.[9] In the nation as a whole, according to the Center for the Study of Social Policy, the number of unemployed black males doubled between 1960 and 1984.

In short, there has emerged among blacks and other minorities a new underclass, as noted by the sociologist William J. Wilson.[10] The characteristics of this urban underclass he further identified in *The Truly Disadvantaged* as particularly an inner-city phenomenon of poor people isolated from employment opportunities.[11] Women and children of minorities are the largest group within this underclass.[12] This is not predominantly a racial phenomenon, according to Wilson, because many whites are also caught in this poverty cycle.[13] In addition, there is a new black middle class that is affluent, well educated, and has taken advantage of new opportunities. In most cases, the latter have moved away from the inner city and have joined their interests with the suburban middle-class whites.[14]

POLICY DEBATE

There are sharp differences of opinion among black leaders as to the cause and way out of this discriminatory situation. Urban reformers on the whole blame the Reagan administration for its cuts in social services and welfare, while a small group of black intellectuals have joined the neoconservative reaction to government intervention. Thomas Sowell, a Stanford University sociologist, believes that moral failure and dependence on government assistance have deprived blacks of initiative, and Clarence Thomas, former chairman of the Federal Equal Employment Opportunity, sees integration programs as perversely increasing black alienation from the mainstream.[15]

The preliminary CORD findings are that affirmative action and black enfranchisement in the south have stirred a minority activist group of whites, predominantly lower middle class, who feel threatened by minorities and whose low educational level reinforces their prejudices. They have formed an alliance with the radical right from the municipal to the national level and are reversing the gains of the 1960s and 1970s through court actions, laws, and administrative intervention with the help of such agencies as the U.S. Justice Department.

The evidence of the effects of government program cutbacks on increasing the disadvantage of the underclass among minorities appears to be overwhelming. The rapid rise in poverty levels in the inner city, the number of homeless who are minorities, the amount of single women with dependents, and the unemployment of minorities in urban areas all correspond to the rapid decrease in government-assisted programs and the attack on affirmative action.

Roger Wilkins, professor of American History and Culture at George Mason University, quoted the calculations of the Center on Budget and Policy Priorities to show that the Reagan administration cut the discretionary assistance programs to low income groups by 54 percent, including housing.[16] Thus Reagan helped segregate more completely the inner cities, despite his intent.

Government equalization measures are the primary remedy. Yet the lack of success of many government interventions needs careful consideration. If bilingual education or desegregation has not led to the equal opportunities anticipated, what can be done to modify their implementation? The way in which the United States addresses this issue will be determinative of progress in the next decade.

One of the critical issues of the 1990s is the continued desegregation of education. This has been successful in many areas, but in others the continued segregation of housing has undermined the basis for nonracial schools. The open school districts of Minnesota are the first of what will be important experiments in open choice for students among schools within a state by 1991.[17] This could provide an answer to a difficult problem if the less affluent schools are helped to compete for quality faculty and students by federal assistance.

The answer is both simple in policy and complex in implementation. A strong majority of Americans support policies of providing the underclass with education, job training, business incentives, parks and play areas, child care, and so on, according to a Louis Harris poll.[18]

A significant shift in public attitudes has taken place, although this has not yet been translated into policies. This shift has been shown in several polls. It took place during the Reagan era and therefore reflects a new orientation on which new policies can be built.

A *Washington Post*/ABC News poll shows that from 1981 to 1988 the largest shift took place among moderates (17 percent), closely followed by conservatives (16 percent), and liberals (15 percent). The higher the income level, the less prejudice, which correlated directly with education level. Important differences emerged between whites and blacks in their views of the nature and extent of prejudice and disadvantage.[19] The general trend is unmistakably toward a recognition of the underclass problems.

A revitalized and reformed affirmative action and war on poverty therefore appears to be possible. Even a Republican administration might reflect this direction, if the push from the public became strong enough. However, priorities can only change with a reclarification of affirmative action goals and a return to the commitment of the American dream for all minorities and the growing underclass. Reform movements go in cycles in American society. We have been through a period of reversal. The preoccupation today with the problems of crime and drugs obscures the need to restructure if discrimination and poverty are to be removed. The problem is who would pay for it, given existing budgetary priorities?

As the military priorities of the Cold War fade, there are signs that a new consciousness is beginning in certain communities. The media, in some areas, has begun to feature the problem, such as the national ''A World of Difference'' campaign. Major foundations have supported programs of research and education on the underclass. New groups such as the Rainbow Coalition and the American Way have made important inroads. What is lacking is the political vision to transform these nongovernmental initiatives into a major new program for the racial underclass.

FREEDOM FROM WANT

The time is right for a Freedom from Want program based on the needs and rights of everyone to be productive members of society. This is what President Franklin Roosevelt had in mind in the Atlantic Charter (1941) for the postwar world. Now the Cold War, which followed World War II, is ending, and the opportunity arises again to assure these freedoms to all peoples, beginning with our own poor. The major public resources of our economic system can be shifted from new military weapons systems to new programs of productivity for the underclass.

The program should not be seen as a drain of social services but as a utilization of the productive capacity of poor and minority Americans as a part of the rebuilding of our infrastructures. This will add to the vitality of the total economy and the common good. Crime and drugs are the result of poverty in the inner cities. A direct attack on the causes of poverty and the racial underclass is the preferable way to deal with human want.

Other principles considered for a Freedom from Want policy are that the programs be primarily directed at the universal poor, not racial groups only; and special consideration needs to be given to the context of minorities such as bilingual education, employment of Native Americans on their reservations, and immigrants with special training needs. These and other policies are given attention in the final chapter of this book.

A NEW CONSCIOUSNESS

A major new priority in American society for the underclass would not have been possible a decade ago, but the shift in public opinion, the leadership of new coalitions of middle-class civil groups, churches, and emerging humanitarian political leaders have made this shift possible.

The National Urban League's proposal for a $50 billion "domestic Marshall Plan to train minority workers to help the United States compete in the international marketplace" is a modest and minimal proposal.[20] They suggest the use of one-third of the savings from demilitarization over the next decade for this purpose. In actual fact, an effective Freedom from Want program over a decade would probably cost far more than this, with funds coming from municipal, state, and federal levels.

The major point is not the cost but the acceptance of the priority and the realization that the entire society and economy can benefit from a reconstruction of American urban life.

It is not too late to restore progress toward equal opportunity for all. The growth of violent racism is still a minor but troubling side show that demonstrates the urgency of renewing the dream that Dr. Martin Luther King, Jr. and others brought alive in the 1960s. This dream faded in the 1980s but could be the triumph of the end of the 1990s.

NOTES

1. Linda Greenhouse, "Marshall Says Court's Rulings Imperil Rights," *New York Times*, September 9, 1989, section I, p. 6.

2. Ronald Walters, "White Racial Nationalism in the United States," *Without Prejudice* 1, no. 1 (Fall 1987): 7–29.

3. Dick Kirschten, "Speaking English," *National Journal* 21, no. 24 (June 17, 1989): 1556.

4. S. I. Hayakawa, National Affairs Section, "Bilingualism in America: English Should Be the Only Language," *USA Today*, July 1989, pp. 32–34.

5. Mark Halton, "Legislating Assimilation: The English Only Movement," *Christian Century*, no. 29 (1989): 1120.

6. Ronald Smothers, "Why the Higher Rungs of Power Elude Black Politicians," *New York Times*, February 26, 1989, section E, p. 4.

7. Kevin Flynn and Gary Gerhardt, *The Silent Brotherhood: Inside America's Racist Underground* (New York: The Free Press, 1989), pp. 171–208.

8. Richard Bernstein, "Twenty Years After the Kerner Report: Three Societies, All Separate," *New York Times*, February 29, 1988, section B, p. 8, quoting Kerner Commission, *Report of the National Advisory Commission on Civil Disorders* (New York. Bantam Books, 1968).

9. Terry Mattingly, "Prayer and Politics," *Rocky Mountain News*, February 12, 1989, p. 57.

10. William J. Wilson, *The Declining Significance of Race: Blacks and Changing American Institutions* (Chicago: University of Chicago Press, 1977).

11. William J. Wilson, *The Truly Disadvantaged: The Inner City, the Underclass and Public Policy* (Chicago: University of Chicago Press, 1987), p. 56.

12. Ibid., p. 27.

13. Ibid., p. 118.

14. These findings have been corroborated by the National Research Council Report, *A Common Destiny: Blacks and American Society* (Washington, DC: National Academy Press, 1989).

15. Bernstein, "Twenty Years After the Kerner Report," section B, p. 8.

16. Roger Wilkins, "The Underside of Progress," *The Progressive*, October 1988, p. 17.

17. "State aid of up to $3600 follows each student to the new school, and the spurned school district loses the money." Gary Putka, *Wall Street Journal*, May 13, 1989.

18. Louis Harris, "Examine These Myths of the 80's," *New York Times*, May 15, 1989, p. A19. See also National Association for the Advancement of Colored People (NAACP) Legal Defense Fund, *The Unfinished Agenda on Race in America* (New York: NAACP, 1989).

19. Richard Movin, ''Fewer Whites Voicing Racial Bias,'' *Washington Post*, October 26, 1989, p. A18.

20. Martin Tolchin, ''50 Billion Sought to Train Blacks,'' *New York Times*, January 10, 1990, p. A12. See also *The National Urban League Annual Report, 1989* (New York: National Urban League, 1990).

CHAPTER 2

The Human Rights of the Underclass

PETER WEISS

WHAT ARE HUMAN RIGHTS?

It is always best to begin with definitions. What are human rights? According to Edmund Burke (who—although a valiant fighter against the excesses of the British Crown in Ireland, the American colonies, and India—never recovered from the shock of the French Revolution), they are "political metaphysics," which are pretexts behind which hide all human vices, uncontrolled "by a power out of themselves."[1] But according to Antigone, determined to bury her brother Polyneices despite Creon's prohibition, they are "the unwritten and unfailing laws of heaven, for their life is not of today or yesterday, but from all time."[2] More than two millennia later, Alexander Hamilton expressed the same view, in words bordering on plagiarism: "The sacred rights of mankind," he said, "are not to be rummaged for among old parchments or musty records. They are written, as with a sun beam, in the whole *volume* of human nature, by the hand of divinity itself; and can never be erased or obscured by moral power."[3]

I myself am not convinced that the hand of divinity ever bothered itself with the drafting of a code of human conduct or that, if it did, the results have been reliably reported to us, although Moses seems to have done a pretty good job of it on Mount Sinai. While I would agree with Edmund Burke that the language of rights can be a mask for hypocrisy, self-interest, and disorderly appetites— as in "I have a right to be a racist, or a sweatshop operator, or an imperialist"— I am firmly on the side of those who regard human rights as overarching precepts of universal validity. It does not matter a great deal whether one views human rights as given by God or deduced by reason from the nature of human beings and human society because, while the starting points of the inquiry are different, the goal is essentially the same. Thus, Thomas Jefferson, good politician that he was, based the right of the American colonists to assume their separate and equal station among the powers of the earth on "the Laws of Nature *and* of Nature's God. . . . "[4]

Moreover, the half century since the founding of the United Nations in 1945 has witnessed the validation and expansion of classic human rights doctrine in the form of countless international, regional, and national treaties; declarations; conventions; constitutions; and laws defining and refining the rights of virtually every conceivable constituent group of society, from human beings as such— what used to be called "the rights of man," before women were acknowledged— to children, the disabled, refugees, workers, minorities, war victims, prisoners, stateless persons, you name it. It is as if, for thousands of years, poets, dramatists, philosophers, and various others in the thick of or on the fringes of statecraft had been taking snapshots of the landscape of human rights, and finally, starting about the middle of the twentieth century, all of that exposed file had been developed, yielding a series of pictures so stark and dramatic in their clarity that they are impossible to ignore. Taken together, they constitute what has been dubbed the international bill of rights and what I prefer to call the emerging constitution of the world.

One result of this extraordinary development is that it has virtually swept away the centuries-old conflict between human rights idealists and human rights positivists, between those seeking to persuade others what human rights ought to be and those who maintain that a human right is whatever is defined as such by a lawmaker -nothing more, nothing less. If doubt exists, take a look at the United Nations publication entitled "Human Rights: A Compilation of International Instruments."[5] It contains the texts of no fewer than sixty-seven such "instruments," from the Universal Declaration of Human Rights (1948) to the Declaration of the Principles of International Cultural Cooperation (1986).

If one is still in doubt, go to Section 701 of the Restatement (Second) of the Foreign Relations Law of the United States, the authoritative text on international law, published in 1986 and representing the consensus of the leading scholars in the field. Section 701 is headed "Obligation to Respect Human Rights" and reads as follows:

A state is obligated to respect the human rights of persons subject to its jurisdiction

(a) that it has undertaken to respect by international agreement;

(b) that states generally are bound to respect as a matter of customary international law; and

(c) that it is required to respect under general principles of law common to the major legal systems of the world.

But if that is the case, why are billions of the world's people hungry and millions homeless when Article 11 of the International Covenant on Economic, Social and Cultural Rights, which has been ratified by ninety-two countries, provides that "The States Parties to the present Covenant recognize the right of everyone to an adequate standard of living for himself and his family, including adequate food, clothing and housing"? Good question. For the answer, one must look to Article 2, which states that "Each State Party to the present Covenant undertakes to take steps, individually and through international assistance and cooperation, especially economic and technical, to the maximum of its available resources, with a view to achieving progressively the full realization of the rights recognized in the present Covenant."

There's the rub, or rather, the two rubs: one, the word "progressively," and two, the phrase "to the maximum of its available resources." No such word, no such phrase, appears in the International Covenant on Civil and Political Rights, which deals with such classic rights as the right to life, freedom from torture and slavery, liberty and security of the person, freedom of movement, equality before the law, and freedom of speech, religion, and association. On the contrary, Article 2 of the Covenant on Civil and Political Rights provides that "Each State Party to the present Covenant undertakes to respect and to ensure to all individuals within its territory and subject to its jurisdiction the rights recognized in the present Covenant . . . ," and Article 4(2) provides that most of these rights may not be abrogated even "in time of public emergency which threatens the life of the nation."

In other words, political and civil rights are real; economic and social rights are to be implemented only to the extent that states, meaning the rulers of states, decide that it is feasible, in their opinion, to take them seriously. One way that lawyers have of expressing this difference is to refer to political and civil rights, at least those which may not be derogated under any circumstances, as peremptory norms, which sounds like something closely related to categorical imperatives, while calling economic and social rights "aspirational" or, worse yet, "merely aspirational." Another semantic distinction sometimes made is between "first generation rights" and "second generation rights," thereby taking all the bite out of the latter, not to mention such "third generation rights" as the right to development or to a safe environment.

WHAT IS THE UNDERCLASS?

Let us now put human rights aside for a while and turn to the underclass. I am not sure where that term originated. It is not to be found in any dictionary or encyclopedia at my disposal. My intuition tells me that the underclass is situated somewhere between what used to be called the proletariat and the lumpenproletariat, before Marx was excommunicated. My intuition also tells me that "underclass" is one of those terms coined by a semanticist for the establishment charged with defanging militant words—probably the same person who substituted "preventive defensive action" for "nuclear strike," "user fee" for "tax," and "underprivileged" for "poor."

"Proletariat," after all, evokes images of underpaid workers storming factory gates and "lumpenproletariat" suggests the great, smelly unwashed. "The underclass," on the other hand, has about it an aura of resignation and docility, like the poor who will always be with us anyway and therefore have little to gain by making trouble.

What, by the way, is the underclass under? Under the horizon? Under the middle class? As good a definition as any probably comes from a cartoon by Rob Rogers, reprinted in the *Times' News of the Week* on March 25, 1990. It shows a census taker consoling a homeless person in the following words: "You'll no longer be the invisible sufferers, the forgotten people, the uncounted Americans. . . . Now you'll be a statistic."[6]

But then, we all know what the underclass is. It's the fifty percent of all Americans over age 65 who, according to Congressman David Pryor's Committee on Aging, lack money for food at some time. It's the 3 million homeless and additional millions living on the edge of homelessness. It's what Senator Daniel Moynihan calls the feminization of poverty and what Dr. Jean Mayer of Tufts University calls the infantization of poverty. It's the 32.5 million of our people who live in poverty and the 23 million who are functionally illiterate. It's the 12 percent loss in household income for the poorest fifth of the population since 1963. It's the 63 percent cut in education block grants to states during the Reagan years and the 81 percent slash in federal funding for subsidized housing. It's America's number twenty rating in infant mortality among the twenty-two principal industrial countries, with black infant mortality twice that of white and black prenatal care one-half that of white. It's the racism and the sexism still endemic in our society, which keeps thousands down while a few rise up.

Let us say that, in the United States, the ignored, the forgotten, the stepped over, the ones who have fallen off the train amount to roughly 20 percent of the total population and 40 to 50 percent of the population of color. For the world at large, the situation is reversed: probably no more than 1 billion, roughly 20 percent of the total—shall we call them the overclass?—can be said to enjoy that quality of life that the aforementioned human rights instruments purport to guarantee to all.

Here are some statistics taken at random from the UN's *1989 Report on the World Social Situation:*

The maternal mortality rate in 1983 was 30 per 100,000 live births for developed countries and 450 for developing countries.

Life expectancy at birth for the period 1985 to 1990 was 51.9 for Africa and 75.5 for North America.

The average daily supply of calories and protein, respectively, for 1983 to 1985 was 1,859 and 38.6 for Bangladesh, compared with 3,343 and 96.4 for Australia.

The lowest decile of 100 countries measured, representing 22.01 percent of the world's population, had a gross domestic product (GDP) of $264 billion; the highest decile, representing 8.89 percent of the world's population, had a GDP of $5,533 billion.

In 1985, 44 percent of the total population of developing countries were living in absolute poverty.

From 1980 to 1985, total central government expenditure for all developing countries declined from 21.32 percent of GDP to 18.22 percent of GDP.

In 1983, the developed market economies (European Economic Community, Japan, the United States) accounted for 72.7 percent of total world expenditures on research and development, compared with 24.2 percent for European centrally planned economies and 3.1 percent for all developing countries.

The world's forests are disappearing at a rate of 15 million hectares per year, with most of the losses occurring in Asia, Africa, and Latin America.

The index of real minimum wages in Tanzania in 1986 was 36 percent of the 1980 level; in Somalia, it was 16 percent, and in Kenya, 75 percent.

The total literacy rate in Africa in 1986 was 50 percent (61 percent for males and 39 percent for females).[7]

And so it goes, not to mention the more than $1 trillion of external debt of developing countries and the nearly $1 trillion of annual worldwide defense expenditures.[8]

THE NEXT STAGE OF HISTORY

Does the underclass have human rights? In one sense, this is a silly question. The underclass, being made up of human beings, has the same rights as all other human beings. In another sense, it may turn out to be the most relevant question of the next stage of history. So far, the only definition of that stage on which there is a consensus is that it is post–Cold War, which doesn't tell us very much about its content. But some shadowy contours are beginning to emerge.

If a ''new world order'' is to be sustainable, an annual expenditure of more than $800 billion on defense is the height of folly.

The debate over whether political and civil rights are a Western luxury or a universal norm is over. The prodemocracy movement has carried the day. While torture, censorship, preventive detention, and other forms of societal brutalization are still practiced in too many countries, hardly anyone defends them anymore on theoretical grounds.

''Quality of life,'' the demand for the satisfaction of human needs, is emerging as the dominant theme of the last decade of the twentieth century and will certainly carry over into the twenty-first.

As Mikhail Gorbachev's increasingly frantic and so far unsuccessful efforts to raise the standard of living of Soviet citizens demonstrate, the formula for achieving social and economic progress remains elusive. Shouting ''market economy'' from the rooftops does not put a chicken in every pot.

Paradoxically, while the developed world gloats over the triumph of its ''system,'' the system is beginning to crumble within the developed world. Witness the increasing pauperization of ever larger sectors of its population and the recent collapse of the Japanese stock market.

From Bensonhurst to Baku, from Soweto to the Sudan, racism and tribalism are flourishing. Pluralism releases all sides of human nature, including the darker ones.

Concern for the environment is no longer the exclusive province of the privileged, liberal few. While Europeans are building the common house of Europe, millions throughout the world fear the collapse of the common house of humankind.

With the exception of the last point concerning the environment, and the continuing threat of nuclear extinction, the problems of the current stage of history are basically problems of the underclass, locally, nationally, and transnationally. What are the chances of the underclass climbing out from under, of achieving the *egalité* that, along with *liberté* and *fraternité*, was one of the goals of the French Revolution; the freedom from want that was one of FDR's four freedoms; the right to "a standard of living adequate for . . . health and well-being" guaranteed to it by Article 25 of the Universal Declaration of Human Rights? At the moment, not very good. Here at home, a spineless Congress and an uninspired president seem concerned only with preserving the status quo while casting about for a new ordering principle to substitute for anticommunism, which served them so well and the people so badly since World War II and of which Mikhail Gorbachev and the long-suffering people of Eastern Europe have so treacherously deprived them.

In Eastern Europe, it looks as if consumerism will have to have a field day before some kind of synthesis is forged between the gentler aspects of socialism—universal health care, social security, education for the masses, minimal unemployment, affordable culture—and the productive forces being unleashed by the wild swing toward the market as the *deus ex machina*.

And the poor Third World, no longer able even to get a pittance from playing off one superpower against the other—no longer entitled to call itself nonaligned—is left swinging in the wind of change, its terms of trade steadily worsening, its raw materials less and less necessary to the developed economies, its burden of debt sitting on its back like a huge, grinning, unshakable monster.

Only Western Europe seems set on a slightly upward course, but even there all is not well. The miracle has gone out of the German economy, Margaret Thatcher's popularity plummeted, leading to her ouster, Belgian unemployment is at an all-time high, and Sweden's middle way is fighting for its life.

So anyone inclined to agree with Francis Fukuyama that we have reached the end of history,[9] and with it the millennium, had better take a look at Paul Kennedy's *The Rise and Fall of the Great Powers*.[10]

The remarkable thing about the current phase of history is the helplessness, the lack of imagination, the apathy with which it is viewed by most of those passing through it. In an issue of *The New Yorker*, Mimi Kramer begins her review of "The Grapes of Wrath," the musical that recently opened in New York, as follows:

> In John Ford's 1940 movie of "The Grapes of Wrath" . . . there is a scene in which Ma Joad . . . goes through a box of old things . . . trying to decide what to throw away and what to take with her to California. There's a postcard from New York, a newspaper clipping about Tom being sent to prison, a pair of earrings. A pot of coffee is boiling on the stove beside her; on the soundtrack, an accordion is wailing "Red River Valley"; and as Ma holds the earrings up to her face and looks at her reflection in the coffeepot she catches sight of what she has become. The precise thing that is happening in the melody of "Red River Valley" at the moment when [her] face changes breaks your heart.
>
> Anyone who attends the Steppenwolf Theatre Company's production of "The Grapes of Wrath" . . . hoping to see this scene (or one very much like it) is in for disappointment. The . . . production . . . is quiet, low-key, and utterly unsentimental. There's nothing in it to pull at your heartstrings; it makes no appeal to nostalgia—no appeal at all to your emotions.[11]

In other words, the census takers have come around, and Ma and Pa Joad have become a statistic.

A CURE FOR APATHY

Is there some hope for putting the wrath back in "The Grapes of Wrath"; for "taking seriously," to use Ronald Dworkin's phrase, the rights of the one-third of a nation and two-thirds of a world ill-clothed, ill-housed, and ill-fed?[12] Let me be bold and suggest that there is.

If what we are looking for is an ideology or, more modestly, a motivating and ordering principle, it is, in the words of the Bard, "invisible, As a nose on a man's face, or a weathercock on a steeple."[13] It is, in fact, right there under our collective noses. It is called, as I have said before, the international bill of rights or the constitution of the world.

The trouble with constitutions—as we know only too well from our own experience, not to mention those of countries that lock people up for demanding their constitutional rights—is that they are far easier to commit to paper than to translate into meaningful action. I am fully aware of the difficulties that beset even the most high-minded legislators and administrators in the face of contending interest groups, growing deficits, and shrinking budgets. But I submit that the outlines of a decent world order have, for the first time, been formulated on the basis of a very broad, to some extent universal, consensus and that this constitutes both a mandate for governors and a powerful tool in the hands of the governed.

How is this to be done? Here are some suggestions.

Exposure

The first step in human rights enforcement is to expose the violations and the violators, who are as dedicated to covering up their misdeeds as to committing them. Nongovernmental organizations like Amnesty International are playing an increasingly important role as observers of and reporters on violations of political and civil rights. The University of Denver's Center on Rights Development's *Africa Rights Monitor* is an example of such activity. There is no comparable, systematic nongovernmental operation in the field of economic and social rights, including periodic reports and country missions. There should be.

Education

A massive effort needs to be made to overcome the invidious distinction between "real" and "aspirational" rights, to which I have referred earlier; to convince judges, government officials, and the public at large that the constant growl of the stomach is as offensive to human dignity as the midnight knock on the door. This must have a political action component to it, like the comprehensive welfare rights movement of the sixties or the various issue-specific, currently functioning organizations concerned with homelessness, hunger, inadequate health care, and other deprivations of human needs. It also requires serious theoretical work, to get beyond such conversation stoppers as, "How are you going to feed everyone when there isn't enough food to go around?" and move on to such questions as, "Why isn't there enough food to go around?" and, "Do the underfed have an enforceable right to some of the nourishment of the overfed?"

Instruments

When it comes to the United States, it is a sad fact that no economic or social rights are specifically guaranteed by the Constitution. We need, therefore, to go on a great scavenger hunt for other morally, politically, and, to some extent, even legally significant sources of such rights, such as

"the pursuit of happiness" in the Declaration of Independence;[14]

the general welfare clause and the mysterious Ninth Amendment to the Constitution of the United States (the latter reads "The enumeration in the Constitution of certain rights shall not be construed to deny or disparage others retained by the People");[15]

various provisions in state constitutions and legislative enactments, for example, the right to health in the constitution of New York and the right of the disabled and elderly to equal access to public transportation in the Mass Transportation Act of 1968;[16]

the common law; and

the various international human rights instruments, both as independent sources of rights and as aids to the interpretation of domestic legislation.

Justice

Judges must be educated to move to higher ground in the area of human rights in the only way that ever moves judges to higher ground, which is a combination of persuasive legal argument and forceful expression of public opinion, including, if necessary, in the streets. India's Supreme Court is a model for other courts to follow in its recognition of economic and social rights, although it has not always been successful in enforcing its writ.

I have referred to the Ninth Amendment to the U.S. Constitution as a sleeper. So is Article 28 of the Universal Declaration of Human Rights, which reads: "Everyone is entitled to a social *and international order* in which the rights and freedoms set forth in this Declaration can be fully realized [emphasis added]." These rights include the right to social security (Article 22), work (Article 23), rest and leisure (Article 24), a standard of living adequate for health and well-being (Article 25), and education (Article 26).

Taxation

Does this mean that the starving children of Ethiopia have a call on the treasury of the United States? Yes. Am I talking about a system of international taxation? Yes. Is this crazy talk? No more so than was talk of a U.S. tax based on income prior to the adoption of the Sixteenth Amendment in 1913, after nearly a four-year ratification process.

Perhaps we should think of this strange, heady, unnerving time through which we are living as time out—time to lick wounds, to catch a little breath, to think about past mistakes, to plan for the next bout. Perhaps when the gong sounds, there will be no opponent in the other corner, except war and famine, global warming and AIDS, illiteracy and poverty. And perhaps the referee, with a tattered copy of the Universal Declaration of Human Rights in hand, will admonish the fighters: "Whereas disregard and contempt for human rights have resulted in barbarous acts that have outraged the conscience of mankind, and the advent of a world in which human beings shall enjoy freedom of speech and belief and freedom from fear and want—I repeat that, *and freedom from fear and want*—has been proclaimed as the highest aspiration of the common people, therefore go to it! Fight clean, and fight hard."

NOTES

1. Edmund Burke, *Reflections on the French Revolution* (London: J. M. Dent & Sons, 1910), pp. 56–57.

2. Sophocles, *Antigone*, lines 411–12.

3. Alexander Hamilton, *The Farmer Refuted* (New York: James Rivington, 1775), reprinted in Harold Syrett, ed.; *The Papers of Alexander Hamilton, Volume I: 1768–1778* (New York: Columbia University Press, 1961), p. 122.

4. Declaration of Independence, 1st preambular paragraph.

5. ST/HR/1 Rev. 3 (1988).

6. For example, see U.S. Census, Special Committee on Aging, *Aging America: Trends and Projections*, 101st Congress, 1st Session, Senate Print 101–59 (Washington, DC: U.S. Government Printing Office, November 1989), pp. 27–28.

7. U.N Department of International Economic and Social Affairs, *1989 Report on the World Social Situation* (New York: United Nations, 1989), Tables 11, 12, 13, 19, 24, 29, 31, and in-text figures, pp. 64–65.

8. For details on this, see Ruth Leger Sivard's annual masterpiece, *World Military and Social Expenditures* (Leesburg, VA: WMSE Publications, various years).

9. Francis Fukuyama, "The End of History?" *The National Interest*, no. 16 (Summer 1989): 3.

10. Paul Kennedy, *The Rise and Fall of the Great Powers: Economic Change and Military Conflict from 1500–2000* (New York: Vintage Books, 1989).

11. Mimi Kramer, "Tender Grapes," *The New Yorker*, April 2, 1990, p. 87.

12. Ronald Dworkin, *Taking Rights Seriously* (Cambridge, MA: Harvard University Press, 1978).

13. William Shakespeare, *The Two Gentlemen of Verona*, act 1, scene 1, line 145.

14. Declaration of Independence, paragraph 2.

15. U.S. Constitution, Article 1, Section 8, paragraph 1 ("The congress shall have the Power to . . . provide for the common Defense and general Welfare of the United States").

16. New York constitution, Article 17, Section 3 (health care), Article 18, Section 1 (housing, including proposed constitutional amendment); and the declaration of transportation policy in 49 U.S.C. 1612.

_____ _PART II_

Racism and the Law _____

CHAPTER 3

Present Remedies and Ancient Wrongs: In Search of a New Civil Rights Jurisprudence

GREGORY KELLAM SCOTT

> Great cases like hard cases make bad law. For great cases are called great, not by reason of their real importance in shaping the law of the future, but because of some accident of immediate overwhelming interest which appeals to the feelings and distorts the judgment.[1]

Having viewed the media attention and response given the *Croson* decision, which "reversed affirmative action," and recently having the opportunity to compare it to the attention and interest expressed for *Metro Broadcasting, Inc. v. FCC*,[2] which "affirmed" governmental preferences based on race, I now realize the wisdom in Justice Holmes's statement, "great cases are called great . . . because [they] appeal to the feelings and distort the judgment."

One of the most important and potentially far-reaching cases decided during the 1988–1989 term of the U.S. Supreme Court was *City of Richmond v. J. A. Croson Company*.[3] Previously, when confronted with cases such as *Brown v. Board of Education*[4] or *Fullilove v. Klutznick*,[5] the Court displayed its ability to arrive at a correct result while following an historically inaccurate and intellectually suspect doctrinal framework.[6] In *Croson*, unfortunately, both the Court's reasoning and the result were neither enlightening nor unexpected. And, somewhat more disappointing than surprising, when confronted with an opportunity to articulate a new affirmative action jurisprudence, the Court, certainly not constrained by precedent,[7] did otherwise. Instead, the justices overlooked an opportunity to realign our civil rights jurisprudence and to establish a foundation upon which to articulate new principles for affirmative action. The Court acknowledged it was following precepts that create "tensions" attributable to the competing interests of affirmative action and equal protection. It is this approach or inability to articulate clearly "the law" that is more distressing than the actual result since, so long as the Court is unable to realign its civil rights jurisprudence, congressional and state affirmative action efforts will be needlessly shackled and burdened by a limiting equal protection doctrine. As a result, the Court, when called upon to review protections and benefits gintended to ameliorate ancient wrongs, will disfavor affirmative action. Moreover, the Court's current course creates a nontrivial risk that the impact of its decision will wreak more havoc than the good intended by the equal protection doctrine. The ancient wrongs of slavery and their present effects, creating for minorities a new form of involuntary servitude, will continue to outweigh individual efforts to overcome discrimination.

Unfortunately, our recent history, including the everyday as well as the notorious racially motivated incident, confirms with all too great frequency that, indeed, racism and discrimination exist today and are freely exercised against African-Americans. To break the 300-year-old chains of slavery and involuntary servitude, governmental intervention remains a priority as the market efficiency of nonlegal controls (the absence of government intervention) has proven to be insufficient to ameliorate the ancient wrongs of discrimination. The private sector marketplace and public morals, yet to fully reflect an integrated society, cannot be reasonably expected to reverse immediately or within the foreseeable future the present effects of past legal and today's illegal discrimination. On the one hand, private efforts too frequently are limited in scope and do not reach a sufficiently broad group of the harmed class. Conversely, public morals, reactive but not proactive, are directed only to isolated, notorious circumstances and events. Both fail to foster a focused, continuous effort, and, as a result, either alone is not a remedy. We live in a society in which a Howard Beach or Forsyth County may not be infrequent exceptions and the lives of judges and attorneys who champion a truly integrated, equal society are threatened by hooligans and criminals.[8] Thus, the need for Congress to exercise its constitutional powers under the Civil War amendments[9] to develop a coherent, comprehensive approach is only exceeded by the urgency with which the Court should respond (i) by developing a new civil rights jurisprudence and (ii) by making it clear there is no refuge in our law nor in our society for those opposed to full citizenship for all.

A close examination of the Court's ruling in *Croson* reveals a decision politically expedient but jurisprudentially deficient. Whatever one may correctly or incorrectly attribute to the Court's decision,[10] it is actually more *unclear* what the Court accomplished in *Croson* than what many are willing to acknowledge. There remains much disagreement as to what was resolved by the decision. However, there should be no dispute that the Court's action, in fact, (i) is not the last (any more than it was the first) word on affirmative action and (ii) implies that our limited successes of the past have, at least in the minds of several of the justices, reduced the judiciary's "unique role in the area of racial equality."[11]

Instead of accepting its traditional role, assumed over the past thirty-odd years beginning with the *Brown* decision, the Court is busy shifting the burden for racial equality from the courts to the legislative branch and into the political arena. As it did with the abortion issue,[12] the Court has, in essence, reduced actions perceived as "judicial activism" and has substituted a form of reluctance that some might refer to as judicial restraint. Such a posture is tolerable only in areas other than race where lowered emotions and the excess baggage of history will permit us to conclude "[s]ome degree of folly is 'legitimate' and the remedy is not the court but the 'political' process."[13] Or, stated another way, "issues of racial justice no longer hold a priority position . . . on the Supreme Court's docket."[14] If this is true, the fact of the Court's restraint is ominous. However, the timing may not be inopportune. Further efforts to effect the election, on a bipartisan basis, of those who are sensitive to the interests of our growing minority population, which is key to preserving our national interests in a more competitive world market, have their benefits. In reality, our lot is not as desperate as we may be led to believe. African-Americans have never had the comfort or luxury of relying upon others to do our bidding nor the right thing, even when it was clearly in the national interest. Nor have advocates who pursue equal justice under the law ever been accused of choosing the easier path. As Derrick Bell has raised the issue in his brilliant "Civil Rights Chronicles," the role of the attorney in the movement for social change may not be for those weak of heart nor for those who are weak of resolve. The battle rages. Minorities are no longer the totally disenfranchised citizenship of the 1950s and before.[15]

However, today there is one unique aspect to our national effort that did not exist previously. Today's battle is for both social *and commercial civil rights.*[16] No longer relegated to seeking only the traditional right to equal education (often confused with school desegregation, which is an end not a means), political influence actually translates into commercial and economic significance. The fight for social and commercial civil rights is fought, however, not solely for personal gain nor to save our collective conscience as a nation; it is inextricably bound to and will be a controlling factor in determining America's future status and position in the shrinking global economy. Constitutional and moral imperatives aside, the changing international political landscape, world economic order, and global competition make it clear the United States can no longer afford the cost and waste of untapped and underutilized human resources that invariably accompany pernicious discrimination.

When little can be done to alter the tides or turn back the hands of time, we need not be captive to a misguided jurisprudence nor our inability to accept the plain language of the Court's ruling. It is well past time that courts abandon the equal protection doctrine that controls our national debate. To that end, this chapter addresses the limitations and inaccuracies resulting from the equal protection doctrine and articulates an alternative basis for our affirmative action jurisprudence. The first section reviews the *Croson* decision. The next section briefly considers the equal protection doctrine and the resultant "tension" between the doctrine's original purpose and its current application and suggests a jurisprudence grounded in recognizing ancient wrongs and remedial actions fostering both distributive and compensatory justice.[17] I do not attempt a substantial examination of the various decisions nor a study of the historical events and legal precepts or factors attendant with the Court's current civil rights jurisprudence, as such a discourse is well beyond the scope of this chapter and the abilities of one not frequently searching in the constitutional law vineyard. What is intended is to introduce a principled and reasoned doctrine, free of the limitations of current precedent, which promotes the inclusion of minorities to full citizenship and the well-being of the United States as a diverse and unified nation.

THE *CROSON* CASE

The *Croson* decision, although establishing a new equal protection test for voluntary race-conscious state action, stakes no new ground and does not, of its own force, outright deny nor advance civil rights jurisprudence. However, in view of the fact that it has resulted in the immediate review or suspension of existing affirmative action programs in over thirty-five jurisdictions, the *Croson* decision has become the focus for determining the constitutional validity of state programs. Thus, its impact may be substantial. However, in the universe of court decisions, a stellar role for *Croson* is unlikely.

The Facts

On January 23, 1989, the U.S. Supreme Court announced its decision in *City of Richmond v. J. A. Croson Company*. We are often reminded that the Court held unconstitutional a state "set-aside" program designed to ameliorate long-standing discrimination in the award of local government contracts.[18] At the same time, and often ignored, *the Court upheld the constitutionality of race-conscious state action.*

Today one must concede that although its impact may not yet be clear, the potential reach of the decision can easily be underestimated. If nothing else, the wake of its aftermath[19] has unnecessarily submerged many existing state affirmative action programs into the costly task of reevaluating existing policies and practices in an effort to meet poorly defined elements of the Court's plurality decision.[20] Rather than a response specifically mandated by the Court's decision, administrative reviews of existing policies were predestined by the public response to the Court's ruling. News accounts of the Court's decision, which reflect a somewhat frightening bias, probably constitute a principal source for much misunderstanding.[21] Even in jurisdictions where it is believed the aftermath will be of little or no effect, the impact may be substantial,[22] but not for the reasons many suspect. The Court's plurality decision does not make set-asides for states unlawful, and it certifies the continuing viability of federal set-asides despite the contrary views of others. Whatever the effect, a review of the facts will prove helpful in determining what the Court decided (and what it did not decide).

The *Croson* decision is, in part, driven by its facts. In 1983, the Richmond City Council, the petitioners, passed an ordinance, the Minority Business Utilization Plan,[23] requiring prime contractors to subcontract 30 percent of the dollar amount of the city's work to minority-owned firms, or minority business enterprises (MBEs).[24] The plan exempted minority-owned prime contractors from the 30 percent set-aside. The plan further defined an MBE as a business at least 51 percent of which is owned and controlled by minority group members or "citizens of the United States who are Black, Spanish-speaking, Orientals, Indians, Eskimos, or Aleuts." There was "no geographic limit" or residency or citizenship requirement for MBEs to participate under the plan, allowing minority group members from "anywhere in the United States" to participate in the 30 percent set-aside. Declaring that it was "remedial" in nature, the plan stated its purpose to be that "of promoting wider participation by minority business enterprises in the construction of public projects." The plan also included an administrative waiver provision by which a firm unable to meet the 30 percent subcontracting requirement could still participate as a prime contractor.

The plan was adopted by the City Council after a public hearing. However, after examining the hearing record, the Court concluded that there "was no direct evidence of race discrimination" on the part of the city or its prime contractors.[25] The record did reflect a disparity between the racial composition of the general population (50 percent African-American not including other minority groups) and the award of contracts to minority-owned business firms (0.67 percent of all contracts awarded) during the five-year period prior to the plan's adoption. Documented also was the lack of full participation by minority-owned firms in city contracting opportunities and also in professional and trade associations in the Richmond area. The record before the City Council included statements by prominent witnesses and city officials "as to the exclusionary history of the local construction industry" and the debilitating effect on minority business enterprise.[26] In addition, the City Council relied upon "evidence in the public domain," including congressional reports disclosing procurement practices that were previously held to perpetuate "the effects of prior discrimination."[27] Opponents spoke of the potential windfall to minority firms located in Richmond as they feared an insufficient number of MBEs to "satisfy the 30% set-aside requirement." Despite the objections, the plan was approved by a 6–2–1 vote, a reasonable legislative response.

On September 6, 1983, the city issued its public invitation for bids on a project for the installation of plumbing fixtures. J. A. Croson Company, a non-MBE, was the only contractor to bid on the contract. After unsuccessful efforts to obtain

bids from MBEs for the fixtures (the only means by which Croson could subcontract 30 percent to MBEs), Croson applied for a waiver.

Croson's efforts to include MBEs appeared substantial and in good faith on
the record. Eugene Bonn, its regional manager, contacted several MBEs identified by state agencies seeking a subcontractor to comply with the plan. Eventually Bonn located a local MBE (Continental) interested in participating with
Croson in the contract opportunity. However, the quotation from Continental
increased the cost of the project to the city by approximately $7,500 (which may
be attributable to the nonminority supplier more so than to Continental) and was
subject to a credit approval that would not be completed until "some 21 days
after the prime bids were due."[28] As a result, Croson requested a waiver of the
30 percent set-aside provisions (as permitted by the plan), a request which the
city denied. Croson then advised the city of the increased cost attributable to
the participation of Continental and asked that it be allowed to raise the contract
price accordingly to accommodate the MBE subcontractor. The city denied the
request and decided to rebid the project.

After being informed there was no appeal of the decision to rebid, Croson
initiated a civil action in the U.S. District Court for the Eastern District of
Virginia under 42 U.S.C. § 1983 arguing the plan was unconstitutional.[29] The
District Court upheld the plan, and a divided panel of the Fourth Circuit Court
of Appeals affirmed "[r]elying on the great deference" that the Court accorded
Congress's findings of past discrimination and the "statistical study concerning
the award of prime contracts in Richmond." The Court of Appeals applied a
"reasonableness" test and concluded the 30 percent set-aside was "narrowly
tailored" when compared to the more than 50 percent minority population. On
appeal the Supreme Court vacated the decision of the Court of Appeals and
remanded the case for further consideration in light of its decision in *Wygant v.
Jackson Board of Education*.[30] On remand, the Court of Appeals, somewhat
misled by the Court's remand, reversed the trial court and held the plan unconstitutional "violating both prongs of [the] strict scrutiny" test under the Fourteenth Amendment.

The Holding

> What is striking is the role legal principles have played throughout America's
> history in determining the condition of [African-Americans and other mi-
> norities]. They were enslaved by law, emancipated by law, disenfranchised
> and segregated by law; and, finally, they have begun to win equality by
> law.[31]

These words reflect upon an experience and life in the law; they were penned
by Justice Thurgood Marshall, who all his life has been a fearlessly principled
defender of the constitutional rights of all Americans. They were written before

Croson, having greater meaning after *Croson* by virtue of the *Metro Broadcasting* decision. However, they reflect a time when the judiciary represented the only branch of government responsive to the interests of minorities. Today, by virtue of the political process now responding under the impact of the Voting Rights Act of 1964, through the Civil Rights Act of 1991 the legislative branch has become responsive as well.[32] And, shortly we may learn whether the executive branch can function as a department of government for all Americans—if President Bush acts regarding a new Civil Rights Act.

The decision of the Court is represented by a plurality opinion written by Justice Sandra Day O'Connor, in which she was joined by Chief Justice William Rehnquist and Justices Byron White, John Stevens, and Anthony Kennedy. However, Justices Stevens and Kennedy joined only as to Parts I, III-B, and IV, which comprise the opinion of the Court.[33] Justice Antonin Scalia, the sixth justice, concurred in the judgment. However, Scalia wrote separately distinguishing himself as the only justice who might hold that a state may not engage in race-conscious, remedial action except when it acts to remedy its own discriminatory actions.[34]

Justice Marshall wrote a dissenting opinion and was joined by Justices William Brennan and Harry Blackmun.[35] With both force and eloquence, Justice Marshall contrasted the current motives and actions of the Richmond City Council with the shift of climate in the Supreme Court, once viewed as in the vanguard of civil rights jurisprudence but now characterized as taking a "giant step backward." This characterization of the Court's action is not without substance. The Court's flirtation with the role of guardian of the rights of African-Americans is a short one. Prior to the Civil War amendments the Court never struck out against slavery. And, following *Plessy v. Ferguson*[36] the ambiance of the *Brown* decision was removed by *Croson*—decided less than forty years after *Brown*. However, more importantly, it is equally clear that at least six, and as many as eight, justices stand by the Court's earlier *Fullilove* decision.

The "Strict Scrutiny" Test. In *Croson*, the Supreme Court held that a state set-aside program established on "race-based" criteria to "ameliorate the present effects of past discrimination" can only withstand constitutional muster if it meets the "strict scrutiny" test. Under the strict scrutiny test applied by the Court, the state must show (i) a "compelling interest" in the use of a race-based quota and (ii) that the "set-aside [is] narrowly tailored to accomplish a remedial purpose."[37] However, perhaps since the Court has not had much opportunity to develop the test and since it is not necessarily the test one may anticipate with much certainty in future rulings,[38] the Court was unable to provide guidance by articulating the specifics of the test. For example, under the Court's strict scrutiny test, it is difficult to determine what constitutes a "compelling interest." On one hand, based on previous decisions, we may safely assume the right to an equal education will meet the test.[39] We may hope and even expect that certain actions to promote the employment of certain teachers that take race into consideration as a comparative factor in order to provide "role models"[40] will constitute a compelling interest.[41] On the other hand, we are advised "[s]ocietal discrimination" alone cannot demonstrate a compelling interest.[42] Meanwhile, a compelling interest exists in the state "preventing its tax dollars from assisting discrimination"[43] so long as the state has taken action to "identify" the discrimination. However, racial and ethnic groups favored under the test must share a nexus with the wrongful conduct. Groups benefiting must not include a "random" selection of racial groups so as to include a group or class that "may never have suffered from discrimination."

The acceptance by the *Croson* plurality of a strict scrutiny test is significant: It is the first time a single test has seemingly satisfied a majority of the justices. However, only five justices, a narrow majority under the facts, agreed that it is the appropriate test. Justice Stevens argued that, consistent with his opinion in *Fullilove*, certain race-based actions are permissible and should be permitted when justified. Stevens, along with the three dissenters, did not apply the strict scrutiny test. He would rather hold that the Court must examine the characteristics of the benefitted and disadvantaged classes to determine whether a preference is justified.[44] In addition, Justice Stevens would rather permit courts, and not legislative bodies, to "fashion a remedy for a past wrong." The obvious difficulty with Justice Stevens's position is that he would thereby limit state action to individual claimants excluding group-based ameliorative responses. If a particular potential beneficiary of state action could not personally prove a discriminatory harm personally suffered, though a member of the group was discriminated against, Justice Stevens might not allow the individual to benefit. To the extent that it permits race-conscious actions, Justice Stevens's approach has merit but is justifiable only if one views the affirmative action to be a remedy and right solely to address past wrongs suffered by actual victims. That is not the case. In fact, affirmative action is as much a class-based response providing certain benefits to individuals who may not have suffered discrimination directly but who achieve the status of beneficiary derivatively.

Apparently, the implicit test as to whether a compelling interest exists is to determine whether the suspect action is (i) "remedial" and designed to address proven instances of discrimination and (ii) intended to benefit victims or persons identified as within the class of those harmed. Such an analysis wrongfully denies the existence of an unfair privilege based solely on membership in the group not suffering discrimination. In a well-written analysis of the *Croson* decision, Michael Rosenfeld, also struck by the equal protection doctrine, develops a theory of "compensatory affirmative action" and "distributive affirmative action."[45] If the wrongdoer is acting to compensate those harmed or others reasonably identified with those harmed, the race-conscious act is "compelling." However, if the state is distributing benefits and acts not as a wrongdoer, the action is probably not compelling unless the particular victim is benefitted. The theory seems plausible and may be used to explain the actions of the court; however, it too is limited and excludes too many victims due to a purely mechanical application under the equal protection genre. It also requires one to accept the premise that "the equal protection clause is designed to uphold the equal worth, dignity, and respect of *every* individual regardless of race."[46] It is this interpretation or concession that complicates judicial analysis of race-conscious actions.

Borrowing a moment from Justice Lewis Powell's opinion in *Fullilove*, as an alternative to the Fourteenth Amendment for the source of our jurisprudence, race-conscious remedial legislation should merely have to survive an analysis weighing the burdens against the benefits.[47] Once the analysis is undertaken in light of the objects and purposes of the Thirteenth Amendment, certain state (or federal) actions may stand even if they initially appear to disadvantage white contractors "based solely upon their race." This is true, in part, since to disadvantage one already in a favored position as a consequence of unjust enrichment (at least when compared to African-Americans) may not necessarily constitute unfair treatment or even denial of equal protection. As the message is not clear, *Croson* will probably require, at some stage, relitigation of the same issues.

Under Wygant states may act to rectify identified private discrimination. In Part II of her opinion, Justice O'Connor reasoned that a state "has the authority to eradicate the effects of private discrimination" and is not limited in its "competence" to reach "practices [of third parties] within local commerce."[48] Contrary to the views of Justice Scalia, who would only permit "States [to] act *by race* . . . to eliminate their own . . . unlawful racial classification,"[49] at least seven[50] and possibly eight[51] justices will permit race-based action by a state to remedy discrimination.

In *Wygant*, the Court previously held that the use of "racial quotas" under an agreement reached between the school board and the local teachers' union to adopt a race-based layoff program rather than the contractual seniority system in place was unlawful without "showing . . . prior discrimination by the governmental unit involved."[52] The Court of Appeals in *Croson II* read the opinion to limit state action solely to instances in which the state was the offending party.[53] The Court acted to disabuse lower courts of such a notion and reversed that portion of the appeals court opinion noting it "erred in following *Wygant* by rote." In *Wygant*, without express authority and in light of the existing collective bargaining agreement, the school board acted improperly. Unlike *Wygant*, in *Croson* the City Council was acting within its organic authority, and was therefore not limited by the Court's ruling in Wygant. Once the state agency is authorized by law to act and it can "identify the discrimination with the particularity required by the Fourteenth Amendment," it may act.[54]

Fullilove affirmed. In substantial portions of Part II, Justice O'Connor distinguished the *Croson* situation, involving state action, from that upheld in *Fullilove* where congressional action established set-asides to address discrimination.[55] Recognizing Congress's special duty and authority under the Fourteenth Amendment, *Croson* does not prohibit federal or federally induced minority set-aside programs.[56]

In *Fullilove* the Court upheld a minority set-aside under the Public Workers

Employment Act of 1977,[57] which was enacted to give the national economy a "boost in a recessionary period." The Congress acted to provide an infusion of federal dollars to fund public works projects; however, it also acted to condition federal assistance upon the expenditure of "at least 10%" of the available dollars in contracts awarded to MBEs. Under the *Fullilove* decision written by then Chief Justice Burger, the Court gave appropriate "deference to the Congress, a co-equal branch charged by the Constitution with the power . . . 'to enforce by appropriate legislation,' the equal protection guarantees of the Fourteenth Amendment."[58] The *Fullilove* Court determined that such congressional action was "within the power of Congress" and that the "limited use of racial and ethnic criteria [is] a permissible means for Congress to carry out its objectives."[59]

Combining Congress's "unique remedial powers"[60] with "the flexible nature of the . . . set-aside," Justice O'Connor concluded a federal race-based action would "pass muster." Including the dissenting justices, at least six justices (O'Connor, Rehnquist, White, Marshall, Brennan, and Blackmun) and probably seven (adding Stevens) agree and recognize such congressional power. However, Justice O'Connor distinguished the factual situation in *Fullilove* (congressionally induced local action) from that in *Croson* (state action) and concluded the Court's "treatment of an exercise of Congressional power in *Fullilove* cannot be dispositive here."[61] Or, in the words of Drew Days,

The *Fullilove* Court unequivocally upheld Congress' power to use race-conscious remedies in its effort to eradicate the effects of past and present racial discrimination and to prevent the recurrence of that discrimination. The Court directly repudiated claims that affirmative action was merely "reverse discrimination" and that the Constitution prohibits any governmental practices that violate the principle of color-blindness.[62]

The Supreme Court's decisions in *University of California Regents v. Bakke* and *Steelworkers v. Weber*[63] affirm the power of the Congress to act to "enforce" the Civil War amendments by "appropriate legislation." Under *Fullilove* and *Croson*, the Court permits federally induced race-conscious state action.[64] Congress can resort to its commerce power (taxing and spending authority) and may appropriately encumber federal assistance to state and local projects by "appropriate means" in order to avoid governmental support or encouragement of illegal conduct.[65]

In April 1989, in a little publicized decision following *Croson*, a federal District Court in Wisconsin[66] appropriately held that "a state program is enacted to implement federal legislation imposing specified requirements on the state and where the legislation is an integral part of the federal-state legislative framework, the state program should be considered a subsidiary element of the federal legislation."[67] In *Fiedler*, Judge Barbara B. Crabb modified an earlier order of the court granting a preliminary injunction to plaintiffs, nonminority highway contractors, against a state contracting program that gave contract preference to minority firms. State defendants argued that the Wisconsin statute establishing the program was the "alter ego" of the federal program established by Congress under federal law providing federal assistance to states under programs administered by the Department of Transportation.[68] Examining the intricate federal statutes and regulations applicable, Judge Crabb modified her prior order and concluded, "The standards articulated in *Croson* do not apply to federal affirmative action programs or to state programs which are subsidiary to them."[69] While the majority in *Croson* was willing to agree that "the sorry history of both private and public discrimination in this country" has "contributed" to denying African-Americans "opportunities," it concluded that fact, "standing alone," cannot justify "a rigid racial quota."[70] The state must engage in fact-finding inquiry exceeding that of "generalized assertion."[71] In *Croson*, the City Council relied upon, among other factors, the small number of minority businesses, conclusionary statements of proponents including a councilperson and the city manager, congressional findings, the disparity between the general minority population (50 percent) and contract awards (.67 percent), and prior judicial determinations.[72] However, according to the majority, the city failed to provide a "strong basis in evidence" or to "identify [the] discrimination, public or private, with some specificity."[73] The Court, rejecting Marshall's view that it was creating an "onerous documentary obligation," determined that "societal discrimination alone" is insufficient.

UNDERLYING CONSTITUTIONAL FACTORS: AFFIRMATIVE ACTION AND INVOLUNTARY SERVITUDE

> The tangled and contradictory logic accrued over the years in *stare decisis* regarding the meaning and interest of the Fourteenth Amendment unavoidably pushed the Supreme Court to the sweeping mandate of Brown.[74]
>
> Harold Cruse

History as well as our own experience reiterates the limitations of our contemporary constitutional theory and civil rights jurisprudence. The results once applied reflect that the prevailing doctrines and our national interests are incompatible, and that is intolerable. For example, in her opinion, Justice O'Connor, almost wearily, discussed this apparent inconsistency when she spoke of the conflict between affirmative action and the equal protection clause of the Fourteenth Amendment.[75] Although recognizing the "tension" between the "guarantee of equal treatment" and "affirmative action" necessary to "ameliorate the effects of past discrimination," Justice O'Connor and the Court failed to confront and address the underlying cause rather than the symptom. It is this very conflict represented by the "tension" between competing doctrines which cries out for attention and should have appealed to the interests of the Court—if for no reason other than their real importance. Instead, relying on "feelings [that] distort judgment," issues worth raising and resolving remain for another day. *Croson* did, no doubt, create difficulties for the six concurring justices, including Justice Stevens, who would extend remedial action to "govern future conduct" as well as a "past wrong,"[76] and Justices Kennedy and Scalia, who would prefer an absolute rule of "racial neutrality." Yet the Court, rather than resolve the conflict and escape the "tension," elected again to weave an important decision with an ecclesiastical fervor for the equal protection doctrine. This is an unacceptable response.

The perceived tension exists from the conflict between the Civil Rights philosophy of "noneconomic liberalism" and economic empowerment. The inability of social advancements to accommodate commercial and economic participation when accompanied by the "legal goals of the Fourteenth Amendment" has resulted in a jurisprudence that could be fairly characterized as hostile. In recent years the development of our affirmative action jurisprudence, as articulated under the equal protection doctrine, requires a new coherent and comprehensive approach to "the race problem." This is especially so since the interests of minorities requiring constitutional protection have shifted from the objective of integration into the cultural and social fabric of American life to full participation, economic and commercial. No longer are African-Americans and other minorities seeking seats in the front of the bus, nor are they satisfied to drive the bus; they want to own and operate the bus company. Theories and doctrines successfully applied under earlier circumstances and readily available to attack public discrimination and social matters have now proven they do not readily transfer to instances involving private unlawful discrimination and economic bigotry.[77]

It is now time that we abandon blind faith in the theology that grants supernatural sanction to the advantaged[78] and ignores the reality of others subjected to the consequences of ancient (and current) wrongs.[79] The precarious and uncongenial Fourteenth Amendment and its equal protection doctrine should be replaced by its companion Thirteenth Amendment as the basis for our affirmative action jurisprudence. It is time our Civil Rights law and lore recognize that matters of race are not inextricably bound to our Constitution solely through the Fourteenth Amendment.

Congress has exercised its authority under the Thirteenth, Fourteenth, and Fifteenth Amendments[80] (the Civil War amendments) to "correct and cure Constitutional defects." Such action has been necessary because, contrary to the position taken by many opponents of affirmative action, our Constitution is not now and has never been colorblind.

As African-Americans are reminded on a daily basis, the myth of a colorblind Constitution is a fiction whose time should have long since been spent. As was forcefully stated by then Chief Justice Roger Taney, writing for a majority of the Supreme Court in *Dred Scott v. Sanford*, even at the outset in the Preamble of the Constitution, with its sweeping "egalitarian language," African-Americans were excluded and were never intended to be included. Chief Justice Taney reasoned, "[A]t the time of the Declaration of Independence, and when the Constitution of the United States was framed and adopted . . . [African-Americans] had no rights which the white man was bound to respect."[81]

An Historical Perspective

Many assert, incorrectly, that the beginning of the permissive use of racial preferences was under the affirmative action decisions of the Berger Court in the *Bakke*[82] and *Weber* cases.[83] That was not and is not the case. Historically, racial preferences have always existed within the very text of our Constitution.[84] This is so despite the care taken by our founding fathers to craft a document protecting the interests of the slave holders without having to tarnish its luster or dim its brilliance by the use of the term "slavery," an obvious enigma. Today, more damning than what Judge A. Leaon Higginbotham, Jr. refers to as "this historically persistent failure of perception"[85] is the apparent inability of many scholars and intellectuals to recognize and accept the truth as history instead of lore. Without making value judgments, we should be able to acknowledge our past and the Constitution and laws that for far too long permitted African-Americans to be treated differently.

These differences existed first in our Constitution. Initially, preferences were only for the benefit of white males who were also property owners.[86] After the Civil War amendments, the Constitution extended the preferences to nonwhite males and, subsequently, to all citizens. For more than twenty years the Court has held that the Constitution permits the use of racial preferences or affirmative action designed to meet a compelling state interest so long as the action is "necessary to the accomplishment of some permissible state objective, independent of the racial discrimination *which it was the object of the Fourteenth Amendment to eliminate* [emphasis added]"[87] Race-conscious actions that were not the target of the Fourteenth Amendment, preferences for slaves and their ancestors or those similarly situated (i.e., those in need of protection), were permissible. European-Americans, those who the Constitution long included in its reach and who are not in need of protection, were never included within the amendment's objects.

The strict scrutiny test applied to race-conscious state affirmative action and set-aside programs in *Croson* was developed under the equal protection doctrine[88] from both *Korematsu v. United States*[89] (which recognized national security as a compelling interest) and as applied in *Wygant*[90] (which required, in addition, that the race-conscious government action must be "narrowly tailored"). Importantly, the *Croson* decision does not adversely impact congressional action. Federal affirmative action programs, unsuccessfully challenged in *Fullilove*, remain intact. At the same time, however, state action induced directly by congressional enactments under the Thirteenth Amendment should also withstand attack. Much like the deference granted the legislature under the Fourteenth Amendment, Congress can act independently or to induce ancillary state action creating "agencies," within and outside the government, to carry out its otherwise lawful actions. The Thirteenth Amendment, with its more precise language as to the intended beneficiaries and its clear object of freeing all citizens from involuntary servitude as well as slavery, would not permit cries or claims made by advantaged nonminorities of "reverse discrimination." As the enforcement clause of the Thirteenth Amendment is intended to be a broad grant of authority permitting the exercise of powers similar to that in the Necessary and Proper Clause of Article I, [91] Congress need only act rationally and in a manner reasonably related to the constitutional objective.[92] This sound logic was accepted by Judge Crabb in *Milwaukee County Pavers Assn. v. Fiedler*.[93]

Prior to the Civil War amendments, the Constitution denied slaves, generally those residents (but not citizens) of "African descent," the full benefits and protections of citizenship. A Civil War and three amendments later, the Constitution was altered intending to empower Congress to act whenever, in the Congress's discretion, it is necessary to fulfill the promise of those benefits previously denied to African-Americans and others subjected to slavery or involuntary servitude. It was generally accepted that congressional action would be necessary to extend full citizenship to African slaves and their descendents and to protect these new citizens from the overt and covert oppression of those who had formerly "exercised dominion over them."[94] Whether it was agreed that appropriate action be taken a hundred years later to rectify manifest injustice is immaterial; so long as one group is overprivileged and another is the object of discrimination or some form of involuntary servitude, prohibited by the Thirteenth Amendment, it must be remedied. However, advocates and the reviewing courts have inappropriately paid too much attention to the Fourteenth Amendment[95] consequently ignoring the Thirteenth Amendment.

Unlike the Fourteenth Amendment, the Thirteenth Amendment was not intended to prohibit state action; it was intended only to abolish slavery and involuntary servitude. Discrimination based on race constitutes a modern badge of slavery and results in "involuntary servitude."[96] As it is under the Fourteenth Amendment, Congress is authorized, and in fact obligated, to "enforce" the Thirteenth Amendment by "appropriate legislation." Unlike the Fourteenth and Fifteenth Amendments, which bar state action in order to create an exclusive domain for enforcement or remedial legislation within the Congress, the Thirteenth Amendment contemplates that *states* may act on their own to ameliorate the present effects of past and present discrimination—modern badges of slavery and a form of involuntary servitude. The obvious absence in the Thirteenth Amendment of any limitation on the states as found in the Fourteenth and Fifteenth Amendments[97] bespeaks the force and effect intended.

Under the Civil War amendments, Congress has the constitutional authority and obligation[98] to ameliorate the conditions of modern involuntary servitude— the arbitrary deprivation of life, liberty, and the pursuit of happiness guaranteed to all citizens but currently denied to citizens of African descent. Such authority exists and may be exercised under Congress's commerce power[99] and its "power to enforce" the Thirteenth Amendment.

In *Bolling v. Sharpe*,[100] the Court appropriately recognized that the rights extended under the Civil Rights amendments to former slaves and others of African descent already existed for all other citizens (nonminorities) under the due process clause of the Fifth Amendment. The *Slaughterhouse Cases* and *Bolling*, when properly read, make it clear that the *Croson* plurality has incorrectly assumed (and thereby continues the legal fiction) that the Fourteenth Amendment was intended to benefit those other than individuals of the "unfortunate race" rather than to remedy the conditions of those subject to "all shades and conditions" of "involuntary servitude."[101]

In any event, despite the *Croson* plurality's reading of the Fourteenth Amendment, the Thirteenth Amendment is the appropriate vehicle for both state and federal action to remove all vestiges of slavery and involuntary servitude in whatever "shades and conditions" it takes in the American fabric and in our daily lives.

The myopic view that our Constitution is colorblind does injustice to our history and the development of a jurisprudence with which to foster the ends all (opponents and advocates) seek: a society in which individuals are "not judged by the color of their skin but by the content of their character." The notion that, today, we all start equally or are competing on a level playing field is at best a fiction, and a dangerous fiction—one which belies the approach of many to "problems of color." To assume that racial equality was part of the framers' original intent or that it was a part of the prevailing circumstances prior to the adoption of the Civil War amendments is unseemly. If this were the case, then the Thirteenth, Fourteenth, and Fifteenth Amendments, which were intended directly to benefit "freedmen" only (and not those already recognized as citizens), would have been superfluous. Today, as a result of extension of the "original intent" doctrine in matters addressing race and discrimination (slavery and involuntary servitude) and notions through judicial pronouncements such as *Croson*, the Fourteenth Amendment, once a shield for those seeking full citizenship, has become a sword in the hands of nonminority plaintiffs with which to attack and dismember public and private efforts intended only to ameliorate discrimination. (The issues raised here go beyond the scope of this work but cannot be ignored.) To assume the amendments were intended to extend rights to those other than African slaves and their ancestors or those similarly situated— including other minorities—requires that the amendments become, as a practical consequence, null and void before they can effect the "correction and cure" of the constitutional defects that necessitated their adoption.

As was stated in *Associated General Contractors v. Altschuler*,[102]

The first Justice Harlan's much quoted observation that the "Constitution [is colorblind] . . . [and] does not . . . permit any public authority to know the race of those entitled to be protected in the enjoyment of such rights," *Plessy vs. Ferguson*, 163 U.S. 537, 554 (1896) (dissenting opinion), has come to represent a long term goal. *It is by now well understood, however, that our society cannot be completely colorblind in the short term if we are to have a colorblind society in the long term.* After centuries of viewing through colored lenses, eyes do not quickly adjust when the lenses are removed. Discrimination has a way of perpetuating itself; albeit unintentionally, because the resulting inequalities make new opportunities less accessible. Preferential treatment is one partial prescription to remedy our society's most intransigent and deeply-rooted inequalities. (Emphasis added.)[103]

Addressing such "intransigent and deeply-rooted inequalities" is certainly within the constitutional province of the Congress. But actions to eliminate the vestiges of slavery and all the rudiments and attributes of involuntary servitude are not Congress's exclusive domain. The states may act and are not prohibited from acting under the Thirteenth Amendment.

Remedies

[W]here there is a legal right, there is also a legal remedy, whenever that right is invaded.[104]

John Marshall

When the Congress has exercised its authority under Section 2 of the Thirteenth Amendment and Section 5 of the Fourteenth Amendment, it has done so to protect groups or classes of persons, not to serve individual interests. The Congress is addressing the institution and legacy of slavery as an ancient wrong and redressing grievances of those presently affected by establishing modern rights.[105]

In a provocative work, George Sher noted that Anglo-American law widely acknowledges that persons may be entitled to compensation for the effects of wrongful acts, private or public, performed even before their birth.[106] This should be the principle underlying our civil rights jurisprudence as the state engages in affirmative action.

In our American jurisprudence we have generally acknowledged that individuals may be entitled to compensation for the effects of actions wrongfully undertaken even before those harmed were born. The compensation provided often results in a redistribution of goods among the affected parties. Thus, as we address the present effects of past discrimination, we are really seeking to "restore a just distribution of goods among the affected parties" or to "nullify the effects of one particular set of inequities"—slavery and involuntary servitude.[107]

CONCLUSIONS

This almost altruistic goal is a means by which an individual or group otherwise privileged as a result of being member of a class will have the benefits nullified. One of the difficulties the Court has wrestled with has been the class-conscious nature of affirmative action programs. Such programs are established as a group rather than an individual remedy. And while it remains impossible to "right all of history's wrongs,'' we can act to nullify certain effects. That is what has become the principal pole-star guiding various affirmative action programs. Yet, in such ancient wrongs, an individual may not experience directly the actual conduct or injustices necessitating congressional action. Thus, actions taken to ameliorate the wrong may not spring from specific instances of discrimination as the ''ancient wrongs'' may predate the beneficiary's existence.

Under the legal doctrine followed in *Croson*, standing firmly upon the suspect jurisprudence of the equal protection doctrine as developed under the Fourteenth Amendment, the Court has created a judicial enigma. At the same time the Court is willing to recognize an ancient wrong, it has failed to permit a viable present remedy. The Court recognizes only a ''hypothetical right.'' This then is the defect of our current civil rights jurisprudence, a defect we now turn to the Congress to correct.

Croson, much like Court decisions that preceded it, must be viewed through the lens of future official action and judicial opinion to fully determine its impact.[108] As stated by William Beaney and his coauthor in 1964 and is appropriate today,

[I]t seems obvious that students of our legal system should not be satisfied with an acceptance of the official theory that court decisions, and particularly Supreme Court decisions that affect important public policy issues, are universally accepted as the law. It is grossly misleading and dangerous to treat law as a significant form of social control by concentrating on the rules handed down by courts. The realist persuasion in legal philosophy, if it has done nothing else, has warned us against ignoring the ways in which law affects or may leave untouched the daily lives of those to whom it ostensibly applies.

When a court decision impinges on an activity of only a few persons, the tracing of impact is a simple and obvious process. . . . But seldom [is] the question and the answer . . . so simple. The impact of decisions affecting behavior [is] difficult to trace because of the difficulty of observing post-decision conduct. If any conclusions are to be reached they must inevitably be based on the judgment of a few well-placed observers, or on the frequency of future cases where a breach of the rule of the earlier decision can be documented.[109]

Croson leaves a good deal to be desired in light of the judicial gloss respecting the purpose and reach of the Thirteenth and Fourteenth Amendments. Moreover, it represents the current status of our civil rights jurisprudence, wherein those singled out for special attention in order to obtain a position of citizenship similar to that already guaranteed to others are in jeopardy of losing any benefits to be so derived by the mere chant of ''reverse discrimination.'' Of course, the impact upon those not assisted by policies determining the distribution of government benefits is significant and even can be painful. However, we have repeatedly been able to accept such inequitable distributions in light of the public good and inherent policy considerations underlying the same. *Croson*, unfortunately, represents our inability to embrace the notion that ''involuntary servitude,'' the present effect of past discrimination, continues to prohibit the full participation of

African-Americans in our national commerce. Unfortunately, our ahistorical view of our own Constitution "appeals to the feelings and distorts the judgment."

However, for everything else it may be, *Croson* represents, sadly, another lost opportunity to realign our civil rights and affirmative action jurisprudence. *Croson* presented the opportunity for the Court to articulate fundamental doctrinal disagreement with the line of cases developed since *Regents of the University of California v. Bakke*,[110] which have created a *de facto* preeminence among the Civil War amendments within the Fourteenth Amendment (and its much heralded equal protection clause) at the cost of subjugating the Thirteenth Amendment to almost dead letter status. The underlying assumption of this misplaced preeminence is, of course, that the hereditaments of citizenship have finally been secured by all. This premise is simply not true. Any legal theory addressing the distribution of wealth, rights, and interests must of necessity consider this in the interpretation of constitutional rights and remedies. As a consequence, unfortunately, judicial actions designed to free all from involuntary servitude or second-class citizenship have become forums for declaring rights of whites platitudes. As a result, parties seeking judicial enforcement of long recognized rights find themselves and their counsel engaged in a labyrinth attempting to follow newly crafted evidentiary routes to a limited remedy. The Court, apparently enamored with statistical certainty, has embraced what one commentator appropriately calls a "process-based approach."[111] This leads to the conclusion that we must seek a substitution of the Fourteenth Amendment jurisprudence, acknowledging the Court's current affirmative action jurisprudence as an "unsatisfactory means by which to circumscribe the constitutional boundaries of affirmative action."[112]

NOTES

The original version of this chapter was presented at the University of Denver Graduate School of International Studies (GSIS) 1990 Spring Public Seminar Series, "The Underclass: Discrimination Against Minorities and State Policy," except this and other minor acknowledgments of the important decision of June 27, 1990, *Metro Broadcasting Inc. v. FCC*, which affirmed much of the legal analysis herein distinguishing federal from state action. The author wishes to express his appreciation to GSIS professors George Shepherd and Ved Nanda, the guiding spirits of the conference; David Penna, without whose efforts much would not have been accomplished; and friends of the university for sponsoring a most worthwhile enterprise. However, I am especially indebted to Carolyn Weatherly Scott, whose intellect and support helped nurture much, and to Lewis and Kathleen Dodds, whose wisdom and insight are matched by few. In addition, I owe a great deal to University of New Mexico professor Alfred D. Mathewson and attorney Earle F. Jones for their comments and engaging discussions over the years during which these issues were repeatedly raised and concepts and ideas shared. I am also greatly indebted to my colleagues who have commented on earlier thoughts, including professors John Carver, Edward Pringle, and John Reese; my secretary, Tori Coker; and other valuable members of the university family without whom faculty scholarship and work effort would not be nearly as productive, including Juli Richardson, Nancy Nones, and Vivienne Burrell. Last, but not least, I am appreciative of the efforts of my research assistants: Dona Chandler, Colin Clarke, and Roberta Wilcox. Without question, however, only I am accountable for the work and opinions expressed, as well as errors and omissions committed.

1. *Northern Securities Co. v. United States*, 193 U.S. 197, 400 (1903), Justice Oliver Wendell Holmes, dissenting.

2. __ U.S. __, 58 L.W. 5053 (1990).

3. 109 S. Ct. 706 (1989).

4. 349 U.S. 294 (1955).

5. 448 U.S. 448 (1980) (upholding the constitutionality of a set-aside program adopted by the Congress).

6. Harold Cruse, in his brilliant work *Plural but Equal* (New York: William Morrow, 1987), properly characterized the *Brown* decision as the zenith of "non-economic liberalism." As was inferred by Cruse, the Fourteenth Amendment, cited by the high court in 1954 to support the *Brown* decision, does not and cannot guarantee or enforce what *Brown* mandated.

7. Despite the Court's decision during the same term to review issues believed resolved in *Runyon v. McCrary*, 427 U.S. 160 (1976), its unlikely precedent controlled the Court's actions in *Croson*. What is unfortunate is the reliance Justice Sandra Day O'Connor placed upon the Fourteenth Amendment, revealing the tenuous position of minorities when total reliance for attaining full citizenship is placed upon the judiciary. Justice O'Connor's infidelity to her reasoning and opinion in *Croson* when dissenting in *Metro Broadcasting, Inc. v. FCC*, __ U.S. __, 58 L.W. 5053, 5067–5075 (1990), is much less amusing than her inconsistent voting whenever the Court is called upon to review civil rights as they pertain to women. If anything, the Court did indicate a willingness to turn from settled precedent in the area of civil rights. However, it is sometimes difficult to determine the impact of precedent upon the Court. Obviously, as easily as the Court can overrule prior decisions when the occasion strikes, as in *Patterson v. McClean Credit Union*, 109 S. Ct. 2363 (1989), the justices may review matters previously disposed of in order to reconsider earlier decisions. In *McClean* the Court reviewed the reach of the Civil Rights Act of 1866 to determine whether it permitted plaintiffs to reach discrimination in private contracts, an issue previously believed well settled by *Runyon*.

8. It is difficult not to draw comparisons between the Colombian drug lords' response of all-out war against the Colombia judicial system and intimidation through assassination of judges, and the letter bomb attacks against southern judges and civil rights lawyers by racist extremists in the United States.

9. 349 U.S. 294 (1955). The term "Civil War amendments" means the Thirteenth, Fourteenth, and Fifteenth Amendments to the U.S. Constitution.

10. Both advocates and opponents of affirmative action have misread this Court. The advocates, fearful of the Court's hesitancy to strike out at racially motivated discrimination against minorities, and the opponents, questioning actions intended to provide a class remedy, have mounted self-styled media actions dominated by newspaper headlines and prime-time news interviews that have only served to confuse the issues and the Court's holdings. This may be due in part to the preoccupation of both with counting victories, as if the decisions of the Court are not incremental and guided as much by what went

before as to what issues are now ripe for determination. As a result, both have exacerbated an already emotion-fueled debate.

11. Daniel A. Farber, "Statutory Interpretation, Legislative Inaction, and Civil Rights," *Michigan Law Review* 87, no. 2 (1988): 19. Although there is some room for disagreement and despite the differing roles between the legislative and judicial branches of government, much can be said for permitting greater legislative responsibility and authority as political participation by minorities increases.

12. *Webster v. Reproductive Health Services et al.*, ___ S. Ct. ___ (1989).

13. J. Tussman, ed., *The Supreme Court on Racial Discrimination* (New York: Oxford University Press, 1963), p. vii.

14. Derrick Bell, "The Supreme Court 1984 Term Forward: The Civil Rights Chronicles," *Harvard Law Review* 99, no. 4 (1984): 4.

15. Ibid. We only need look to November 7, 1989, when the state of Virginia elected its first African-American as governor, and the cities of New York and Seattle, among other political subdivisions, elected the descendants of slaves to mayoral positions. Interestingly, the first elected governor of African-American descent will lead his state from Richmond, the former capital of the confederacy. This followed, among other notable events, the impact of the Voting Rights Act of 1964 as evidenced by the confirmation hearings on the nomination and vote for confirmation of Robert Bork. We cannot now overestimate the importance of the Voting Rights Act of 1964, and we should realize the political forum should not sound the death knell for affirmative action. (Unfortunately, the jury is still out as to whether Justice Kennedy, who was confirmed without significant opposition, will be more harmful to fulfilling the promise of the Constitution and its bounty of rights for all Americans. I must agree with many scholars who now are exceedingly concerned about the junior justice, especially in light of his opinion in *Croson*. Some see the victory over the Bork confirmation as misplaced optimism similar to the initial euphoria over the *Brown* decision. As then NAACP attorney Thurgood Marshall estimated, after *Brown* it would take five years for the school desegregation case decision to be implemented. Thus, many assumed the defeat of the Bork nomination represented progress. In fact, neither represented progress for African-Americans. The *Brown* decision was no more significant than the "Bork victory." Bork's appointment to the Court could not have done more harm than the direction of the civil rights movement after *Brown*. Today, integration cases are still pending, and the condition of African-Americans has not improved dramatically.)

16. Previously, notions of the bundle of interests constituting "civil rights" inappropriately excluded business or commercial activities, generally being limited to traditional areas such as public accommodations, education, housing, and political franchise.

17. In his work regarding the *Croson* decision, Michael Rosenfeld defines distributive justice as "the fair distribution of benefits and burdens among members of a society" and can "denote both the *process* of distribution and the *product* of distribution." He also says compensatory justice "means the voluntary or involuntary exchange of equivalents designed to restore the equilibrium between two" or more persons. Michael Rosenfeld, "Decoding *Richmond*: Affirmative Action and the Elusive Meaning of Constitutional Equality," *Michigan Law Review* 87, no. 9 (June 1989): 1729, 1730.

18. 109 S. Ct. 706 (1989) at 717 (Justice O'Connor).

19. As used here "aftermath" means "everything taking place after a specified event," and "impact" refers to "all policy related consequences of a decision." Theodore

L. Becker and Malcolm M. Freeley, *The Impact of Supreme Court Decisions* (New York: Oxford University Press, 1969), pp. 211–13.

20. According to a report of the Minority Business Enterprise Legal Defense and Education Fund, Inc., since June of 1989, (i) nine state or city agencies have elected to "voluntarily terminate or suspend" existing programs, (ii) four agencies are contemplating major modifications, and (iii) twenty-one have programs "under re-evaluation." The report, "Visions: Strategies for Minority Business Development" (Minority Business Enterprise Legal Defense and Education Fund, 1990), is available from the author.

21. The bias, not different from that accompanying the Court's decision in *University of California Regents v. Bakke*, 438 U.S. 265 (1978), can be observed in the headline treatment given the story by the national media. Despite including substantial excerpts of the various opinions, the *New York Times* headlines incorrectly characterized the decision as one involving employment issues. The January 24, 1978, edition of the *Times* read, "Court Bars A Plan To Provide *Jobs* To Minorities" (emphasis added). Although it would be incorrect to assume *Croson* will not influence equal employment cases, it is a greater wrong to characterize the decision as defining the reach of federal law in job or employment circumstances being controlled more by statute than solely an interpretation of constitutional principles.

22. As reported in the January 25, 1989, edition of *The Indianapolis Star*, Mayor William Hudnut, indicating set-asides "are illegal in Indiana," distinguished the Indianapolis program from the Richmond Plan by noting Indianapolis uses goals while Richmond utilized a quota. *The Indianapolis Star*, January 25, 1989, p. 1. Despite the distinctions drawn by the mayor regarding "goals" and "quotas," under *Fullilove*, as affirmed in *Croson*, Congress may act to induce local and state agencies to establish affirmative action or set-aside programs in order to qualify for specific federal assistance, including funds and grants. See *Milwaukee County Pavers Assn. v. Fiedler*, 710 F. Supp. 1532 (W.D. Wis. 1989). Under certain federal assistance programs, such as those administered by the Department of Transportation (DoT)—including those providing federal assistance to all airports within our nation's air transportation system, such as Indianapolis's Weir-Cook International Airport or our national highways, grantees, states and their agencies—may be required to establish goals or set-asides to reach the participation of minority business firms necessary to qualify for certain federally assisted projects. See section 105(f) of the Airport and Airway Safety and Capacity Expansion Act of 1987, Pub. Law 100–223; or section 106(c) of the Surface Transportation and Uniform Relocation Assistance Act of 1987, Pub. Law 100–17. *Fiedler*, supra. Enforcement of such requirements are easily effected through the withholding of federal assistance under DoT regulations, 49 C.F.R. Sec. 23.83, and the Civil Rights Restoration Act of 1987, Pub. Law 100–259, 102 Stat. 28–32 (1988) (codified at various sections of 20 U.S.C., 29 U.S.C., and 42 U.S.C.).

23. Ordinance No. 83–69–59, codified in Richmond, Virginia, City Code Section 12–156(a) (1985).

24. *Croson* at 712–13.

25. Ibid. at 714.

26. Ibid. at 740–43, Justice Marshall, dissenting. As Justice Marshall noted, several witnesses, including those representing trade associations, a former mayor, and the city manager, testified as to local discrimination in the construction industry of Richmond. All this "against the backdrop of systematic nationwide racial discrimination which Congress has so painstakingly identified." Ibid. at 743.

27. Ibid. at 741–42.

28. Ibid. at 715.

29. Ibid. at 716.

30. 476 U.S. 267 (1986).

31. Justice Thurgood Marshall, "The Supreme Court 1986 Term—Commentary: Reflections in the Bicentennial of the United States Constitution, *Harvard Law Review* 101, no. 1 (1987): 5.

32. Certainly one clear monument to that response is the Civil Rights Act of 1990 (S. 2104/H.R. 4000) introduced on February 7, 1990, which but for a presidential veto would have altered procedural rules previously relied upon in civil rights cases, with the clear intent of reversing Supreme Court decisions during the 1988–1989 term. (However, conspicuous by its absence is the inclusion of a response to *Croson*, a subject for later discourse.)

33. The chief justice and Justice White joined in the entire opinion, while Justice Stevens only joined in Parts I, III-B, and IV, 109 S. Ct. at 730, and Justice Kennedy was unable to join in Part II, opining that the reach of congressional action was an issue not before the Court, ibid. at 734. Justice Scalia wrote separately concurring only in the judgment.

34. 109 S. Ct. at 735, Justice Scalia, concurring.

35. Ibid. at 739–57, Justice Marshall, dissenting.

36. 163 U.S. 537, 554 (1896).

37. 109 S. Ct. at 717.

38. *Croson* was the first time a majority of justices could agree as to a particular test to be applied. However, the majority is a slim and delicate one as Justice Stevens may not actually be a disciple of the O'Connor approach. 109 S. Ct. at 732.

39. See *Brown v. Board of Education*, 349 U.S. 294 (1955); *U.S. v. Montgomery Board of Education*, 395 U.S. 225 (1969); and *Swan v. Charlotte–Mecklenburg Board of Education*, 402 U.S. 1 (1971).

40. *Wygant v. Jackson Board of Education*, 476 U.S. at 274–76 (1986).

41. Justice Stevens acknowledged such a "public interest." 109 S. Ct. at 731.

42. *Croson* at 727. This, though, is a curious reading of the Constitution by the Court. It seems clear that societal discrimination was the target of the Civil War amendments, giving Congress in the Thirteenth Amendment the power to address both slavery and involuntary servitude and in the Fourteenth and Fifteenth Amendments the power to assure equal protection (impact?) of the laws and the right to vote, a most cherished and important element of citizenship.

43. Ibid. at 726–28.

44. 109 S. Ct. at 732–33, Justice Stevens.

45. Rosenfeld, "Decoding *Richmond*," pp. 1735–38, 1751–55.

46. Ibid., p. 1749. Rosenfeld attributes this belief to all justices—a belief that, as a conclusion, reads too much into the equal protection clause.

47. 448 U.S. 514–15, Justice Powell.

48. *Croson* at 720.

49. Ibid. at 737, Justice Scalia.

50. Justice O'Connor, joined by Chief Justice Rehnquist and Justice White, would find agreement in this point from the dissenters, Justices Marshall, Brennan, and Blackmun. Ibid. at 743, as well as 730–31, Justice Stevens.

51. It is unclear as to whether, on this issue, Justice Kennedy would join Justice

O'Connor. While not joining Part II and stating a preference for Justice Scalia's position, Kennedy rejected "a rule of automatic invalidity" in deference to precedence. *Croson* at 734.

52. *Wygant*, 476 U.S. at 274.

53. This is the position Justice Scalia took in his concurring opinion. *Croson* at 737.

54. Ibid. at 720.

55. *Fullilove* is consistent with the recent decision in *Metro Broadcasting*.

56. 109 S. Ct. at 726. Justice O'Connor wrote,

If the statistical disparity between eligible MBEs and MBE membership were great enough, an inference of discriminatory exclusion could arise. In such a case, the city would have a compelling interest in preventing its tax dollars from assisting these organizations in maintaining a racially segregated construction market. See *Norwood [v. Harrison]*, 413 U.S. at 465 [1973]; *Ohio Contractors [Assoc. v. Keip]*, 713 F. 2d at 171 [1983] (upholding minority set-aside based in part on earlier District Court findings that "the state had become a joint participant with private industry and certain craft unions in a pattern of racially discriminatory conduct which excluded black laborers from work on public construction contracts").

57. Pub. L. 95–28, 91 Stat. 116 (codified at 42 U.S.C. § 6701 et seq.).

58. 448 U.S. at 472.

59. 109 S. Ct. at 717. At 718–19, Justice O'Connor reasoned: "Congress' commerce power was sufficiently broad to allow it to reach the practices of prime contractors on federally funded local construction projects. [*Fullilove*] at 475–476. Congress could mandate state and local government compliance with the set-aside program under its § 5 power to enforce the Fourteenth Amendment. *Id.*, at 476 (citing *Katzenbach v. Morgan*, 384 U.S. 641, 651 [1966])."

60. 109 S. Ct. at 718–19. "Not only may [Congress] induce voluntary action to assure compliance with existing federal statutory or constitutional anti-discrimination provisions, but also, where Congress has authority to *declare certain conduct unlawful*, it may, as here, authorize and induce state action to avoid such conduct. Id., at 483–484. (Emphasis added.)"

61. 109 S. Ct. at 719.

62. Drew Days, "*Fullilove*," *Yale Law Journal* 96 (January 1987): 453, 454. Then a member of the Civil Rights Division of the Justice Department, Days participated in the presentation of the *Fullilove* case before the Supreme Court.

63. *Steelworkers v. Weber*, 443 U.S. 193 (1979).

64. *Jones v. Alfred H. Mayer Co.*, 392 U.S. 409 (1968).

65. *Croson* at 726, Justice O'Connor; *South Carolina v. Katzenbach*, 338 U.S. 301 (1966).

66. *Milwaukee County Pavers Assn. v. Fiedler*, 710 F. Supp. 1532 (W.D. Wis. 1989). In *Fiedler*, on motion of the state, the trial judge modified her earlier order enjoining the state set-aside program. Recent decisions in other circuits have also followed this logic.

67. Ibid. at 1545.

68. Pub. L. 97–424, 96 Stat. 2097, 2100.

69. 710 F. Supp. at 1539.

70. *Croson* at 724.

71. Ibid. at 724–25.

72. Ibid. at 748.

73. Ibid. at 727.

74. Cruse, *Plural but Equal*, pp. 29–30.

75. *Croson* at 712.

76. Ibid. at 730–31. Remember, Stevens did not embrace the "strict scrutiny" test.

77. What is agreeable is that the right of association under the First Amendment permits association by choice so long as it is social and does not create an economic privilege in one group or an economic disadvantage in the other. What many Americans forget or ignore is that school busing was not about the right of association; it was and is a temporary remedy until a remedy is found for housing discrimination and quality education.

78. As used here, a person is "advantaged" or assumes a position of privilege if others, based on race or irrelevant distinctions, are disadvantaged—that is, denied rights or benefits by law or *de facto*.

79. The term "ancient wrongs" should not be interpreted to assume discrimination is an artifact of history; it unfortunately is alive and well today. However, for convenience, unless otherwise stated, "ancient wrongs" includes current or present discrimination. It is only ancient based on the length of its life.

80. The Thirteenth Amendment provides

Section 1. Neither slavery nor involuntary servitude . . . shall exist within the United States, or any place subject to their jurisdiction.

Section 2. The Congress shall have power to enforce this article by appropriate legislation.

The Fourteenth Amendment provides, in material part, that

Section 1. All persons born or naturalized in the United States and subject to the jurisdiction thereof, are citizens of the United States and of the State wherein they reside. No state shall make or enforce any law which shall abridge the privileges or immunities of citizens of the United States; nor shall any state deprive any person of life, liberty, or property, without due process of law; nor deny to any person within its jurisdiction the equal protection of the laws.

Section 5. The Congress shall have power to enforce, by appropriate legislation, the provisions of this article.

The Fifteenth Amendment provides

Section 1. The right of citizens of the United States to vote shall not be denied or abridged by the United States or by any State on account of race, color, or previous condition of servitude.

Section 2. The Congress shall have power to enforce this article by appropriate legislation.

81. 60 U.S. 393 at 407 (1857).

82. 438 U.S. 265 (1978) (admission to medical school may be based, in part, on racial preference).

83. 443 U.S. 193 (1979) (affirming a voluntary preference by private employer).

84. As noted by Bell, the historian William Wiecek listed "ten different provisions" accommodating slavery and denying certain privileges and immunities to those of African-American ancestry. Some of the provisions are: Article I, Section 2, apportioning representatives in the House by counting three-fifths of the slaves but denying the slaves the right to vote; Article I, Section 9, prohibiting the abolition of slavery before 1808; and Article IV, Section 2, prohibiting the emancipation of fugitive slaves who were to be returned to their owners. Bell, "The Supreme Court," p. 34.

85. A. Leon Higginbotham, Jr., *In the Matter of Color: Race and the American Legal Process: The Colonial Period* (New York: Oxford University Press, 1978), p. 7.

86. The Fifteenth Amendment, ratified February 3, 1870, permitted all *men* regardless of "race, color or previous condition of servitude," the right to vote. The Nineteenth Amendment, which was ratified August 18, 1920, gave women the right to vote.

87. *Loving v. Virginia*, 388 U.S. 1, 11 (1967).

88. As discussed below, the equal protection doctrine is insufficient to address affirmative action. The limitations were eloquently exposed by Bell in his book *And We Are Not Saved: The Elusive Quest for Racial Justice* (New York: Basic Books, 1987), pp. 162–65. Although set forth in several chronicles, it does not appear more eloquently than in "The Chronicle of the Amber Cloud." This chronicle sets forth how a malady that strikes African-Americans is only worthy of national attention and the dedication of resources when it also afflicts the white populace. Also, if a cure is found and resources limited, the available treatment is distributed by the state within the communities dominated by whites almost to the exclusion of minorities. Finally, and coincidentally, the emergency is coterminous with the application within the white community.

89. 323 U.S. 214 (1944).

90. 476 U.S. 267 (1986).

91. *Ex Parte Virginia*, 100 U.S. 339 (1880).

92. *Katzenbach v. Morgan*, 384 U.S. 641, 651 (1966); *Civil Rights Cases*, 109 U.S. 3, 21 (1883).

93. 710 F. Supp. 1532 (W.D. Wis. 1989).

94. *Slaughterhouse Cases*, 83 U.S. 36 (1873).

95. The judicial gloss which has developed around the Fourteenth Amendment since the *Slaughterhouse Cases*, unfortunately, has caused that amendment to carry with it the excess baggage of protecting *all* citizens and not the African slaves and their descendants as originally intended.

96. *Slaughterhouse Cases*, 83 U.S. at 71–72.

97. See Section 1 of the Fourteenth Amendment.

98. *Croson* at 718–19 (citing *Fullilove* at 475–76).

99. U.S. Constitution, Article 1; see *Fullilove* at 475–76.

100. 347 U.S. 497 (1954). *Bolling*, the companion case to the infamous *Brown* decision, addressed discrimination in public education within the District of Columbia.

101. 83 U.S. 36 (1873).

102. 490 F. 2d 9 (1st Cir. 1973) *cert. den.* 416 U.S. 957 (1973).

103. Ibid. at 16.

104. *Marbury v. Madison*, 1 Cranch 137, 163 (1803).

105. See George Sher, "Ancient Wrongs and Modern Rights," *Philosophy and Public Affairs* 10, no. 1 (Winter 1981): 3.

106. Ibid.

107. Ibid., p. 5.

108. As noted earlier, while "aftermath" refers to judicial decisions taking place immediately after *Croson*, "impact" refers to responses within and outside the judiciary (including political reaction from both the legislative and executive departments of the various states and federal government), is yet unknown.

109. William Beaney and Edward Beiser, "Prayer and Politics: The Impact of Engel and Schempp on the Political Process," *Journal of Public Law* 13 (1964): 374.

110. 438 U.S. 265 (1978) (race may be considered as a comparative factor, among others, when determining admission to a state university).

111. Rosenfeld, ''Decoding *Richmond*,'' p. 1729 (June 1989).

112. Ibid.

CHAPTER 4

Free Speech and Ethnic Intimidation: A Preliminary Inquiry

DAVID PENNA AND JOSE BLAS LORENZO

Human rights can be defined most simply as those rights that individuals have solely by virtue of their membership in the human race. These rights are not those of a particular nationality, sex, class, or gender but rather those of all human beings without distinction. What, then, does it mean to speak of the human rights of the underclass?

It certainly does not mean that the human rights possessed by members of the underclass are something more or less than the human rights belonging to members of other classes, at least in theory. It may, however, mean that the human rights of this group may need special protective measures due to the disadvantageous situation of the underclass in modern society. At the same time, these special measures must not destroy the human rights of other individuals or, indeed, individual members of the underclass. This chapter focuses on the appropriate special measures for implementing the human rights of the underclass to be free of racist speech while at the same time preserving the rights of all individuals to free speech.

The recognition of even a basic list of human rights suggests that no single human right can be absolute since, when stated broadly, human rights often conflict with one another. The conflict between the right of free speech and the right to be free from racist speech presents itself more starkly than is common. Both of these rights are recognized under international law, and both of these rights are of particular importance to the underclass. The right to free speech is important in that it provides a means for members of the underclass to articulate their demands for the change of a system they do not control and in which their social, political, and economic participation has been marginalized. The guarantee of free speech alone, however, obviously does not guarantee that their demands will be acted upon.

The right to be free from racist speech is also of particular importance to the underclass, who, composed in large measure of racial and ethnic minorities, are often the subject of such speech. Racist speech can be used not only to injure individual class members in an emotional sense (as well as the possibility that such speech may lead to physical violence) but may also serve as an underlying rationalization among the dominant classes for the maintenance of conditions that produce an underclass. Additionally, racist speech within the underclass can be used as a divisive wedge to prevent the unification of diverse racial and ethnic elements in demanding an end to exploitative economic, social, and political conditions.

Freedom of speech is guaranteed by both international legal instruments and by the U.S. Constitution.[1] Freedom from racist speech—that is, the "advocacy of national, racial or religious hatred that constitutes incitement to discrimination, hostility or violence"—is protected under international law,[2] but the U.S. Constitution has no analogous provision. The U.S. Senate, in considering the ratification of the International Convention on Civil and Political Rights, has indicated its understanding that in the event of a conflict between the provisions of the Convention and the Constitution, the Constitution (i.e., free speech) rules.

Even given the dubious attitude of the Senate and the executive administration toward the right to be free from racist speech, and despite settling the conflict in favor of free speech, the government still has duties to fulfill this right. We argue in this chapter that while we believe the U.S. Constitution (with or without the stipulation included in future ratification of the Convention) would prevent the state from banning racist speech, such a prohibition would not be effective public policy. However, the prohibition of racist speech is only one method of dealing with the problem of racist speech. The state can fulfill its international requirements under the Convention by taking other measures to prevent racist speech. Indeed, we submit that these measures are not only good policy but are required as special protective measures to assure the provision of human rights to the underclass. These measures are indeed required by the special circumstances of the underclass. We now turn to a consideration of these circumstances.

THE PROBLEM OF RACIALLY OFFENSIVE SPEECH IN THE UNITED STATES

The great strides made in the civil rights movements of the 1950s and 1960s stalled in the 1980s.[3] The cause of the halt in the march toward racial equality in the United States is the subject of much debate. Some credit neoconservative leaders such as Ronald Reagan, while others see the problem as one of the resistance of threatened middle- and lower-class whites.[4] Regardless of the cause, this phenomenon has been called the white backlash to affirmative action.

Associated with this backlash are increasing incidents of violence against racial, ethnic, and religious minorities. Coupled with such violence is heightened racial tension. In such an atmosphere, racial, ethnic, or religious remarks of a derogatory nature often precede and/or follow such violent incidents. It is unclear whether these remarks can be considered a cause or an effect of the violence itself. Still, there is an apparent link between words and deeds.

The use of overtly racist remarks is often seen as contributing to the atmosphere of tension, thereby contributing to the circumstances that encourage the actual outbreak of violence. Symbolic speech is also significant, considering the feelings people of different races may attach to symbols such as the Confederate flag.[5]

A particularly volatile situation has arisen where speech has traditionally been the freest: on college campuses.[6] At least part of the problem seems to be related to perception and sensitivity. According to one campus survey, 20 percent of minority students had experienced personal harassment. Further, 74 percent of members of some minority groups were aware of racist incidents on campus, compared to less than 35 percent of the nonminority students.[7] Insensitivity to the concerns of minorities was also illustrated in a recent national poll of blacks and whites. When asked if blacks were treated equally by the justice system, only 30 percent of whites thought blacks were treated less equally, while 65 percent of blacks felt they were treated less equally. Similar results were also evident in the perception of the treatment of blacks with regard to employment opportunities.[8]

This has resulted in a variety of approaches to deal with the increase in racial tension and violence, including attempts to prohibit racist speech in different fora. These attempts to restrict permissible speech are discussed in a later section of this chapter.

For the purpose of this chapter, it is useful to distinguish among different types of racist speech. One type of racist speech we call a slur. It can be viewed as a generalized derogatory comment about an individual or group. A second general category can be called threats. These remarks carry with them the promise of action. Finally, a third category is words that are accompanied by action. These three types of racial remarks can either be directed at an individual or at a group, resulting in a typology of six classes of racial remarks. While these distinctions among different types of remarks are not always as clear in practice, this classification scheme will prove useful in both understanding the legal basis for permitting or criminalizing racist speech and evaluating the desirability of restricting racist speech.

One way to restrict racist speech is to criminalize such speech. Criminalization would subject the speaker of racist remarks to a criminal trial and, if convicted, to face fines, imprisonment, or other punishment. A second alternative is to permit the victim of the racist remark to seek compensation for injuries caused by the racist remarks. This alternative can be employed in addition to criminalization, but the burden and costs of enforcement would fall upon the victim and not the state. This alternative would restrict racist speech through imposing financial costs upon those who choose to utter racist remarks; the added financial burden would serve as an incentive to refrain from making racist remarks. Finally, a program of education can be pursued to attempt to change the attitudes of racists, thereby removing their desire to utter racist remarks. Again, this strategy is not exclusive of the others.

RESTRICTING RACIST SPEECH

Foreign Attempts to Limit Racist Speech

Speech that is derisive of an individual's racial, religious, or ethnic heritage is proscribed by several international legal instruments.[9] States are given a positive duty to protect individuals from such speech, and such speech is not considered to be within the free speech guarantees provided by the other articles of these human rights instruments.[10] Therefore, in the broadest sense, international law avoids the conflict between free speech and racial intimidation by explicitly defining the conflict out of existence. Racist speech is simply not considered "speech." Unfortunately, these same instruments have neglected to specifically define what speech is properly to be considered as racist. Still, the international instruments have served as the basis for national legislation prohibiting racist speech in many countries.

Many Western European nations have group libel laws that prohibit the slander or mockery of groups of people based upon race, ethnic background, or religion.[11] Other nations, including Australia, West Germany, Greece, Italy, and the states of Eastern Europe, prohibit racist organizations.[12] Some nations' laws are modeled directly on Article 4 of the Convention on the Elimination of Racial Discrimination, such as those of Spain and the Philippines.[13]

The law in force in Sweden and throughout Scandinavia limits free speech through prohibiting the defamation of identifiable groups.[14] This type of law prohibits slurs, even when directed against a group rather than an individual. Recently, a news report from Sweden indicated that a Moroccan man had been sentenced to six months' imprisonment for "disparaging and deeply offending" comments about Jews on a radio station.[15] However, such laws are rarely used, and this was only the second conviction under the Swedish law. In fact, a 1983 Swedish government commission warned that overemployment of such provisions risked narrowing the "scope for objective public debate even on the frequently sensitive matters related to minority groups."[16]

Another nation with such laws is Canada. Canada recognizes the crimes of public incitement of hatred and willful promotion of hatred.[17] The former provision is linked to actions in that it is only punishable when "likely to lead to a breach of the peace,"[18] while the latter punishes speech that "willfully promotes hatred against any identifiable group."[19] Therefore, the second provision punishes slurs against groups.[20]

While space does not permit a full discussion of the Canadian laws, it suffices to note that these and similar laws have been the subject of vigorous constitutional and academic debate over the last several years, in both the courts and law journals.[21] Several comments are in order. First, the permissibility of these provisions given the Canadian Charter of Rights and Freedoms, the Canadian equivalent of the U.S. Bill of Rights, is called into question.[22] Second, these provisions, as the ones in Sweden, have rarely been invoked. One source contends that there have been no more than six prosecutions under these offenses since their adoption in 1970 in Canada.[23] Finally, the criminalization of hate propaganda in Canada has not resulted in a decrease in such propaganda there. Instead, there has been a reported substantial increase.[24]

Related to laws prohibiting racist remarks are antiblasphemy laws in other countries, though often these laws are designed to protect the sensibilities of the majority from attacks by the minority. Still, such laws rest on the same principles as the laws prohibiting racist speech: the maintenance of public order, the protection from mental anguish, and the elimination of discrimination. Blasphemy laws remain in England and India and have recently been brought up in discussions of the Salman Rushdie affair.[25] It should be noted, however, that while such blasphemy laws have been criticized,[26] they have been upheld by the European Commission on Human Rights to be in accordance with the European Convention on Human Rights' guarantee of freedom of thought and expression. While these laws do not technically prohibit racist remarks, by protecting religious doctrine, they attempt to curtail religious and ethnic hatred.

Perhaps the most spectacular case of criminalization of hate propaganda has been in Israel. Antihate propaganda laws were developed there in large part as a response to the activities of Rabbi Meir Kahane who had been elected to Parliament in 1984 on an extremist, anti-Arab platform. A law was passed preventing racist parties from standing for election to the Knesset as well as laws criminalizing the publication or possession of racist literature.[27] This would include literature that contains racist slurs directed at either groups or individuals. The Israeli laws, taken as a whole, seriously restrict political debate, as they permit the silencing of a member of Parliament. While the majority of people in a democracy may indeed be disgusted by the views expressed by Kahane and his party, the implications of such laws must be examined more closely.

Two comments should be noted in this regard. First, the same law that is used to silence Kahane can be used to silence those in Israel that express pro-Palestinian sympathies. Second, if such laws were to be adopted by other Third World nations, they may in fact be used to silence any support for Israel, given that the United Nations has passed a resolution equating Zionism with racism. Therefore, it is clear that these laws can be said to generate differing levels of support depending upon whose ''racist'' is being silenced.

There are several points that need to be highlighted here. First, the criminalization of racist speech has not been shown to be an effective method of curbing racist speech. Nor has criminalization been effective at eroding the underlying ideology of racism that pervades most modern societies. The reason for this ineffectiveness may be linked to a second shortcoming of criminalization: Those nations that have enacted antiracist laws rarely use them. This may be due to several factors. Institutionalized racist values may mitigate against the punishment of racism per se. Priorities in spending scarce enforcement finances may prohibit expending the necessary funding to investigate and prosecute cases of racist speech since the dominant class or group is likely to see the harm in most cases of racist speech as *de minimis*. Third, the standards that are to be used in defining racist speech are either nonexistent or vague. This vagueness only complicates the task of the prosecutor and often calls into question the validity of the criminalization attempt itself. Poor definitions of racist speech often permit the racist to continue to spread his or her racist views through operating in the gray areas that are likely to be uncovered by the law. Therefore, it can be contended that these laws may give a society a false sense of security against racism.

Finally, these laws can be seen as presenting a positive danger to society. By permitting the government to curb speech through vaguely defined laws against racism, the government can interpret these laws to suit its political convenience. This is not an unlikely extremist scenario; a similar scenario has already taken place in the recent conservative Supreme Court decisions on discrimination that employ constitutional provisions to strike down affirmative action plans as discriminatory against whites.

While this survey of foreign laws may be useful to indicate how other nations deal with racial incitement, it is doubtful that any of these laws can be directly transplanted to the United States. The reason for this is the protection to free speech given in the First Amendment of the U.S. Constitution. Free speech protection in the United States is arguably more extensive than in any country surveyed thus far. The contours of that protection are explored in the next section.

CONSTITUTIONAL PROTECTION FOR RACIST SPEECH IN THE UNITED STATES

There are several important principles of First Amendment doctrine that are relevant to attempts to restrict racist speech. It should be noted that content-based regulation is treated unfavorably under the First Amendment since this is seen as a hindrance to the search for truth.

The Constitution of the United States declares "Congress shall make no law abridging the freedom of speech, or the press." Freedom of speech has been seen as essential not only to the democratic process itself but also to protecting the other liberties in the Bill of Rights.[28] The freedom to voice opinions and learn from differing views is considered essential to the American political system. However, not all speech receives constitutional protection; case law establishes limits on what speech is protected by the Constitution. Still, there is a strong presumption that it is better to permit speech than to restrict it.

The idea of free trade of ideas is implied by the Constitution.[29] Truth has been historically perceived as a social goal, resulting from a free exchange of ideas.

Therefore, any but the most necessary restrictions of speech are seen as contrary to the purpose of the Constitution.

The freedom to think and speak as one thinks is accepted as an indispensable means to the discovery and spread of political truth.[30] Thomas Jefferson noted that it is safer "if others are left free to demonstrate errors, especially when the laws stands ready to *punish the first criminal act produced by the false reasoning*" (emphasis added).[31] Courts in the United States have stressed that "fear breeds repression; that repression, in hand, breeds hate; that hate menaces stable governments; that the path of safety lies in the opportunity to discuss freely supposed grievances and proposed remedies."[32] These fears of restricting speech are not without exceptions. These exceptions seem to be more numerous during times of increased national stress such as war. During peacetime, however, the scope of constitutionally protected speech is very broad.

Regulation of Content

Despite the presumption favoring free speech, most commentators concede that speech can be justifiably curtailed in situations of grave danger. This conception was expressed in this most popular form by Justice Oliver Wendell Holmes in 1919: "The question in every case is whether the words used are used in such circumstances and are of such a nature as to create a *clear and present danger* that they will *bring about the substantive evils* that Congress has a right to prevent [emphasis added]."[33] If so, the speech can be restricted according to Justice Holmes.

Freedom of speech has been curtailed most when it is considered to impair the social interest of national security. A state is empowered to curtail that which *incites or produces imminent lawless action and is likely to incite or produce such action*. In order for the state to have such power, the circumstances must be such that they justify the apprehension that action will occur.[34] This advocacy must be related to the probability of the speech producing violent action.[35] Those to whom the advocacy is addressed must be urged to do something and not just believe in something.

The clear and present danger test has been modified. The elements to consider before speech is prohibited are (1) whether the advocacy is directed to inciting or producing imminent lawless action and (2) whether the advocacy is likely to incite or produce such action.[36] This clarification specifically established that mere abstract teaching of a violent action is not the same as preparing for such action.[37]

The purpose of the First Amendment is to ensure the free exchange of ideas; arguably speech that does not further this goal is not protected. Traditionally, regulation of speech has centered around a series of sometimes bewildering questions. Several dichotomies have become significant in determining if speech is protected. As Rodney A. Smolla notes:

Free speech jurisprudence often seems a collage of confusing bipolar choices: Is it speech or conduct? Does it communicate thought or emotion? Does the regulation state facts or opinion? Is the regulation content-based or content-neutral? Is the government property a forum or non-forum? Is the speech political or nonpolitical? Commercial or noncommercial? For adults or children?[38]

While most of these jurisprudential dichotomies were originally fashioned to protect speech considered essential to the rationale underlying the First Amendment, rigid application of these distinctions can lead to anomalous results.

One example may be the "fighting words" exception to protected speech. States can punish outbreaks of violence; they can also seek to prevent such outbreaks. Therefore, if an individual, in a face-to-face confrontation with another, speaks words that would ordinarily provoke a violent response, the state can punish such speech in an effort to keep the peace.[39] However, in a different context, for example in a political speech before a crowd, such a doctrine may provide for a "heckler's veto" or even a veto of hecklers. This results in the limitation of unpopular ideas and hinders the search for "truth." The difficulty is in drawing a meaningful line between those instances where speech contributes to this search and where it does not. The problem becomes more complex when individuals or groups wish to air provocative or even hateful messages that the majority denies are a legitimate part of the political debate. An example of this scenario was present when the National Socialist Party marched in the predominantly Jewish suburb of Skokie, Illinois.[40] It was argued that when a speaker intrudes on the privacy of an individual, such intrusion is not protected speech. Others maintained that if the receiver of the speech has the opportunity to avoid the speech, his or her privacy has not been intruded upon. This imposes on the victim the burden of avoiding exposure, especially if exposure is likely to incite violence.

Along with this proviso, speech that is coupled with action may be considered symbolic speech and is protected by the First Amendment. Such actions can include dramas, salutes or refusals to salute, or burning a flag or a cross. It is the action of violence leading to injury that is not protected. Thus, there is a distinction between "pure speech" and "conduct as speech." The latter may be considered as a symbolic expression and thus protected by the Constitution.

However, where "nonspeech" and "speech" are combined in conduct, a government can regulate the nonspeech so long as it has important or substantial governmental interest.[41] For example, burning a flag cannot be prohibited unless such burning endangers or involves bystanders, the destruction of government property, or the property of others. When such action physically injures, criminal laws regarding intimidation, assault, and battery become effective.

Having considered the importance of speech to society itself, it must also be noted that unregulated speech can be a burden upon the members of society. That which is written, printed and seen, or spoken and heard may constitute a legal wrong under which an individual may recover damages.[42] In order to do so, there must be malicious intent to disseminate a false statement that injures the reputation of another and does not further the exchanges of ideas nor seek the truth. Hence, a defamatory racial statement must meet this criteria.

Unless the language of a defamatory publication is directed at a small group such as to apply to every member of the group without exception, it may be that no member of a group has a cause of action. A defamatory statement must be directed at a specific individual in order for there to be redress. This is because injury must be specifically proven in most instances. Courts require a good deal of particulars, especially in the slander and libel cases: The complaint must set forth precisely in what way the special damage resulted from the spoken or written words. It is not sufficient to allege generally that the plaintiff has suffered special damages or that the party has been put to great costs and expenses.

The Supreme Court decision *Beauharnais v. Illinois*, however, noted that a statute prohibiting propaganda that portrayed lack of virtue of a class of citizens was valid.[43] The Court's characterization of the words prohibited by the statute as those "liable to cause violence and disorder" paraphrases the traditional justification for punishing libels criminally, namely their "tendency to cause breach of peace."[44] In *Beauharnais*, the speech in question attacked the mayor's policies favoring integration, invoking racist images in its circulars.

The Court in *Beauharnais* assumed that speech that defames race or religion may be considered as inherently productive of violence, so it is unnecessary to show that it is used in a personally provocative manner. Courts today might decide contrary to *Beauharnais* because the speech was politically oriented toward the mayor's policies. Thus, the speech itself had political appeal. It was concerned with the effect that the mayor's policies were having in Chicago. In essence, *Beauharnais* attempts to restrict what should be considered political. Since *New York Times v. Sullivan*, the soundness of *Beauharnais* has been questioned.[45] *Sullivan* establishes the requirement of malicious intent when the defamed individual is a public figure. Thus, the criticism of public officials is protected to allow for genuine public debate on political issues and pertaining to an official's public conduct.

Court decisions repeatedly state that "if there is a bedrock principle underlying the First Amendment, it is that the Government may not prohibit the expression of an idea simply because society finds the ideas itself offensive or disagreeable."[46] However, if this is so, what can be said about group libel, especially since racist remarks are directed at the underclass?

The marketplace of ideas approach is a guiding constitutional principle in Supreme Court jurisprudence. This does not, however, mean that other First Amendment principles cannot be found that conflict with the seemingly absolute protection of speech. For example, almost every advocate of limiting speech has quoted the Holmes example that freedom of speech does not protect those who would yell "Fire!" in a crowded theater. Since this example is so well known, it will be useful to examine it more closely while keeping in mind the limits of reasoning by analogy.

Did Justice Holmes mean that no one could scream "Fire!" in a crowded theater? Certainly not. Obviously if there were actually a fire, a person would be justified in sounding the alarm, even though this would likely panic the patrons and endanger their lives in a rush to the exits. The cry of "Fire!" is justified since it seeks to alert the audience to an actual and probably greater harm. Justice Holmes obviously envisioned a case where the speaker knew there was no fire and sought to panic the theater patrons for his or her own enjoyment. These are the two polar examples.

On a continuum between these examples we may envision other cases. What if the speaker smells smoke, but there is, in fact, no fire? If he screams to alert others can he or she be held responsible, under Holmes's rationale, for a stampede of patrons? It would seem not, since the speaker's actions were reasonable under the circumstances.

Another situation would exist where the speaker's words would not seem so reasonable. Imagine a speaker with an irrational fear of fire, perhaps due to an unpleasant childhood experience. The speaker is convinced he or she smells smoke and shouts "Fire!" thus panicking the audience. Is the speaker's speech protected? This case is certainly much different from the one envisioned by Justice Holmes where the amused speaker watches chuckling as the crowd rushes to the exits. Here the speaker is probably a part of the panic-stricken crowd seeking to flee. It would be difficult to argue that the speaker's cry is not protected in this case.

At the risk of stretching this analogy, we can apply it to racist speech. While we cannot accept the racist's words as true, the fact is that he or she probably is thoroughly convinced of their verity. Perhaps the belief is due to emotional or psychological problems. Punishing racists will be unlikely to deter them from speaking their "truth" in the future, unless some sort of reeducation is instituted that helps the racist overcome his or her irrational fear or hatred. Therefore, criminalization of racist speech is contrary to principles underlying First Amendment jurisprudence, and it is likely to be ineffective in deterring future racist speech.

Recent Efforts at Curbing Racial Intimidation

There have been several recent efforts at the state level to criminalize racial intimidation. None has been entirely successful; some provisions have been tested and sustained by lower courts, but the majority of the statutes have failed to pass constitutional challenges.

Much of the attention has focused on racial intimidation on college campuses.[47] Traditionally, college campuses have tolerated a wide range of speech officially, though unofficial sanctions and pressures may have presented a limiting influence on the spectrum of speech actually tolerated. The recent trend has been officially to prohibit racist speech. Restrictions on racial remarks on campuses have been reported at Tufts, Emory, Penn State, Brown, Trinity College, and the Universities of Connecticut, Michigan, North Carolina (Chapel Hill), Wisconsin, Massachusetts (Amherst), California (Berkeley), and Pennsylvania.[48]

A recent example is the case of the University of Michigan.[49] A law prohibited verbal and physical behavior that "stigmatizes or victimizes an individual" on a number of bases, including race and national origin. In *Doe v. University of Michigan*,[50] a student charged under the statute claimed the statute was an unconstitutional violation of protected speech. The court ruled that part of the statute reached protected speech in violation of the First Amendment and was also unconstitutionally vague in violation of the due process clause. The judge ruled that the university could not "establish an anti-discrimination policy that had the effect of prohibiting certain speech because it disagreed with [the] ideas or messages" communicated in that speech.[51] The court did, however, find that the statute was constitutional with regard to the prohibition of physical conduct and behavior.

Even more recently, the New York Court of Appeals, the highest state court in New York, struck down a law on abusive language. The law was not specifically targeted at ethnic or racial intimidation but at abusive and obscene language generally. A woman had been convicted under the law for calling a retarded neighbor a "bitch" and her son a "dog" and threatened to "beat the shit out of them." The 17-year-old woman was convicted on the basis of her words alone under the statute. Her words did not have to be construed to constitute a "serious" threat of physical harm. The New York Court of Appeals overturned the conviction and held that the statute reached protected speech and permitted defendants to be prosecuted for their words alone. The court found that another part of the statute that allowed conviction for physical acts such as striking, shoving, or kicking was constitutional because the prohibited acts were more than a crude outburst of speech.

In the past, the New York statute had been used to arrest the homeless and had also been employed against demonstrators who shouted "pig" or cursed at police.[52] The Michigan and New York cases indicate that courts are likely to find unconstitutional most attempts to criminalize slurs, while justification can be found to punish speech that amounts to threats or is linked with otherwise criminal action.

In 1989 the State University of New York also sought to control racial tensions on its campuses. Rather than relying on an approach of banning abusive or intimidating language, however, it planned a program of education and dialogue to defuse tensions after the occurrence of racial incidents. The plan included more financing for the promotion of ethnic holidays, the development of "racial climate" committees, and task forces that were to be sent to campuses after racial incidents. These task forces were to work with local committees to organize activities to promote racial understanding.[53] Since this program has been only recently implemented, it is too early to evaluate its results.

Similar types of education and understanding programs have been undertaken after racist incidents on the campus of the University of Colorado.[54] Still, racial incidents continue; a black C.U. coed was placed under police protection after receiving harassing racist phone calls. Her apartment had been burglarized, and racist slurs were scribbled on her bed sheets.[55] In another incident, another black female C.U. student was confronted by a white Boulder resident who allegedly made racial slurs at her and then attempted to hit her.[56] The man was charged under Colorado's felony ethnic intimidation law.[57]

The case, however, has not been pursued, at first because the defendant fled the state, and then because it was reported that the defendant suffered from paranoid schizophrenia and was receiving hospital treatment.[58]

The Colorado law provides for a misdemeanor offense if, with intent to intimidate another due to the victim's race, color, religion, ancestry, or national origin, a person knowingly places the victim in fear of an imminent lawless action. This action must threaten the victim's person or property, and the words or conduct of the attacker must be likely to produce such an injury or such damage.[59] It is clear, therefore, that this law does not punish all racist remarks. It requires that the defendant knowingly intimidate the victim through threats to the person or property and that the defendant be likely to be able to carry out the threat. Finally, such a threat is only punishable as a misdemeanor offense. It is submitted that this offense in reality does not reach conduct that is not otherwise punishable under other provisions of the criminal code. It does not punish the slur alone.

ANALYSIS

It seems clear that in the foreign countries surveyed, it has become acceptable to punish racial slurs. Since the criminalization of slurs is the most controversial aspect of limiting racist speech, these nations have banned the entire spectrum of racist speech.

The situation in the United States is much more complex. The prevalent view is that most unsavory types of speech, including racist slurs, are protected by the Constitution. This is not true of speech that constitutes threats or is linked with action. The different types of crimes linked to the different types of speech are indicated in Table 4.1.

Criminalization is not the only way to attack racist speech. Civil remedies may lie in some cases to compensate individuals injured by racist speech. These actions are still subject to constitutional limitations, but since these actions often have more stringent requirements regarding injury and malice than the criminal provisions discussed so far, they can withstand constitutional scrutiny in most cases. Such actions would include libel and slander for racial slurs, intentional infliction of emotional distress or outrageous conduct for both slurs and threats, and perhaps intentional torts for words linked with actions. The variety of civil remedies potentially available to the victims of racist speech in the United States is illustrated in Table 4.2.

In all cases, some injury, whether physical or financial, must be proven as a

Table 4.1
Criminalization of Racist Speech in the United States

	Directed at Individuals	Directed at Groups
Slurs	Criminal Libel (?)	Crim. Group Libel (?)
Threats	Intimidation Assault	Intimidation
Plan/Action	Assault, etc.	Assault, Genocide

Table 4.2
Civil Remedies for Racist Speech in the United States

	Directed at Individuals	Directed at Groups
Slurs	Libel, Slander	Group Libel (?)
Threats	Intentional In-fliction of Emotional Distress	?
Plan/Action	Intentional Torts	?

result of the defendant's conduct. There is a traditional reluctance to extend protection to injuries or mental distress that do not have physical manifestations.[60] A problem with the utilization of civil actions to curtail racist speech is that the compensation awarded is likely to be minimal in most cases,[61] and, considering the costs of litigation and documenting injury and causation, widespread use of these actions is likely to be precluded.

CONCLUSIONS

According to international law and practice, it is acceptable, and perhaps obligatory, to prohibit racist slurs.[62] It is equally clear that in most instances the curtailment of such speech would likely be considered an impermissible content-based restriction on free speech. Is there any way to reconcile international and U.S. practice, and, if not, is the high level of protection given to racist speech in the United States merited?

What are the objectives of banning racist speech? If one considers racist slurs, the justifications for their prohibition are at least twofold. First, the suppression of racist slurs can be seen as a way of combatting racism and its most obvious manifestation, discrimination. The most hated crimes of the twentieth century have been justified through racist ideologies. These crimes include genocide, apartheid, and colonialism. While these crimes are themselves outlawed, it is felt that insufficient protection is provided by waiting to attack these crimes until racism is manifested in action.

Certainly racist beliefs present formidable dangers to the international community and the United States in particular. However, it also seems clear that the banning of racist speech, such as slurs, is an ineffective method of combatting the underlying ideology of racism. Ideas are not banished by outlawing them but by demonstrating their falsity. Therefore, in order to combat racist beliefs, open expression of beliefs should be encouraged. The solution to this dilemma is more speech, not less.

A second and more compelling justification for prohibiting racist slurs concerns their effect on individual members of racial groups who are subject to racist slurs. An individual's sense of self-worth as well as his or her conception of his or her relationship to society can be seriously affected by repeated racial slurs.[63] This problem is complicated by the differential effect on individuals; not all individuals react in the same way to racist speech. Some may internalize the problem, while others may react with visible anger and hostility.[64] Some may strive to overcome racism through confrontation, while others may withdraw in order to avoid being subjected to racist insults.[65] It is likely, however, that criminalization is not the answer here either. Since racist insults can take a great variety of forms, and these forms are constantly changing, it is unlikely that an acceptable definition of racist speech can be constructed. Further, to leave the government to apply a vague standard is to invite encroachment on liberty. One lawyer remarks:

We live in a racist society, which is why you can't trust the people in power to make distinctions about which speech should be permitted. We just got through eight years of a national government that believed affirmative action was reverse discrimination against whites. . . .

Ours is still a white society defending its historical racism. We can't control how they will interpret these rules. No one should have any confidence in our law-enforcement apparatus. To rely on the Supreme Court and the dominant political majority to make good decisions about restricting speech is to live in a dream world.[66]

This chapter, however, does not conclude that inaction is appropriate. Several steps should be taken that may have the ultimate effect of curtailing racism and racist speech, though not through directly banning either speech or belief. As indicated above in the discussion of the Colorado law on racial intimidation, threats and racist remarks linked with action are already punishable under existing provisions of law. Given the increasing problem of racism in the United States, it would seem justified to increase the penalty for either threats or actions that are racially motivated. This does not necessarily involve changing any of the elements of the offense but merely finding the motivation of race hatred as an aggravating factor so that a conviction will entail a longer sentence or a higher fine.

Another alternative would involve defining racial assault or racial intimidation as a separate crime from assault or menacing, as has been done in Colorado. While the resulting imprisonment and fines are identical to the first alternative, the enumeration of a separate crime can have value in itself. It may encourage prosecutors to punish such offenses more often than under a generic statute. It will also send a signal to racists that such conduct will not be tolerated as well as inform victims of such attacks that the law will protect them.

Under either of these alternatives, additional measures would also be warranted. Increased public education programs concerning not only legal rights but also ones that provide for intercultural and interracial understanding would seem to be appropriate, particularly after incidents that raise racial tensions.[67] Furthermore, there must be an empowerment of minority groups through the encouragement of their active participation in the economic and political community.[68]

The probable effect of these measures, if properly implemented, would be a reduction of racist speech. This reduction would occur not through the mere silencing of racists but through their conversion or in many cases the prevention of people from becoming racists. While this may be an optimistic scenario, it seems to us to be one that has a better chance of curtailing racism than the criminalization of racist speech and is well worth working toward.

The real problem is the institutionalization of racism. Too much of a focus upon eradicating racist speech is likely to result in only minor gains for those opposed to racism. Even if it were possible to ban racist speech, racist attitudes and racist conduct will remain, albeit in more subtle forms. Therefore, any victory in banning racist speech is likely to be hollow, particularly if it has the unintended effect of eroding other rights—in particular that right which is likely to be one of the most useful tools in attacking the deeper roots of racial prejudice.

NOTES

1. See International Convention on Civil and Political Rights (ICCPR), adopted December 16, 1966, in force March 23, 1976, General Assembly Resolution 2200 (XXI), 21 UNGAOR Supp. (no. 16), UN Document A/6316; and Constitution of the United States, First Amendment.

2. ICCPR, Article 20(2). See also B. S. Murty, *The International Law of Propaganda* (Dordecht: Martinus Nijhoff, 1989).

3. One survey in the late 1980s found that 50 percent of Americans thought that blacks were less well off in terms of education; 65 percent thought blacks were less well off in terms of criminal justice treatment; and 69 percent thought blacks were less well

off in terms of employment opportunities than the rest of the population. See NAACP Legal Defense Fund, *The Unfinished Agenda on Race in America* (New York: NAACP, 1989), pp. 10–11.

4. Ronald Walters, "White Racial Nationalism in the United States," *Without Prejudice* 1, no. 1 (Fall 1987): 7–29.

5. See Peter Applebome, "South's Race Relations: Violence Amid Progress," *New York Times*, November 21, 1989, p. A13, column 1, quoting Charles Reagan Wilson.

6. See J. Wiener, "Words that Wound: Free Speech for Campus Bigots?" *The Nation*, February 26, 1990, p. 272.

7. Marilyn Soltis, "Sensitivity Training 101," *ABA Journal*, July 1990, p. 47, quoting survey by National Institute Against Prejudice and Violence.

8. NAACP Legal Defense Fund, *The Unfinished Agenda*, pp. 10–11, 22.

9. International Convention on the Elimination of All Forms of Racial Discrimination, adopted December 21, 1965, in force January 4, 1969, 660 UNTS 195, Article 4; ICCPR, Article 20.

10. ICCPR, Article 19(3).

11. See, for example, France, Act. no. 72/546 of July 1, 1976; and Belgium, Law on the Suppression of Certain Acts Prompted by Racism or Xenophobia. Denmark, Iceland, Norway, Sweden, and the Netherlands also have such laws. See Natan Lerner, "Group Libel Revisited," *Israel Year Book of Human Rights* 17 (1987): 184, 192–93; and Henning Jakhelln, "Freedom of Speech and the Prohibition of Racial Discrimination," *Scandinavian Studies in Law* 26 (1982): 97.

12. Lerner, "Group Libel Revisited," p. 193.

13. Ibid.

14. See Jakhelln, "Freedom of Speech."

15. *Denver Post*, November 15, 1989, p. 12A, column 1.

16. Justitie-Departementet, *Defend the Freedom of Expression: Recommendations of the Swedish Government Commission on the Freedom of Expression*, Summary of Report SOU 1983:70 (Stockholm: Liber, 1985), p. 16.

17. Canada Criminal Code, chapter c-46, section 319 (1) and (2).

18. Ibid., section 319 (1).

19. Ibid., section 319 (2).

20. However, the willful promotion offense is subject to several defenses, including truth, establishment of an opinion on a religious subject, public relevance and a reasonable belief that the statements were true, or if in good faith the speaker intended to use the statement in an attempt to reduce feelings of hatred toward a group. Ibid., section 319 (3).

21. See *Re Taylor et al. v. Canadian Human Rights Comm. et al.*, *Dominion Law Reports* (4th Series) 37 (1987): 577; and *R. v. Keegstra*, [1988] 5 W.W.R. 211 (Alta.). See also "Language as Violence v. Freedom of Expression: Canadian and American Perspectives on Group Defamation," *Buffalo Law Review* 37 (1988–1989): 337; Ronda Bessner, "The Constitutionality of the Group Libel Offences in The Canadian Criminal Code," *Manitoba Law Journal* 17 (1988): 183.

22. See Bessner, "The Constitutionality," pp. 187–208.

23. Ibid., p. 209.

24. Compare ibid., p. 184 (citing a 1960s-to-early-1970 study by the Cohen Committee) with p. 209 (citing a 1984 report by the Parliamentary Task Force on the Participation of Visible Minorities in Canada).

25. See Fali S. Nariman, "Freedom of Speech and Blasphemy: The Laws in India and UK," *International Commission of Jurists Review* 42 (1989): 53.

26. "Blasphemy—The Case for Abolition," *New Law Journal* 131 (April 1981): 156; "Time to Drop Blasphemy," *New Law Journal* 138 (September 1988): 539.

27. See Eliezer Lederman and Mala Tabory, "Criminalization of Racial Incitement in Israel," *Stanford Journal of International Law* 24 (1987): 55.

28. Alexis de Tocqueville, *Democracy in America*, vol. 1 (New York: Modern Library edition, 1981 [1835]), p. 103.

29. *Abrams v. United States*, 250 U.S. 616 (1919).

30. *Whitney v. California*, 274 U.S. 357 (1927).

31. Quoted by Charles A. Beard, "The Great American Tradition: A Challenge for the Fourth of July," *The Nation* 123 (July 7, 1926): 8.

32. *Whitney*, supra.

33. *Schenck v. United States*, 249 U.S. 47 (1919).

34. *Dennis v. United States*, 341 U.S. 494 at 507 (1951), imposing a stricter standard than *Whitney*, supra.

35. *Yates v. United States*, 354 U.S. 289, 320–24 (1957).

36. *Brandenburg v. Ohio*, 395 U.S. 444 (1969).

37. *Noto v. United States*, 367 U.S. 568 (1942).

38. Rodney A. Smolla, "Rethinking First Amendment Assumptions About Racist and Sexist Speech," *Washington and Lee Law Review* 47 (1990): 171, 178.

39. *Chaplinsky v. New Hampshire*, 315 U.S. 568 (1942).

40. *Collins v. Smith*, 578 F. 2d 1197 (7th Cir., 1978).

41. *Texas v. Johnson*, 41, 109 S. Ct. 2533 (1989).

42. See Richard Delgado, "Words that Wound: A Tort Action for Racial Insults, Epithets and Name-Calling," *Harvard Civil Rights and Civil Liberties Review* 17 (1982): 133.

43. 343 U.S. 250 (1952).

44. Ibid. at 254.

45. *New York Times v. Sullivan*, 376 U.S. 254 (1964).

46. *United States v. O'Brien*, 391 U.S. 367 (1968).

47. See Wiener, "Words that Wound."

48. Claire Martin, "Conflict on Campus," *Contemporary Magazine/The Denver Post*, November 19, 1989, p. 12; and Patricia B. Hodulik, "Prohibiting Discriminatory Harassment by Regulating Student Speech: A Balancing of First Amendment and University Interests," *Journal of College and University Law* 16, no. 4 (1990): 573, n. 1.

49. See Wiener, "Words that Wound," for a discussion of the background to the Michigan case, as well as descriptions of other cases of racial hatred and violence on campus. See also Wiener, "Racial Hatred on Campus," *The Nation*, February 27, 1989, p. 260.

In the Michigan case, a student had been disciplined for offering the opinion in a class that homosexuality was a disease and was treatable by therapy. Wiener, "Words that Wound," p. 272.

50. 721 F. Supp. 852 (E.D. Mich., 1989). See also the note in "Recent Cases," *Harvard Law Review* 103 (1990): 1397.

51. Wiener, "Words that Wound," p. 274.

52. "Top New York Court Voids Law on Abusive Language," *New York Times*, December 20, 1989, p. A16, column 2.

53. "SUNY Adopts New Strategy to Ease Its Racial Tensions," *New York Times*, December 24, 1989, p. 23, section 1, column 1.

54. Martin, "Conflict on Campus," p. 14.

55. "Black Student Carries Beeper After Racist Incident," *Denver Post*, December 5, 1989, p. 1B, column 2.

56. "Racial Slur Incident in Boulder Could Be Filed as a Felony Charge," *Denver Post*, December 1, 1989, p. 5B, column 3. For a thorough discussion of racist incidents and the arguments against attempts to minimize the effects of these incidents, see M. Matsuda, "Public Response to Racist Speech: Considering the Victim's Story," *Michigan Law Review* 87, no. 8 (1989): 2320.

57. Colo. Rev. Stat. sec. 18–9–121; the law was passed in July 1988.

58. "The Test of Boulder Racial Intimidation Law in Doubt," *Denver Post*, February 3, 1990, p. 4B, column 3.

59. Colo. Rev. Stat. sec. 18–9–121.

60. See *Restatement, 2nd of Torts* § 4, comments b and d (Washington, DC: American Law Institute, 1965).

61. Dean M. Richardson, "Racism: A Tort of Outrage," *Oregon Law Review* 61 (1982): 267.

62. Matsuda, "Public Response," p. 2341.

63. Ibid., pp. 2336–37.

64. Richardson, "Racism."

65. Matsuda, "Public Response," p. 2337. The production of such effects is analogous to other problems in modern society. It is a problem not limited to racist speech but to any derogatory generalizations. Overweight people, blondes, and short people all may feel their self-worth questioned by various remarks and representations common in the modern world.

66. Wiener, "Words that Wound," p. 274, quoting Ira Glasser, national director of the American Civil Liberties Union.

67. Such a program has been in instituted in the Bensonhurst neighborhood of New York City, which was the scene of the killing of Yusuf Hawkins. Report on National Public Radio, "All Things Considered," March 17, 1990. Interestingly, it would appear that such education programs would be prohibited under laws that criminalize racist speech since students are encouraged to articulate their reasons for distrusting people from different ethnic and racial groups.

68. Wiener, "Words that Wound," p. 276.

PART III

Racism and Policy

Immigration Reform and Barriers to Immigrant Integration: Enhancing Acculturation by Impacting U.S. Policy

DEBRA KREISBERG VOSS, JOY SOBREPEÑA, AND PETER W. VAN ARSDALE

The United States, since its founding, has prided itself on being a nation of immigrants. It is a nation that has espoused the belief that people of all races, religions, and cultures could come to seek a new and better life. The ''American dream'' is the ideal that all people will enjoy freedom of choice, economic opportunity, and upward mobility. In other words, in this ''great melting pot,'' a person's heritage should not limit his or her opportunity to obtain success and happiness.

Beneath the rhetoric of freedom and equality for all lies a disquieting truth. It is a truth of new times and changing attitudes: the American dream is not enjoyed by all. Despite numerous success stories, immigrants are not always welcomed with open arms; they are often met with discrimination and distrust. Thus, for many, the tedious and painful journey in search of the American dream ends in the realization that the dream is reserved for the few and withheld from the many. The land of plenty has become a land of scarcity, a battleground in which the fight for obtaining scarce resources becomes the key to upward mobility, success, and happiness. Power and wealth become the means to freedom and equality, and diversity among people becomes a mechanism by which to discriminate as to who are the ''most deserving.''[1]

Relationships between majority and minority groups are influenced as much by structural conditions as by differences in culture. The nature of those conditions and differences influences not only the distribution of power resources (economic, social, and political) but also the accessibility to those resources by groups who are seeking upward mobility. During times of expanding economic and social conditions, the fabric of society stretches to make room for increased opportunities for minority group members. Yet, during periods of economic stagnation (perceived or real), there is a tendency for society to restrict access to necessary resources, thereby thwarting efforts by immigrants and minorities to improve their economic and social status.

Sociologists have found that people become more hostile toward others when they feel that their security is threatened.[2] Thus many social scientists conclude that social and economic competition can breed conflict and prejudice. Negative stereotyping, prejudice, and discrimination clearly increase whenever competition for limited resources increases. As frustration heightens, as a result of relative deprivation[3] in which expectations remain unsatisfied, aggression toward others is amplified, causing people to strike out against the perceived cause of their frustration. When the true source of frustration is not easily identified, the frustrated individuals or groups may redirect their aggressiveness toward a more visible, vulnerable, and socially sanctioned target. Immigrants and other minorities have long been the recipients of displaced aggression and xenophobic behavior.[4]

When feelings of prejudice and racism become institutionalized, the result can be policy decisions that protect the interests of the majority group and curtail the mobility of minority groups. These types of policies create barriers against the integration of minority groups and, in particular, recent immigrants, resulting in the formation of persistent subcultures.[5]

Throughout the 1970s and the 1980s, immigration, particularly the flow of illegal immigrants, once again became a pressing policy issue in the United States. The extent of the illegal flow, although difficult to quantify, caused sufficient alarm among policymakers to warrant a review of existing immigration laws. After a decade and a half of debate and controversy, the United States initiated the most sweeping immigration reforms in its history by signing the Immigration Reform and Control Act (IRCA) into law in November 1986.

IRCA was the product of a sustained congressional movement to ''gain control of the United States' borders,'' yet it also contained a unique legalization provision granting amnesty opportunities to certain illegal aliens. Although IRCA allowed for the implementation of some innovative policies, it also implicitly suggested potentially deleterious regulatory and socioeconomic constraints as well as xenophobic attitudes that have affected the implementation of the legislation. Thus many immigrants wishing to integrate into mainstream society have been deterred.

There are a number of important issues associated with IRCA. The most important of these are the impact of the legalization program on the allocation of resources and access to public benefits (both federal and state), the administration of the State Legalization Impact Assistance Grants (SLIAG) program, and employer sanctions and their impact on minority workers.

This chapter assesses the impact of the implementation of IRCA. The first section looks at immigration policy within a historical context. It examines how immigration legislation has responded to shifts in the nation's political and socioeconomic conditions and its implications for the integration of immigrants into society. The next section examines how socioeconomic constraints, perceptions, and attitudes have affected policy formulation and, therefore, the legislative outcome (IRCA). The third section identifies the statutory and regulatory constraints of IRCA's three major provisions and how they combine with socioeconomic constraints and attitudes to impact the allocation and accessibility of resources by both immigrants and service providers. The evidence is then summarized in terms of its implications for policy. The fourth and final section traces how accessibility to resources impacts the acculturation of people moving through the IRCA policy environment. An important concern of this section is to demonstrate the way in which IRCA influences the acculturation process that hinders or enhances the immigrants' movement through the system. An overview of the sections is seen in Figure 5.1. Differential access to resources (economic, political, and social) by immigrants can ultimately cause them to become trapped in the underclass of society.[6]

Of primary importance is this question: How can immigration policies become an effective mechanism for controlling both legal and illegal immigration without creating barriers to acculturation?

THE HISTORICAL CONTEXT OF IMMIGRATION

Historically, immigration legislation has responded to perceived changes in socioeconomic and political interests. The relative restrictiveness of immigration policy has reflected competing national concerns to control borders yet ensure a secure labor supply. Until the late nineteenth century, the United States did not have comprehensive restrictions on immigration. Its policies restricted only particular nationalities that entered the United States in large numbers. This open-door policy ended with the enactment of the 1924 National Origins Act. This was the first comprehensive legislation effectively curtailing immigration from entire regions. This act imposed numerical restrictions on immigration from Southern and Eastern Europe but set no quotas on immigration from the western hemisphere.[7]

Foreign laborers (mainly Mexicans) were needed to ease labor shortages during World War I and thus were not excluded under the new act. This resulted in a large flow of Mexican workers.[8] With the end of the war and the onset of the Great Depression, the priority of seeking laborers to fulfill wartime shortages was replaced by a climate of competition for dwindling resources, leading to the massive deportation and forcible repatriation of Mexican laborers.[9]

The situation was again reversed in the 1940s as military requirements associated with World War II and related manufacturing manpower needs led to labor shortages in the agricultural sector. These wartime pressures resulted in a bilateral immigrant labor agreement between the United States and Mexico. In 1942 the two governments negotiated a formal treaty permitting the entry of Mexican farm workers under contract to American employers. These contracts

Figure 5.1
Overview of Immigration Reform and Barriers to Integration

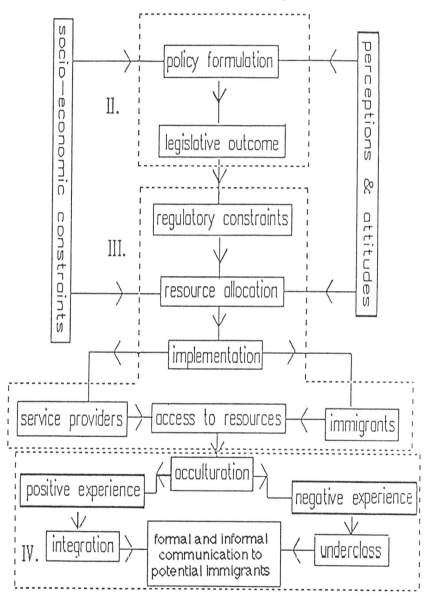

were guaranteed by the U.S. government. This program legally allowed temporary Mexican workers to enter the United States for agricultural work. This emergency wartime measure was the beginning of what is commonly known as the Bracero Program.

With the lapse of special wartime legislation at the end of 1947, the agreement expired. However, the Bracero Program continued under various legal authorizations, many of which contributed to abuse and exploitation of Mexican laborers. With the use of immigrant labor from Mexico formally established, former Bracero workers continued to come to the United States even after the termination of their contracts. This resulted in a parallel flow of illegal workers. Opinions on the impact of the continued use of Mexican labor in American agribusiness reflected competing concerns: inadequate protection of domestic farm labor and the need to supplement the agricultural labor supply. In all, the Bracero Program continued for twenty-two years and involved 5 million Mexican workers. The Bracero Program and reliance on Mexican labor illustrates historical sources of Mexican immigrant flow to the United States.[10]

As the numbers of illegal immigrants continued to increase, the U.S. government employed drastic measures "to clean up the borders." The method employed was a massive deportation campaign with the unfortunate title "Operation Wetback." Under this area sweep operation the United States expelled over a million immigrants in the American southwest in 1954 alone.[11] These expulsions helped diminish the illegal immigration problem of the mid-1950s. It led, however, to a growing sentiment that in the future it would be better to prevent illegal aliens from entering rather than utilizing an expulsion process of which Operation Wetback was an example.

On June 27, 1952, the U.S. Congress enacted the Immigration and Nationality Act (INA), which was a major recodification of existing immigration law. The INA restricted quota immigration and carried forward the essential elements of previous immigration law. It was a restrictionist document that reflected the Cold War climate in which it was written. In contrast to the atmosphere of the 1920s, the INA was not based on the concept of Nordic superiority. Instead, it was based on preserving the sociological and cultural balance of the American population and ensuring the successful assimilation[12] of immigrants.[13]

By 1960 a new climate of public opinion had emerged. It was one that rejected the criteria of nationality and ethnic considerations as a basis for determining numerical restrictions for immigration policy. In 1965 Congress passed the Immigration and Nationality Act Amendments, which repealed the National Origins Quota System, substituting a system of preference based on skills and family unification for the establishment of numerical ceilings on immigration. The 1965 Amendments reflected the liberal views of the 1960s as the 1952 Act reflected the Cold War climate of the 1950s.[14]

Despite the more liberal atmosphere in the nation and new policies, the illegal immigration problem continued. With the termination of the Bracero Program in 1964, legal channels for temporary employment were closed, causing an even greater increase in illegal entrants. Now, undocumented Mexican workers were no longer limited to the agricultural sector as they moved to industry, manufacturing, and service sectors of the economy. This expansion in the use of undocumented workers was a result of low unemployment and a tight labor market.[15] The success of these workers encouraged even more illegal aliens to come.

As the political climate and structural conditions changed in the 1970s and 1980s, economic security and resource scarcity became important policy issues. Increased competition for limited resources heightened tensions between immigrants and natives. This resulted in the perception that immigrants were diverting resources away from natives and were becoming a threat to economic security. A new theme emerged in the American political environment: America had reached its limits in terms of immigrants. "We have scarce resources, and we are in trouble domestically in terms of solving our own problems. If we can't solve our own problems—unemployment, inflation, federal deficits and so forth—how can we possibly attempt to solve other countries' problems by admitting a large number of immigrants?"[16]

In this atmosphere illegal aliens became a convenient scapegoat for collective frustration. They were ideal targets because they were perceived as a threat to the American way of life.[17] The common outcry became "U.S. immigration policy is out of control!" It was within this political and socioeconomic environment that the Immigration Reform and Control Act of 1986 emerged.

THE GENESIS OF IRCA

Public clamor for immigration reform led federal and state governments in 1971 to begin exploring policy alternatives to regulate the flow of illegal aliens. The prevailing sentiment among policymakers was that existing laws were ineffective in addressing the problems of illegal immigration.

It took fifteen years (from 1971 to 1986) of congressional debate to produce new legislation to control illegal immigration. The Nixon administration put forth the first of a series of bills to address this problem. In response to this bill, and reports by the Special Study Group on Illegal Immigration, the House Committee on the Judiciary began investigations on the problems of illegal immigration in the United States. Hearings by the committee concluded that "the adverse impact of illegal aliens was substantial and warranted legislation both to protect United States labor and the economy, and to assure the orderly entry of immigrants into the United States."[18]

These hearings raised pertinent issues relating to illegal aliens and other immigrants such as prohibiting the knowing employment of illegal aliens, allowing the legalization of undocumented aliens, prohibiting the discrimination of individuals on the basis of alienage or citizenship, and the eligibility of aliens for federal benefits. In addition, assessment of the impact of illegal immigrants on the economy, social services, job displacement, and wages remained controversial. Consensus could not be reached on the exact provisions to include in the new legislation. Succeeding administrations continued the debate, appointing commissions and study groups to pursue the problem. Legislative remedies came to be seen as the only solution to prevent illegality from breeding illegality.

National interest continued to be the bottom-line criterion underlying proposals for new legislation: "Our policy—while providing opportunity to a portion of the world's population—must be guided by the basic national interests of the people of the United States."[19] Most of the proposed bills included one or more of the following: increased border enforcement, deterrents against hiring, and legalization of illegal aliens already in the country.

President Jimmy Carter's Select Commission's report on immigration recommended the legalization of certain undocumented workers. The commission believed that to allow them to remain in a second-class status would have tremendous social costs. Removing the population through massive deportations would be expensive, politically unacceptable, and difficult to implement. The legalization of the population, the commission argued, would benefit the country as a whole as it would reduce the potential for depressed wages related to undocumented workers. Furthermore, this population could then participate more freely and contribute more to society.[20]

Building on the recommendations put forth in the Carter Commission's report, the Reagan administration appointed a special task force to further study the issue. This led to a proposal for immigration policy reform in July 1981. Both the Reagan proposal and the commission report were subjected to extensive congressional hearings in the fall of 1981 and early 1982. In March 1982, identical bills were proposed by the subcommittee chairmen, being jointly referred to as the Simpson-Mazzoli Bill. This, rather than the administration's bill, became the vehicle for legislative action.

Over the next four years debates concerning the final makeup of the new immigration legislation continued. The primary obstacle to passage of the new law was the opposition expressed by the Hispanic Caucus, the Black Caucus, civil rights organizations, state and local governments, labor unions, and the Chamber of Commerce. These organizations contended that the law was inherently discriminatory. Representative Don Edwards summarized the opposition to the bill saying, "I believe the employer sanction provision is discriminatory on its face. With the prospects of fines and criminal penalties looming over each employer, what employer would be willing to talk about employment to someone who looks or sounds foreign or bears a foreign surname?"[21]

Beyond these objections, many policymakers would not consider employer sanctions without a provision for the legalization of illegal aliens as well. Others believed that legalization could be damaging because it condoned lawbreaking and would be extremely costly. This debate also raised controversy over the issue of reimbursement to state and local governments to offset expenditures of servicing eligible legalized aliens, highlighting the importance of resource allocation and accessibility in the policymaking forum. Despite the remaining controversy, IRCA was signed into law in November 1986. IRCA was to usher in a new era of immigration reform in the United States. The complex and confusing legislation, however, carried with it serious complications for implementation as many had speculated.

THE PROVISIONS OF IRCA

Difficulties immediately arose among key actors (the Immigration and Nat-
uralization Service [INS], federal and state governments, and state and local
public assistance programs) due to the complexity of implementing a federal law
at state and local levels. As one observer noted, the federal government "is
silent on the state's role of implementing immigration reform. It seems that
IRCA envisioned a limited role for states, primarily as a fiscal watchdog and
'pass through' agent for federal funds. There is no clear state role in planning
program delivery or managing the long-term impact of IRCA on a state's educational system and its economy."[22] Yet it is at the state and local levels where
the impact of the newly legalized population is being felt the most.

Legalization

There are three major provisions of IRCA, the first of which is the legalization
program. The legalization provision was designed to adjust the legal status of
illegal aliens already in the country, allowing them to "come out from the
shadows" and permitting them to function freely as members of society. However, regulatory constraints inherent in the act, along with deterrents imposed
by the policy environment, have hindered the process of effectively allocating
and accessing necessary resources.

The first of a series of problems in the legalization program was confusion
over the definitions of terms for eligibility. The legalization provision of IRCA
is a two-step procedure. The first stage would grant temporary residency to those
illegal aliens who could establish that they have continuously resided in the
United States since before January 1, 1982 (pre-82s), and for special agricultural
workers (SAWs) who establish a work record of ninety days between May 1,
1985, and May 1, 1986. Interpretation of the term "continuously resided" proved
controversial. In addition, INS eligibility criteria required that amnesty applicants
remain in the United States from the date of IRCA's enactment to the date of
application for legalization. Only absences controversially described as "brief,
casual, or innocent" would be authorized by the INS on the grounds that they
were legitimate emergencies or for humanitarian purposes and not longer than
forty-five days.[23]

It was difficult for applicants to abide by these terms since the families of
undocumented workers often resided outside the United States. It was not unusual
for undocumented workers to return to their home countries for visits. The result
of the restrictive interpretation of these terms was the exclusion of a substantial
portion of the otherwise eligible population. Furthermore, little notice was given
to potential applicants that *any* absence without prior INS approval would make
them ineligible for amnesty.[24]

Beyond the controversy over terms was the difficulty illegal aliens had in
establishing their eligibility. Thus, one of the primary concerns surrounding the

legalization process became the problem of documentation. To prove eligibility the INS accepted only seven types of documents to establish evidence of identity and continuous residence. These were to be submitted in their original forms or otherwise certified by proper authorities. Many of the required types of documentation raised problems of time, cost, employer cooperation, and accessibility to records that often did not exist.[25] It is ironic that a population that had previously been forced to bury evidence of their presence in the United States to avoid detection was now required to document their continuous residence. Immigrants' fears surrounding their inability to do so deterred many potential applicants from applying.

The cost of the legalization process was high considering the incomes of many of the applicants. The basic application fee for an individual was $185, $50 for each minor, and $420 for a family of four.[26] In addition, the applicant incurred costs for medical examinations, legal fees, photographs, fingerprints, and loss of work time. The application fee could not be waived. Given the uncertainty of qualification, these fees seemed especially high. Some estimated the total cost of legalization to be $1,000 for an individual and $3,000 for a family of four.[27]

Another significant deterrent for applying for legalization was the issue of family unity. It was not unusual for one member of the family, often the father, to be eligible for legalization, having resided and worked in the United States since before January 1982, while his wife and family (who had not joined him until a later time) were not eligible for legalization. In such situations many of those eligible did not seek amnesty for fear of exposing their families. An INS survey in 1987 found that 35 percent of potential applicants did not seek amnesty on these grounds.[28]

The restrictive regulations of IRCA's legalization provision also deterred potential applicants by excluding those persons who had accepted certain forms of public cash assistance. This exclusion particularly affected single women with children. Many women felt that they would rather not apply for amnesty than forfeit the security of assistance. For some, it was a decision to best ensure the welfare of their children.[29]

The onerous documentation requirements, extensive costs, the issue of family unity, and public charge exclusion dissuaded otherwise eligible aliens from applying. At the same time, many who did apply were rejected on the basis of technicalities. Reports during the early implementation of IRCA recorded the difficulty potential applicants were having in documenting their claims.[30] One immigration lawyer stated that up to 80 percent of those eligible would have moderate to severe document problems.[31]

To assist in the process of legalization and to maximize participation in the legalization program, Congress included a provision in IRCA that allowed voluntary organizations to provide outreach, application assistance, counseling, and initial application processing. These organizations were given the title Qualified Designated Entities (QDEs). The role of the QDE was believed to be essential to the success of the legalization process as it provided a buffer for the illegal population who might fear direct contact with the INS. Unfortunately, participation of voluntary organizations as QDEs was limited due to high administrative costs. This reduced the number of groups that aliens could approach for assistance.[32] Without access to QDEs the danger that applicants would turn to uninformed sources to assist with their applications increased.[33] Although QDEs were established to provide key services throughout the legalization process and were thought to be the "underlying infrastructure for legalization,"[34] poor allocation of resources by policymakers prohibited QDEs from performing their functions effectively.

Because of the stringent requirements for the first phase of legalization, and the related resource constraints, the number of potential applicants was significantly reduced. Out of an estimated total of 4 million illegal aliens who were thought to be eligible, only 2.1 million were given temporary residency status.[35]

To complete the regularization of status to permanent residency, those granted temporary residency are required to enter a second stage in the legalization process. Applicants for second-stage legalization must fulfill English language and civic requirements to retain their eligibility or, at minimum, must show they are pursuing instruction to gain this knowledge. If eligible legalized aliens (ELAs) fail to meet this requirement or otherwise become ineligible for permanent residency, or fail to apply, they revert back to undocumented status. Although there were initial concerns with Stage II requirements to regularize status, such as lack of outreach and confusion about deadlines, almost all ELAs have been successful in gaining permanent residency.[36]

State Legalization Impact Assistance Grants

The State Legalization Impact Assistance Grants is the second major provision established under the new immigration bill. In part, SLIAG is the result of a compromise between groups who believed that illegal aliens would become legal residents and abandon employment in order to live on welfare, and state and local groups who feared that the impact of unknown numbers of ELAs would drain already limited resources. In response, Congress barred ELAs for a five-year period from federally funded assistance programs such as Aid to Families with Dependent Children (AFDC), Medicaid, and food stamps. Instead, they provided SLIAG funding that was to reimburse state and local agencies for increased costs associated with servicing ELAs under already existing programs. The result of this compromise shifted some costs from federal budgets to already overburdened state and local human services budgets.

Congress initially appropriated nearly $1 billion a year in SLIAG funds (in fact, this figure has been substantially reduced) for four consecutive years to help states offset costs incurred in providing public assistance, public health, and educational services to ELAs. This funding did not address costs of servicing thousands of family members who are not eligible for legalization but who legally reside in the United States under INS fairness policies.

Under SLIAG, reimbursement categories were created dividing allowable and nonallowable services. By separating the availability of services an artificial split was created in the types of services provided. The division of services into reimbursable and nonreimbursable services fails to convey the important inter-relationship among all of the needs of ELAs. For example, SLIAG money under its education provision may be used for English as a Second Language (ESL) and civics courses but may not be used for vocational courses. Both types of courses are necessary, however, to assist ELAs to gain critical skills for successful employment and integration in the job market. Clearly, the artificial segmentation of services could hamper attempts to meet the needs of ELA clients.

State agencies are also faced with the task of developing a service plan that fits SLIAG reimbursement services into an overall approach. Because of the limitations placed on SLIAG reimbursements, this is difficult to accomplish. Low utilization rates of public services by ELAs in the past, due to their previous immigration status, exacerbate the problem. State agencies must carefully eval-uate whether their current approach to public health, public assistance, and education is culturally appropriate and effective with specific, targeted groups of legalized aliens. Making this evaluation continues to be difficult despite recent studies on the characteristics of the undocumented population.[37] Plans must remain flexible since it is difficult to predict the level of services ELAs will use and the amount of reimbursement states will actually receive.

Further complicating the situation, outreach activities designed to ensure that ELAs adjust successfully to permanent resident status initially were excluded as an unacceptable use of SLIAG funds. Given the confusing and complex nature of IRCA and SLIAG regulations, it is important to make ELAs aware of the services available to them and the extent to which receiving such services will affect their legal status.

Another regulation that constrains effective service delivery is the federal requirement that many programs must identify and track the number of ELAs using services in order to claim reimbursement. This is accomplished in several ways, two of which are most commonly used. The agency may ask clients to present documentation of their alien registration number or collect Social Security numbers. In order to trigger reimbursement all numbers must be verified through a federal computer database. This process raises questions of practicality and cost-effectiveness since the primary reason to collect this information is for SLIAG reimbursement, which in many cases may not translate into significant resources for state and local agencies.

One of the most pressing concerns is that of "Public Charge" determination. Legalization applicants can become ineligible for amnesty or permanent residency on a "Public Charge" determination if they or a member of their family receives certain forms of public cash assistance. As a result, aliens seeking legal status and ultimately citizenship may inadvertently sacrifice those long-term goals by receiving cash assistance payments in the interim. The list of programs from which ELAs are excluded has been amended several times throughout the implementation of IRCA. Poorly publicized changes have resulted in misinformation between the INS and service providers. This leaves both service providers and ELAs confused as to what services may be utilized. For fear of jeopardizing their eligibility, many legalized aliens show unwarranted caution against receiving any kind of assistance. This has caused many ELAs to forego essential services such as Special Food Programs for Women, Infants, and Children (WIC); prenatal care; and other health care services that do not affect their eligibility status. Others may not apply for legalization since they believe past receipt of innocuous benefits makes them ineligible.

This has led to an unanticipated low participation rate in the use of public services despite immediate and critical needs of ELAs for these services. This jeopardizes the SLIAG program as future funding allocations are dependent on current use. As a result, resources might be reallocated to other programs.

Employer Sanctions

Employer sanctions are the third major provision and are at the heart of IRCA. Their purpose is to remove employment incentives through creating hiring constraints, thereby dissuading illegal immigrants from seeking employment in the United States. This provision makes it illegal to hire undocumented workers knowingly and establishes sanctions ranging from fines to jail sentences for repeated violations. However, to date, employer sanctions have neither removed these incentives nor stemmed the flow of illegal immigration to this country. Instead, their implementation has raised many civil rights issues that affect not only the rights of illegal aliens but also those of legalized aliens and minority citizens.

Statutory provisions of IRCA require that all employers verify the work authorization of all new hires. The employer sanctions provision of IRCA is to be enforced through INS I-9 (work status verification form) inspection visits or audits. These visits were conceived solely as document examinations and not as a method of locating illegal aliens. According to Congress, "The bill is designed to ensure that this information [I-9] will not be used by the INS in its alien enforcement activities."[38] Despite these assurances, it is regular practice in many regions for INS officials to combine inspection visits with raids on the workplace.[39]

Many employers and civil rights groups have become concerned over the enforcement techniques employed by the INS. The INS, according to some, has been so overzealous in enforcement that it has violated employer privacy rights and disrupted the workplace and production by conducting visits and raids without warrants or sufficient notice.[40] One manufacturer said, "Why do they raid when employers need employees desperately? Someone should be making sure these people aren't exploited, that's all. What does the INS think they are doing, pest control? These people aren't termites."[41]

Many civil rights and minority groups expressed strong opposition over the possible discriminatory impact of employer sanctions. In response, Congress incorporated an antidiscrimination provision that prohibits employers from discriminating in the hiring or firing of U.S. citizens and authorized workers.[42] In addition, Congress created the Office of Special Counsel (OSC) to hear and act upon discrimination complaints. Despite the inclusion of the antidiscrimination provision, the implementation of employer sanctions has caused a widespread pattern of discrimination. Evidence of this discrimination is illustrated in the third oversight report of the General Accounting Office (GAO 1990)[43] and other independent researchers.[44]

A significant problem surrounding employer sanctions is the controversy over the adequacy of the definition of discrimination. Conventionally, discrimination in the workplace is perceived as "a situation where individuals with equal characteristics and experiences receive unequal rewards. The rewards are measured either by earnings or by proportion of hirings."[45] Debate surrounds the issue of whether unequal employment outcomes are sufficient evidence of discrimination or whether intent must accompany the discriminatory act.

The definition of discrimination utilized by IRCA is narrow, as it addresses solely the issues of hiring and firing and requires that employers show purposeful intent. In his testimony to Congress, Special Counsel Lawrence J. Siskind said that IRCA *must* make this distinction between disparate outcomes and intent, otherwise "we might find that practically every employer in the country was potentially liable" under the antidiscrimination provision (Section 101) of IRCA.[46]

The potential for discrimination arises out of the difficulty employers face in verifying the work authorization status of potential employees. Says Siskind, "It is very difficult for many employers in this country to figure out all the different documents they can and can't accept. Frankly, many employers are making mistakes. Unless they have a lawyer, and an immigration lawyer at that standing by their side, many of them are going to misapply the Section 101 employer verification requirement."[47] The misapplication of Section 101 guidelines could be reduced if employers were better informed of the legitimacy of various documents. The second GAO report found that budgetary restrictions imposed on outreach programs provided by the OSC were severely affected, and thus many employers were unaware of the antidiscrimination provision.[48]

Aside from those employers who unknowingly misapply verification procedures, there are those who deliberately exceed IRCA verification requirements by accepting only green cards or U.S. passports as proper documentation. They do not recognize other forms that may be legitimate.[49] An example of this practice is related by a Massachusetts food plant owner who said, "Ninety-nine percent of our employees don't know we aren't supposed to do that [accept only green cards or U.S. passports]. When one of them realizes it and decides to challenge our policy, then maybe we'll decide to change it. Until then, we'll keep insisting on whatever documents we want."[50] Other employers simply reject certain applications rather than take the risk of offering employment to illegal aliens.[51] This practice disproportionately impacts legal immigrants and minorities.

In order to avoid employer sanctions, employers discriminate against potential employees who "look foreign" or bear foreign surnames, regardless of their legal status. Even though the second GAO report did not state that a widespread pattern of discrimination resulted from employer sanctions, it did record that out of 3.3 million employers interviewed, 1 out of every 6 (528,000) had employed the practice of asking only "foreign-looking" persons for work authorization or resorted to hiring only U.S. citizens.[52]

These practices severely restrict the ability of authorized workers to secure employment. The antidiscrimination provision of IRCA does not effectively protect these people's rights to employment. From October 1987 to May 1989, the OSC found only sixty-nine cases of discrimination to be meritorious. This number undoubtedly does not begin to reflect the extent of discrimination occurring in the workplace. Special Counsel Siskind acknowledged that "the charges that we see is [sic] just a limited segment of the total picture." Furthermore, "[m]any injured parties just suffer in silence. Either they don't want to risk filing a charge or they don't know."[53] Cecilia Muñoz of La Raza points out that it is common in other civil rights situations that upward of 99 percent of discriminatory acts go unreported.[54] Immigrants, as a rule, are particularly reluctant to speak out for fear of reprisals. Linguistic barriers and unfamiliarity with the law intensify their reluctance.[55]

IRCA's antidiscrimination provision does not address the issue of terms and conditions of employment. This has resulted in continued and ever greater exploitative conditions for immigrant labor. Previously illegal workers who are now authorized to work often request that their employers update their records with correct names and Social Security numbers. This request has resulted in the loss of seniority status or salary benefits.[56] The most vulnerable, however, are illegal aliens.[57] They are provided no protection under IRCA, which protects only citizens and legalized aliens. When illegal aliens are able to obtain work, they are often forced to accept low wages and poor work conditions. Given their tenuous legal status, illegal aliens are unlikely to complain. This vulnerability invites exploitation from employers.[58] In her written testimony to Congress, Shirley Lung of the Center for Immigrants' Rights illustrates the plight of unauthorized workers under IRCA:

Increased apprehension and fear of chronic unemployment causes a greater reluctance among unauthorized workers to protest abuse, to file complaints, or to participate in unions. Some employers seek to capitalize on this atmosphere of fear by imposing more oppressive work conditions and committing increased violations of the laws governing wages and hours. The intensified illegality and vulnerability of the unauthorized workers imposed by employer sanctions creates greater, not fewer incentives to hire and exploit undocumented workers.[59]

In the minds of many, IRCA has created the perception that the government condones discrimination on the basis of national origin. This discrimination has a spillover effect in areas outside the workplace including housing and public accommodation.[60] Jennifer L. Gordon of Centro Presente in Massachusetts documents this problem by relating the story of one El Salvadoran woman:

"Emilia" had two young sons who were diagnosed with lead poisoning from the paint in their apartment. Their landlord refused to comply with the housing code by repainting, claiming that "Emilia" had no resources because she was "illegal". It was only after she applied for asylum and her lawyer intervened that the landlord agreed to take the necessary steps.[61]

Gordon also relates that landlords refuse to return security deposits "because they believe their undocumented tenants have no rights."[62]

Employer sanctions have made the illegal population in the United States more vulnerable.[63] Furthermore, they have contributed to a situation whereby citizens and permanent residents are detrimentally affected. As one author describes it, IRCA is a law that "although politically expedient [it] . . . cannot fulfill one of its own purposes: namely the elimination of the vulnerable status of undocumented employees whose position in the labor force affects legal workers' employment conditions."[64]

Summary

In sum, IRCA has created a new set of problems for policymakers, immigrants, and the American public. Key points include:

- Regulatory constraints inherent in the legalization process have led to confusion regarding the required process for legalization. In addition, the provision has put unnecessary requirements on applicants to prove their eligibility.

- Confusion over the requirements of the legislation as well as restrictive interpretation of the law have resulted in the exclusion of a substantial portion of the otherwise eligible population.

- Resource constraints on voluntary organizations have diminished the effectiveness of the legalization process. This has also affected the ability of many illegal aliens to regularize their status and many ELAs to gain permanent status.

- Excluding ELAs from federally funded services, and at the same time restricting the allocation of funding for SLIAG services, creates resource scarcity and thus limits the immigrant's accessibility to necessary resources. Furthermore, by attaching a misunderstood "Public Charge" exclusion to the use of certain services, the ELAs' legal status is unnecessarily put at risk.

- Despite the implementation of IRCA, many employers continue to hire illegal aliens either because they do not fully understand their legal obligations or because they choose to ignore them. The evidence shows that many employers still appear able to draw on the same labor pool that they used before IRCA.

- As a result of sanctions, employers are discriminating against ELAs and other minorities. This represents a new form of national origin discrimination that did not exist prior to IRCA.

- Although the employer sanctions provision has made jobs more difficult to get, the undocumented population is still growing. This contributes to a situation wherein the undocumented worker is more willing to accept substandard working conditions and wages, creating exactly the kind of easily exploitable underclass that IRCA was designed to eliminate.

- The lack of legal protection provided to illegal aliens ultimately affects the availability of employment and work conditions for the legal work force.

- IRCA has had spinoff effects outside of the workplace, creating multiple social costs for the individual and both social and economic costs for society.

Despite provisions to assist and protect legalized immigrants and other minority groups, regulatory and socioeconomic constraints along with structural barriers have made it difficult for these immigrants to get jobs and obtain services. Xenophobic attitudes have exacerbated the problems of integrating immigrants into mainstream society. Furthermore, IRCA has neglected the reality of the presence of a lingering illegal population in the country as well as the continuing arrival of new illegal immigrants. As a result, immigrants, both legal and illegal, are consistently pushed into persistent subcultures and are forming a growing underclass in the United States. The following section illustrates this potential for marginalization.

SYSTEMS EFFECTS ON ACCULTURATION

Certain social scientists have said that policy is a guideline for the allocation of scarce resources.[65] Since the allocation and accessibility of resources determine the quality of life of all individuals, the human dimension of policy, its impact on people, and the way in which these people communicate their experiences to others have serious implications for policymaking.

The way in which resources flow is governed not only by regulatory and socioeconomic constraints but also by the way in which the policy evokes responses from the general population. This determines the policy environment. It is the interface of these human responses with constraints and deterrents, often beyond the control of acculturating immigrants, that can hinder their integration into society. The responses and choices of acculturating immigrants often are outweighed by other policy-related factors.

Figure 5.2 illustrates this dynamic interaction in the legalization process by identifying the paths open to illegal immigrants. The main process flow is represented by a direct incremental path from illegal status to citizenship. At any time, however, internal and external factors may influence the direction of the immigrant's movement through the system. In some cases these influencing factors may have a negative impact, thus causing the acculturating migrant to

Figure 5.2
The Legalization Process

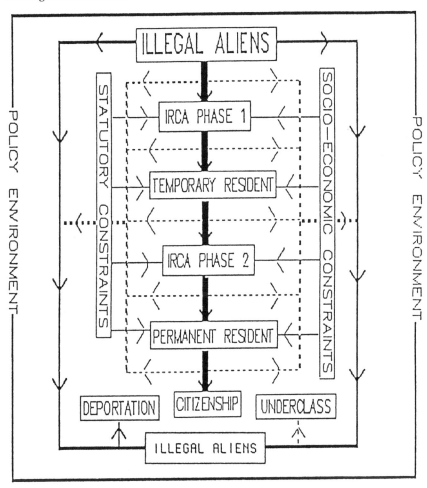

```
———    MAIN PROCESS FLOW              ---    FALLOUT FLOW
```

be forced out or voluntarily fall out of the legalization process. It is this potential for marginalization that contributes to the formation of persistent subcultures or an underclass.

Figure 5.3 illustrates this same pattern of potential marginalization as it relates to the allocation of and accessibility to particular resources. The process flow indicates which federal services are excluded and which SLIAG services are both available and required. Although SLIAG provides public assistance, edu-

Figure 5.3
State Legalization Impact Assistance Grant Process

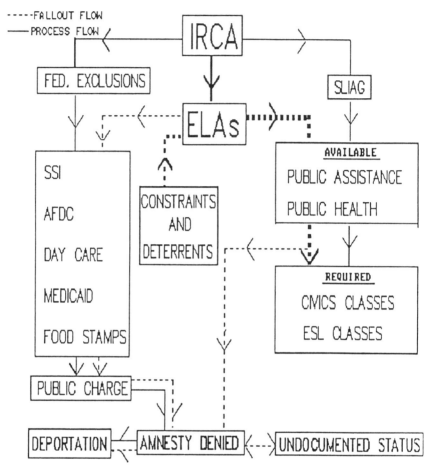

cational programs, and health services, these services often become inaccessible to acculturating immigrants. This happens when policy restrictions are poorly understood, resulting in misinformation and inadequate resource allocation. These constraints and deterrents affect the choices made by service providers and immigrants.

Regulatory constraints and unresponsive human service situations can create fear and confusion, resulting in the use of excluded services or decisions not to access required services. In all, the result is often diminished service utilization and unfulfilled needs that both psychologically isolate individuals and effectively diminish their ability to secure resources.

Employer sanctions as illustrated in Figure 5.4 show three flows. The first

Figure 5.4
Employer Sanctions Provision Process

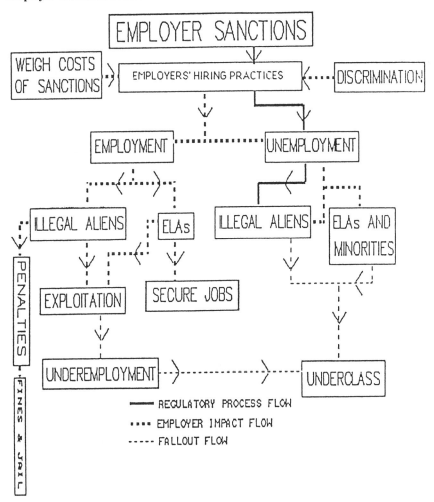

shows the regulatory process that corresponds to the intended flow of illegal
aliens under the sanctions provision. The second flow is the employer impact
flow. This traces the impact of the employer sanctions provision on employers'
hiring practices. Following the flow from hiring practices to employment, it can
be seen that some employers will weigh the cost of sanctions against the perceived
value of hiring undocumented workers and will choose to risk invoking penalties.
If they hire undocumented workers and avoid detection, exploitation can result.
Those eligible to work may be hired and secure good jobs. However, because
ELAs are still in the process of securing permanent status, they are often fearful

to speak out against poor work conditions. They are thus left vulnerable to exploitation.

Employers may refuse to hire illegal aliens. Due to fear and confusion surrounding employer sanctions, employers may also adopt discriminatory hiring practices toward anyone who "looks foreign" despite their legal status. Thus, as indicated on the chart, ELAs and other minorities can also face unemployment.

The third flow in Figure 5.4 represents the "fallout" flow. It traces how employers' hiring practices can impact both legal and illegal workers. When illegal as well as legal immigrants are hired under these conditions, low wages and poor working conditions can result. As indicated, some are forced out of mainstream employment into unemployed situations. This may lead to their marginalization.

Anecdotal evidence of the overall impact of IRCA on individuals highlights the human aspect of their increased marginalization. One plant manager said, "We're Italians, we're immigrants. Used to be [*sic*] the first generation came and worked like hell; second generation went to high school and worked like hell, then took over the business; third generation worked in the business and went to college; fourth generation went to Harvard Law School. Not with this law, not anymore. It doesn't seem fair."[66]

Our analysis, along with many others addressing issues surrounding IRCA, raises serious questions for policymakers. Does IRCA as a whole hinder or enhance the acculturation of an immigrant moving through the IRCA and post-IRCA environment, taking into consideration both positive aspects (such as civics and English classes) and negative aspects (such as employer sanctions)? Given this outcome, what are the spinoff effects of these acculturating immigrants on other potential newcomers? How will those already here communicate their aspirations and successes, or fears and failures, to other potential immigrants? Will this communication, in turn, enhance, hinder, or make no difference to the experiences other newcomers have? Will it encourage or discourage the arrival of more new immigrants? Most importantly, given all that pertains in the IRCA and post-IRCA eras, what are the implications for U.S. policies relating to illegal immigration for 1993–1994 and thereafter?

As these problems continue to escalate, the "great melting pot" is reaching the boiling point. Resource scarcity, exemplified by rising unemployment rates and cuts in public service budgets, along with heightened xenophobic attitudes toward a growing immigrant population within the country all contribute to the situation's escalation.

CONCLUSION AND RECOMMENDATIONS

IRCA was implemented June 1, 1987. This chapter has shown that the consequences of implementation are widespread with implications for today's society as well as for that of tomorrow. The challenges for policymakers are many and can be categorized as follows:

1. Resource scarcity, exemplified by rising unemployment rates and cuts in public service budgets, along with heightened xenophobic attitudes toward the growing immigrant population will continue to pervade the policymaking environment.

2. Since immigration flow is a dynamic phenomenon created from an array of complex problems, effective solutions must address these complexities in integrative fashion.

3. Reasons for migration flow also are many, deriving from both domestic and foreign sources.

4. Many service providers and analysts are not optimistic about the effectiveness of IRCA in fulfilling its intended goals of controlling illegal immigration and minimizing the impact of illegal aliens on the labor market and federal assistance programs.[67]

As the flow of illegal aliens continues, despite recent immigration reform, effective solutions appear further from our grasp. How then can immigration policies become an effective mechanism for controlling both legal and illegal immigration without creating barriers to acculturation?

First, immigration law must take into consideration the pressures for family reunification. In the initial implementation of IRCA, the status of nonqualifying spouses and minors living in the United States was unclear. Oftentimes, deportation proceedings for these dependents would be initiated at the discretion of INS officers. It was not until February 1990 that INS Commissioner Gene McNary announced that the dependents of legalized aliens living in the United States prior to the implementation of IRCA would not be deported and would be granted work authorization. Despite the fact that many family members arrived after their spouses had secured such status, the "family fairness" policy excludes spouses and children entering after 1986. This has resulted in a new population of illegal immigrants unable to secure their status under current legal preference categories.

Second, immigration policy must also recognize the complex push and pull factors that cause people to migrate. In conventional analysis, these social forces are usually described as the pull of political freedom and economic opportunities and the push of repression and poverty. IRCA's narrow interpretation of the causes of illegal immigration fails to take into account how push factors may outweigh pull factors. We believe this can be better understood when the relationship between resource scarcity and quality of life is placed in culturally relative contexts. "Victor," an illegal alien, illustrates this by saying, "People come here [the United States] because they can't live at home. No law is going to stop them. It hasn't stopped them from coming. It won't stop them. The reason we can stand it is that things are worse at home."[68] This describes a situation where push factors seemingly force people to immigrate to this country independent of any pull factors. This is one reason that people continue to come.

Third, immigration policies have traditionally ignored the role of U.S. economic and foreign policies over the years, despite their roles as causal factors for current immigration patterns. For example, U.S. foreign policy toward El Salvador during the 1980s should be analyzed in conjunction with immigration policies toward Central America. The traditional use of undocumented labor (particularly Mexican) in the United States has historically been exploitative as immigration legislation has often been designed to benefit the interests of American agriculture and industry. It has provided a pool of cheap labor and at the same time enabled the government to expel undesirable immigrants. Previous policy of this type is partly responsible for the large immigrant work force in the United States today. Thus, the relationship between American foreign and economic policy and the flow of immigrants entering this country must be addressed in future reform legislation if policies are to be effective.

In an endeavor to identify the underlying causes of continued immigration and create effective reform legislation, independent analysts and government commissions have repeatedly stressed that U.S. immigration legislation must include provisions for foreign aid to sending countries to stimulate their economies and increase their employment opportunities. In doing so, natives of these countries would feel less need to seek a better life abroad. Yet there is little evidence that policymakers are willing to recognize the connection between foreign policy and immigration flows.

By allowing many immigrants to continue to fulfill the role of cheap exploitable labor, IRCA contributes to the immigrants' double bind: the pressures for immigrant labor triggered by the needs and attitudes of American economic and political interests and the pressures of oppressive economic and political situations that pertain in immigrants' homelands. In a sense, the "national origins" concept—manifested through its structural characteristics—has never died. U.S. immigration policy does not reflect the spirit of friendliness and generosity many had intended.

In acknowledging this reality, we raise the question of whether this country has an ethical and moral obligation to promote immigration reforms that take into account the basic human rights of immigrants, especially those whom we have chosen to legalize. We believe that immigration reforms should reflect the same democratic standards and human rights principles that American citizens enjoy. Every immigrant and legalizing alien deserves equal treatment under the law and protection against violations of their rights.

As currently interpreted and implemented, IRCA has the potential to marginalize immigrants further by indirectly limiting the quality of life they can achieve. Despite innovations, immigration policies *de facto* treat newcomers differently from the majority, the established citizenry. Subcultures with separate sets of rights are being perpetuated and discouraged from full integration into mainstream society.

At the present time, however, it seems unlikely that any specific changes will be made in IRCA despite calls for the repeal of employer sanctions.[69] Policymakers fear that any tinkering with IRCA could open "Pandora's box," resulting in disastrous repercussions. Thus, despite the fact that the illegal immigrant population is as large today as it was prior to IRCA, policymakers continue to deny the failure of the immigration reform bill.[70]

Instead, policymakers are once again focusing on broad-based strategies for new immigration reform. Under consideration in 1990 were several bills dealing with immigration reform legislation.[71] Near the end of the year, the Immigration Act of 1990 was passed. Many of the same issues discussed during the formulation of IRCA have reemerged in current immigration debates, such as: (1) whether the United States can absorb still more immigrants; (2) the economic impact of immigrants on domestic employment; (3) the impact of immigrants on social cohesion; and (4) the impact of immigrants on the social welfare system.

In Congress these issues as well as new ones have resulted in interesting compromises: While immigration quotas will be increased, particular preference categories (specifically high-skilled slots) will be greatly expanded.[72] The goal is to move away from family reunification as the basis for immigrant visa allocations to high-skilled employment categories.[73]

Policymakers and analysts across the political spectrum have presented an array of other ideas regarding immigration reform strategies, yet virtually all agree that comprehensive reform is imperative to controlling the American labor force and improving the economy. The greatest controversy arises over the type and number of immigrants to be allowed in.[74]

One perspective is to open the borders, allowing virtually anyone to enter. According to those holding this view, concerns over population increases by the inflow of large numbers of immigrants are unfounded. The United States is extremely resilient and will be able to absorb the influx. Furthermore, it is ultimately beneficial economically to the United States by improving its comparative advantage.[75] A contrasting perspective raises the concern that "immigrants from Third World nations threaten to undermine the essentially European cultural values of the United States."[76] According to those holding this view, too many new immigrants threaten domestic labor, and therefore inflow should be curtailed.

In developing future policy, we recommend the following precepts. First, we must be morally and ethically committed to policies that do not violate basic human rights, ones that acknowledge and build upon the socioeconomic and cultural contributions immigrant workers have made to this country. Most immigrant workers are upwardly mobile, risk-taking individuals. Very few represent the old, stereotypical "bottom of the barrel."[77] Second, immigration reform must recognize the importance of social networks in the migration process[78] and their subsequent potential for easing acculturational stresses. We must, therefore, adopt an approach based on facilitative codevelopment rather than one based on social engineering.[79] This means finding ways to facilitate the transition of immigrants into mainstream society. This can be done by ensuring access to opportunities in education and vocational training and encouraging participation in the political process. Third, we must promote immigrant integration that is network based.[80] We recommend, no later than 1993, the creation of an independently funded task force that combines scholars with agency-based program developers and immigrant representatives.[81] This task force should be in regular consultation with immigrant advocacy groups so that by the mid-1990s more effective post-IRCA immigration reforms can emerge.

NOTES

Special thanks to Patrick Lyness, Chuck Stout, and Bart Givens for insights offered to the authors as this paper was being finalized.

1. Vincent N. Parrillo, *Strangers to These Shores: Race and Ethnic Relations in the United States*, 2d ed. (New York: Wiley & Sons, 1985).

2. Ibid.

3. According to David F. Aberle, *The Peyote Religion Among the Navaho* (New York: Wenner-Gren Foundation for Anthropological Research, 1966), relative deprivation is the self-appraisal by members of a reference group of their situation in relation to the circumstances of another group. For example, members of an immigrant group might perceive their socioeconomic circumstances as being significantly worse than those of members of an established Anglo-American group, but as significantly better than those of members of another U.S. minority group.

4. John W. Berry, "The Acculturation Process and Refugee Behavior," in *Mental Health in Resettlement Countries*, ed. Carolyn L. Williams and Joseph Westermeyer (Washington, DC: Hemisphere Publications Corporation, 1986).

5. John H. Bodley, *Victims of Progress* (Menlo Park, CA: Cummings Publishing, 1975).

6. There are many definitions of "underclass." See, for example, Ken Auletta, *The Underclass* (New York: Random House, 1982); William J. Wilson, *The Truly Disadvantaged: The Inner City, the Underclass and Public Policy* (Chicago: University of Chicago Press, 1987); and Fred R. Harris and Roger W. Wilkins, eds., *Quiet Riots: Race and Poverty in the United States* (New York: Pantheon, 1988). Although these definitions vary, they share several characteristics including: marginalization, underemployment/unemployment, and poverty, each factor as manifested within the United States.

7. Department of Justice, Labor and State, *Staff Report: Interagency Task Force on Immigration Policy* (Washington, DC: U.S. Government Printing Office [GPO], March 1979).

8. Manuel García y Griego, "The Importation of Mexican Contract Laborers to the United States, 1942–1964: Antecedents, Operation, and Legacy," in *The Border that Joins: Mexican Migrants and U.S. Responsibility*, ed. Peter G. Brown and Henry Shue (Totowa, NJ: Rowman and Littlefield, 1983).

9. Geoffrey Rips, "The Simpson-Mazzoli Bill: Supply-Side Immigration Reform," *The Nation* 237, no. 10 (October 8, 1983): 289.

10. Alejandro Portes and Ruben G. Rumbaut, *Immigrant America: A Portrait* (Berkeley, CA: University of California Press, 1990); and George J. Borjas, *Friends or Strangers: The Impact of Immigrants on the U.S. Economy* (New York: Basic Books, 1990).

11. Rips, "The Simpson-Mazzoli Bill."

12. Peter W. Van Arsdale, "New Immigrants to Colorado: Impact of the Amnesty Program," lecture presented to the Society for International Development, Denver, Colorado, October 25, 1989 (unpublished manuscript); and Berry, "The Acculturation Process and Refugee Behavior," use the term "assimilation" differently. Underlying the

present chapter is the belief that ''assimilation'' is useful only as a theoretic abstraction but does not, in fact, occur to immigrants in reality. The notion of assimilating immigrants is rejected both because of its biological connotation as well as the seemingly unidirectional change implied. The term ''acculturation'' is preferred as it includes the notion that immigrants and society are affected by interaction and that immigrants do not divest themselves of all indigenous cultural traits. Acculturation theory does have difficulty in handling such issues as ethnocide.

13. Congressional Research Service, *U.S. Immigration Law and Policy: 1952–1986* (Washington: GPO, 1987).

14. Ibid.

15. Barry R. Chiswick, *Illegal Aliens: Their Employment and Employers* (Kalamazoo, MI: W. E. Upjohn Institute, 1988).

16. Manuel García y Griego, ''Immigration, the 'National Interest' and Public Policy,'' in *The Report of the U.S. Select Commission on Immigration and Refugee Policy: A Critical Analysis*, ed. Ricardo Anzaldua Montoya and Wayne A. Cornelius (La Jolla, CA: Center for U.S.-Mexican Studies, 1983), p. 6.

17. Edwin Harwood, ''American Public Opinion and U.S. Immigration Policy,'' *Annals of the American Academy of Political and Social Sciences* (September 1986): 201–12.

18. Quoted in Congressional Research Service, *U.S. Immigration Law and Policy*, p. 87.

19. Select Commission on Immigration and Refugee Policy, *U.S. Immigration Policy and the National Interest*, Final Report and Recommendations of the Select Commission on Immigration and Refugee Policy to the Congress and the President of the United States, March 1, 1981, pp. 2–3.

20. Thomas Cordi, ''The Select Commission and the Law Enforcement Approach to Immigration Control,'' in *The Report of the U.S. Select Commission on Immigration and Refugee Policy*, ed. Montoya and Cornelius.

21. Congressional Research Service, *U.S. Immigration Law and Policy*, pp. 94–95.

22. Linda Wong, testimony in *Immigration Reform and Control Act of 1986*, hearings before the Subcommittee on Immigration, Refugees, and International Law of the House Committee on the Judiciary, 101st Congress, 1st Session (Washington, DC: GPO, 1990), p. 84.

23. Peter Schey, ''The Immigration Reform and Control Act of 1986: INS Misinterpretation and Misapplication,'' in *Continuing Oversight of the Immigration Reform and Control Act of 1986*, hearings before the Subcommittee on Immigration, Refugees, and International Law of the House Committee on the Judiciary, 100th Congress, 1st Session (Washington, DC: GPO, 1989).

24. Charles K. Kamasaki, testimony in *Review of the Early Implementation of the Immigration Reform and Control Act of 1986*, hearings before the Subcommittee on Immigration and Refugee Affairs of the Senate Committee on the Judiciary, 100th Congress, 1st Session (Washington, DC: GPO, 1987).

25. James C. Paras, testimony in *Review of the Early Implementation of the Immigration Reform and Control Act of 1986*, supra.

26. ''INS Legalization Program Opens to Mixed Reviews,'' *Refugee Reports*, May 15, 1987, p. 12.

27. Kamasaki, testimony in *Review of the Early Implementation of the Immigration Reform and Control Act of 1986*, supra.

28. Maurice Belanger, "Family Fairness: A Success Story," *The Advisor* 1, no. 3 (March/April 1990): 1–6.

29. Diane M. Bessette, "Getting Left Behind: The Impact of the 1986 Immigration Reform and Control Act Amnesty Program on Single Women with Children," *Hastings International and Comparative Law Review* 13 (Winter 1990): 287–304.

30. "Lure of Amnesty Takes Painful Toll on Families," *Dallas Times Herald*, March 24, 1987, p. 7; "The Paradox of Amnesty," *Dallas Times Herald*, March 22, 1987, p. 6.

31. Jonathan Lamb, cited in Peter Applebome, "Amnesty Sending Fearful Aliens for Help, Only Some of It Useful," *New York Times*, January 15, 1987, p. B7.

32. Msgr. Nicholas DiMarzio, letter to Hon. Edward M. Kennedy in *Review of the Early Implementation of the Immigration Reform and Control Act of 1986*, supra.

33. Ibid.

34. Kamasaki, testimony in *Review of the Early Implementation of the Immigration Control and Reform Act of 1986*, supra, p. 67.

35. Figures provided to the Department of Health and Human Services by the INS as of February 25, 1990.

36. National Immigration, Refugee and Citizenship Forum, "Special Edition on Employer Sanctions," *Immigration Bulletin*, March 22, 1990.

37. Leo R. Chavez, Estevan T. Flores, and Marta Lopez-Garza, "Here Today, Gone Tomorrow? Undocumented Settlers and Immigration Reform," *Human Organization* 49, no. 3 (Fall 1990): 193–205; and Chiswick, *Illegal Aliens*. See also Portes and Rumbaut, *Immigrant America*; and Borjas, *Friends or Strangers*.

38. Quoted in Josie Gonzalez, testimony in *Immigration Reform and Control Act of 1986*, supra, p. 205.

39. Jennifer L. Gordon, "Out of the Spotlight and into the Shadows: Life after the Immigration Reform and Control Act of 1986 for Undocumented Central Americans in Boston," unpublished manuscript (Cambridge, MA: Centro Presente, 1989).

40. Gordon, "Out of the Spotlight"; and Gonzalez, testimony in *Immigration Reform and Control Act of 1986*, supra.

41. Quoted in Gordon, "Out of the Spotlight," p. 8.

42. Authorized workers include permanent residents, aliens, refugees, asylees, or newly legalized aliens. In order to be protected under the antidiscrimination provision of IRCA, they must file a notice of intent to become a citizen.

43. General Accounting Office, *Immigration Reform: Employer Sanctions and the Question of Discrimination* (Washington, DC: GPO, 1990).

44. For example, the California Fair Employment and Housing Commission, the New York Task Force on Immigration Affairs, the City of New York Commission on Human Rights, the U.S. Commission on Human Rights, Center for Immigration Rights, Centro Presente, the Coalition for Humane Immigration Rights, and the New York Bar Association. See Dick Kirschten, " 'Citizens-Only' Hiring," *National Journal*, January 27, 1990, p. 194.

45. Robert L. Bach, "Immigration: Issues of Ethnicity, Class and Public Policy in the United States," *Annals of the American Academy of Political and Social Sciences* 485 (May 1986): 141.

46. Lawrence J. Siskind, testimony in *Immigration Reform and Control Act of 1986 Oversight*, supra, p. 38.

47. Ibid., p. 37.

48. Ibid.

49. Shirley Lung, "Employer Sanctions: An Update on Its Impact upon Authorized and Unauthorized Workers in the New York Metropolitan Area," in *Employment Discrimination under the Immigration Reform and Control Act*, hearings before the Subcommittee on Employment Opportunities of the House Committee on Education and Labor, 101st Congress 1st Session (Washington, DC: GPO, 1989).

50. Quoted in Gordon, "Out of the Spotlight," p. 6.

51. Andrew M. Stojny and Lisa K. Channoff, "IRCA's Antidiscrimination Provision: A Three Year Perspective," *Immigration Journal* 13, no. 1 (January 1, 1990), p. 5.

52. General Accounting Office, *Immigration Reform: Status of Implementing Employer Sanctions After Second Year* (Washington, DC: GPO, 1988).

53. Siskind, testimony in *Immigration Reform and Control Act of 1986 Oversight*, supra, p. 36.

54. Cecilia Muñoz, testimony in *Immigration Reform and Control Act of 1986*, supra, p. 59.

55. City of New York Commission on Human Rights, "Tarnishing the Golden Door: A Report on the Widespread Discrimination against Immigrants and Persons Perceived as Immigrants which has Resulted from the Immigration Reform and Control Act of 1986," in *Employment Discrimination under the Immigration Reform and Control Act*, supra.

56. Lung, "Employer Sanctions."

57. Estevan T. Flores, Raul Hinojosa, and Carlos Holguin, "Immigration Reform: An Analysis of Employer Sanctions," paper presented at the Seminario sobre la migración internacional en Mexico; estado actual y perspectivas, October 4–6, 1989, Cococyoc, Moreles, Mexico.

58. Lung, "Employer Sanctions."

59. Ibid., p. 98.

60. City of New York Commission on Human Rights, "Tarnishing the Golden Door," p. 35.

61. Gordon, "Out of the Spotlight," p. 16.

62. Ibid.

63. Flores, Hinojosa, and Holguin, "Immigration Reform."

64. Catherine L. Merino, "Compromising Immigration Reform: The Creation of a Vulnerable Subclass," *Yale Law Journal* 98 (1988): 417.

65. Van Arsdale, "New Immigrants to Colorado."

66. Quoted in Gordon, "Out of the Spotlight," p. 8.

67. Patrick Lyness, Colorado Administrator of State Legalization Impact Assistance Grant Program, personal communication, May 15, 1990; Portes and Rumbaut, *Immigrant America*; Borjas, *Friends or Strangers*; and Chavez, Flores, and Lopez-Garza, "Here Today, Gone Tomorrow?"

68. Quoted in Gordon, "Out of the Spotlight," p. 12.

69. See for example Senate Bill S-2797 and H.J. Res. 534.

70. Lyness, personal communication, 1990.

71. Including H.R. 4300, H.R. 4165, and S-358.

72. See H.R. 4300; and Ben J. Wattenberg and Karl Zinsmeister, "The Case for More Immigration," *Commentary*, April 1990, pp. 19–25.

73. See Cecilia Muñoz, panel discussion on Family Sponsored Immigration: Symposium on Legal Reform, *Georgetown Immigration Law Journal* 4 (1990): 201–20.

74. Dick Kirschten, ''Come In! Keep Out!'' *National Journal*, May 19, 1990, pp. 1206–11.

75. James Cook, ''The More the Merrier: An Interview with Julian Simon,'' *Forbes*, April 2, 1990, pp. 77–81.

76. Kirschten, ''Come In!'' p. 1209, referring to an editorial in Rockford Institute of Illinois *Chronicles*.

77. Peter W. Van Arsdale, ''Secondary Migration and the Role of Voluntary Agencies in the Resettlement Process,'' paper presented at the Conference on the Mental Health of Immigrants and Refugees, March 23, 1990, Houston, TX.

78. See Portes and Rumbaut, *Immigrant America*.

79. Social engineering is the selective elimination of traits and customs. See Bodley, *Victims of Progress*.

80. See James T. Fawcett, ''Network, Linkages, and Migration Systems,'' *International Migration Review* 23, no. 3 (1989): 671–80.

81. See for example Robin M. Wright, ''Anthropological Presuppositions of Indigenous Advocacy,'' *Annual Review of Anthropology* 17 (1988): 365–90. She gives examples of the effectiveness of networking of and by indigenous advocacy groups.

Who Benefitted from the Gains of Asian-Americans, 1940–1980? _____

JOHN GROVE WITH JIPING WU

Most scholars agree that some Asian-Americans have overcome discriminatory barriers and have not only reached parity with white Americans in the early 1960s but have now overtaken the majority whites. This process of crossover is not well understood because there have been few examples in which minorities have actually caught up with and overtaken the superordinate group. Asian-Americans have often been called a success story because they have heavily invested in education and have taken full advantage of equal opportunity strategies. They have moved increasingly into previously restricted jobs and have become economically upwardly mobile. But have all Asian-Americans prospered through this process?

Most studies have pictured Asian-Americans as "model minorities" with little concern for who has actually benefitted from the processed of catching up.[1] The cultural explanations for their success run from the strength of the Asian culture and how it reinforces middle-class values of a commitment to work[2] to kinship networks and ethnic enclaves.[3] Charles Hirschman and Morrison Wong, however, caution that the cultural variables must be interpreted in light of the structural conditions that give rise to them and maintain them over time.[4]

Within these competing explanations, no one denies that progress has been made by Asian-Americans. What is unclear is whether their progress can best be characterized as a "double" minority: whether they fit both a privileged "overminority" as well as a disadvantaged "underminority."[5] If there is an emerging underminority, who are they? As far as we know, no studies have looked at whether this progress has been distributed evenly within the Asian community. Victor Nee and Brett de Bary Nee mentioned the emergence of

Figure 6.1
Asian-Americans: Educational Differentials

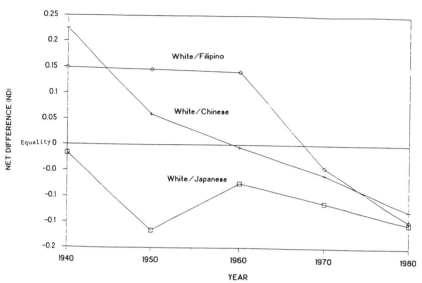

distinct social classes in San Francisco's Chinatown but did not go into any detail.[6]

This chapter examines the extent to which the success of Asian-Americans has created two distinct minority communities: one consisting of families slipping deeply into poverty and the other consisting of upwardly mobile families overtaking their white counterparts. To determine who benefits from the catch-up process, this study examines the socioeconomic census data for the three largest communities within the Asian-American community—Chinese, Japanese, and Filipinos—over the forty-year period from 1940 to 1980.

EDUCATIONAL AND OCCUPATIONAL ATTAINMENT

Education has long been associated with status and respect in most Asian societies, and the Asian-American community is no exception. In charting out the educational success of Asian-Americans, we first compare their achievement with the majority population through Stanley Lieberson's index of net difference (ND).[7] An index of .25 means that the educational attainment of whites exceeds the Asian level by 25 percent more often than the educational attainment of the Asians will exceed the level of whites, and a negative sign means that the Asian group overtakes whites. Figure 6.1 shows that the Japanese have had some educational advantage over whites since 1940; the Chinese reached parity with whites in 1960; while the Filipinos reached parity around 1970. Over 50 percent

Figure 6.2
Asian-Americans: Occupational Differentials

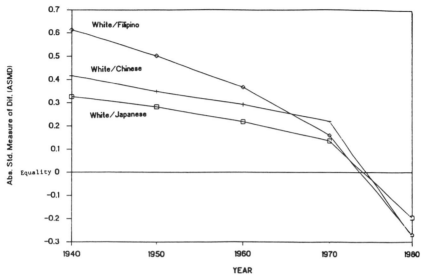

of that advancement by all three groups is due to a larger proportion of Asian-Americans entering higher education than their white counterparts. This finding is generally consistent with the work of Hirschman and Wong (see Table 6.A1 in the appendix).[8]

When the levels of attainment are disaggregated by place of birth for the period 1960–1980 (see Table 6.A2 in the appendix—the census data do not give place of birth for the three groups before 1960), a greater proportion of native-born Chinese-Americans and Japanese-Americans had achieved some level of higher education than their Chinese and Japanese national counterparts. Surprisingly, foreign-born Filipinos have consistently achieved more education than native-born Filipinos. By 1980, 54.9 percent of foreign-born Filipino-Americans had achieved university education compared with 32.5 percent of native Filipinos.

Has this investment in education enabled Asian-Americans to become more occupationally mobile? In measuring the occupational differentials over time, we use Jack Gibbs's absolute standardized measure of differentiation (ASMD), as it controls for structural effects by treating all occupations as if they were of equal size.[9] The closer ASMD scores get to zero, the more similar the two occupational distributions become. The extent to which the occupational upgrading of the three Asian-American groups has become similar to the white community is shown in Figure 6.2. The ASMD scores over forty years show that in each of the three comparisons, the occupational differences between the

Table 6.1
Qccupational Specialization of Asian-Americans, 1940–1980

Representational Proportion

Ethnicity	Professional /Technical	Administrative /Managerial	Farmer/Farm Managerial	Clerical /Sales	Craft /Foremen	Operatives	Service	Labor
1940								
Japanese	0.833	1.541	1.709	1.215	0.645	2.797	0.575	1.253
Chinese	0.833	1.986	0.151	1.290	0.452	0.893	1.490	0.181
Filipino	0.250	0.161	0.198	0.140	0.258	0.161	1.220	2.094
White	0.361	1.162	1.279	2.140	3.742	0.739	0.351	0.394
Black	0.778	0.149	1.686	0.194	1.000	0.414	1.355	1.083
1950								
Japanese	1.218	0.833	1.618	1.246	0.844	0.949	0.649	1.283
Chinese	1.291	2.357	0.176	1.311	2.125	0.457	1.359	0.157
Filipino	0.418	0.202	0.779	0.369	0.641	0.746	1.299	1.833
White	1.455	1.381	1.074	1.697	2.141	1.493	0.279	0.475
Black	0.600	0.214	1.368	0.385	0.828	1.362	1.320	1.263
1960								
Japanese	1.183	1.057	2.235	1.335	1.348	0.791	0.602	0.718
Chinese	1.557	1.814	0.177	1.244	0.565	0.920	1.065	0.137
Filipino	0.817	0.257	0.559	0.591	0.902	0.975	1.086	2.089
White	1.052	1.671	1.265	1.384	1.500	1.098	0.532	0.597
Black	0.409	0.214	0.824	0.445	0.663	1.202	1.715	1.452
1970								
Japanese	1.011	1.319	2.071	1.087	1.365	0.736	0.636	0.951
Chinese	1.374	1.417	0.357	1.398	0.633	0.535	0.800	0.402
Filipino	1.313	0.347	0.357	0.830	0.788	0.896	1.206	1.524
White	0.827	1.583	1.714	1.025	1.298	1.181	0.648	0.683
Black	0.464	0.319	0.429	0.664	0.865	1.646	1.715	1.427
1980								
Japanese	1.031	1.280	2.000	1.137	1.075	0.562	0.776	1.107
Chinese	1.340	1.290	0.143	0.901	0.602	0.901	1.121	0.393
Filipino	1.201	0.770	0.286	1.038	0.892	0.868	1.000	1.089
White	0.830	1.130	2.143	1.072	1.441	1.050	0.691	0.911
Black	0.593	0.520	0.429	0.856	0.968	1.612	1.400	1.536

Asian-Americans and the white majority community become more similar, and by 1980 all three groups had overtaken the occupational position of whites.

Over the forty years, Table 6.1 shows that the occupational specialization of Japanese-Americans had become more evenly distributed.[10] Note that scores higher than 1.0 mean overrepresentation and under 1.0 mean underrepresentation. In 1940 the Japanese were concentrated in managerial-administrative positions and clerical, sales, and skilled operative jobs. Forty years later, the upgrading of the Japanese occupational order spread out to most other sectors, although they still retained their dominance in managerial and administrative positions. Much of this overrepresentation was due to the entrance of the foreign-born Japanese into managerial positions (see Table 6.2).

Chinese-Americans in the 1940s had a much more distinctive polarized occupational pattern. Like the Japanese, they tended to concentrate in managerial-administrative and clerical positions, but they also clustered in service sectors. By 1980, Chinese had entered the professional-technical jobs in greater numbers while maintaining their overconcentration in managerial positions. In 1980 there was still a slight overrepresentation in the service sectors, but much of this was due to foreign-borns (see Table 6.A3 in the appendix).

The occupational order of the Filipinos in the 1940s was skewed toward the bottom; Filipinos clustered in the service and unskilled labor category. Forty years later, Filipinos had moved into most of the previously underrepresented sectors and especially into the professional-technical positions where they have now become an overrepresented group. A greater proportion of those entering the professional jobs were foreign-born (see Table 6.2).

WHO BENEFITS FROM SOCIAL MOBILITY?

We can now tackle the question of whether the beneficiaries from the social mobility of the three Asian-American communities have been distributed evenly among the various economic classes. To determine who has benefitted from economic mobility, we will use D. John Grove and Robert Hannum's inequality (I) measure, which is disaggregated into a threefold classification of the top 10 percent, middle 50 percent, and bottom 40 percent.[11] The application of this measure in Table 6.3 shows that there was a reduction in personal income differences between all three Asian communities and whites from 1950 to 1980 (ΔI scores less than zero); Japanese-Americans overtook whites in 1970, while the Chinese and Filipino-Americans achieved it in 1980. In all three cases the process of overtaking started at the bottom and then extended to the middle to upper income groups. Similarly, in all three cases, the crossover was led by the upper income groups who made over two times the overall gains (top 10 percent/ overall I changes), while middle income Asian-Americans made slightly above average gains. The Japanese and Filipino poor (bottom 40 percent) hardly improved their relative position, while the Chinese bottom 40 percent actually lost ground. As Table 6.3 shows, the top-down catch-up process of Asian-Americans is different from the more even progress of blacks and Chicanos whose advancement is due to middle income groups; upper income blacks and Chicanos actually lost ground compared to their white counterparts.

The findings in Table 6.3 suggest that the progress of Asian-Americans has been highly skewed in favor of the upper to middle income groups. This skewness can be demonstrated in a different way by measuring the overall income inequality

Table 6.2
Occupational Distribution of Asian-Americans by Nativity, 1960–1980

	Professional /Technical	Administrative /Managerial	Farmer/Farm Managerial	Clerical /Sales	Craft /Foremen	Operatives	Service	Labor	Not Represented
1960									
Japanese									
total	13.6	7.4	7.6	21.9	12.4	12.9	11.2	8.9	4.0
for. born	9.6	8.8	13.3	9.4	5.6	14.2	19.7	16.6	2.8
nat. born	14.5	7.1	6.3	24.8	13.9	12.7	9.3	7.1	4.3
Chinese									
total	17.9	12.7	0.6	20.4	5.2	15.0	19.8	16.6	6.5
for. born	16.3	14.5	0.6	13.1	2.9	19.5	28.3	1.3	3.5
nat. born	20.0	10.4	0.6	29.6	8.1	9.4	9.3	2.3	10.3
Filipino									
total	9.4	1.8	1.9	9.7	8.3	15.9	20.2	25.9	6.9
for. born	10.0	1.9	2.3	6.1	7.1	15.3	23.2	31.3	2.8
nat. born	7.9	1.4	0.7	19.2	11.4	17.6	12.3	11.7	17.8
1980									
Japanese									
total	20.0	12.8	1.4	29.9	10.0	6.8	12.8	6.2	-
for. born	18.0	15.6	0.7	21.7	7.3	10.6	20.8	5.2	-
nat. born	20.6	12.0	1.6	32.5	10.8	5.6	10.3	6.5	-
Chinese									
total	26.0	12.9	0.1	23.7	5.6	10.9	18.5	2.2	-
for. born	25.4	12.3	0.1	19.7	5.2	13.4	21.8	1.9	-
nat. born	27.4	14.6	0.2	33.9	6.4	4.4	10.3	2.7	-
Filipino									
total	23.3	7.7	0.2	27.3	8.3	10.5	16.5	6.1	-
for. born	26.2	7.7	0.2	26.0	7.3	10.4	16.4	5.6	-
nat. born	12.3	7.7	0.2	32.2	11.8	10.7	16.9	7.9	-

Sources: 1960 U.S. Census, Special Reports: Nonwhite Population, Tables 43, 44, and 45. 1980 U.S. Census, Subject Reports: Asian and Pacific Islander Population, Tables 21, 27, and 33.

within each Asian community by the Gini coefficient, a measure of income concentration. Figure 6.3 plots the Gini and the Grove-Hannum inequality scores over time. In order to compare the rates of change with other American racial minorities, the Gini and *I* scores were also computed for blacks, Chicanos, and Native Americans. As Figure 6.3 indicates, the polarized form of progress of Asian-Americans was much more marked than the other three racial minorities. The Gini scores for all three Asian groups rose (the lines move downward to the lower righthand corner of the figure) by .1, from .38 to .48. The implication

Table 6.3
Beneficiaries from Changes in Income Inequalities, 1950–1980

	Overall Changes	Average Gains/Losses of Income Groups		
	^I	^Bottom 40%	^Middle 50%	^Top 10%
White/Chinese	-.0727	.0083	-.1208	-.1550
White/Japanese	-.0721	-.0039	-.1082	-.1660
White/Filipino	-.0738	-.0049	-.1103	-.1420
White/Black	-.0611	-.0630	-.1218	.2510
White/Chicano	-.0842	-.0543	-.1362	.0570
White/Indian	-.2554	-.1443	-.3790	-.2020

Note: Absolute change in I (^I) = I_t -I_{t-1}. For example, ^I for Japanese/White = I_{80} -I_{50}. Thus - means convergence, + means divergence. The average change in an income group = ^I in bottom 40%/0.4.

from this downward movement of Asian-Americans, away from the "model minority" upper lefthand corner indicating egalitarian progress, is that the Asian poor have not shared in the success of middle to upper income Asian-Americans.

THE ASIAN POOR

How extensive is Asian poverty in America? Our discussion here shifts from personal income to family/household income where most of the poverty analysis has been conducted. Some dimensions of the problem can be seen when we compute the ratio of family income to the poverty line for 1970–1980 (previous periods are not comparable). Chinese-Americans who earn 74 percent or less than the poverty line rose from 6.5 percent to 9.6 percent of the total Chinese-American population, while for Japanese-Americans the percentages only slightly increased (from 4.5 percent to 4.8 percent). For Filipinos they declined from 7.5 percent to 4.5 percent. Comparable figures show that the poverty ratio increased for whites from 5.5 percent to 6.1 percent, and the ratio for blacks increased from 21 percent to 21.5 percent. Thus, poverty for Chinese-Americans outstripped the increases in black poverty (see Table 6.4).

To understand why poverty has increased so dramatically within the Chinese community, we observe 1980 family income, which is disaggregated into foreign- and domestic-born. The percentage of Chinese in the bottom income category from 1960 to 1980 increased from 3.3 percent to 7.6 percent (the comparable figures for whites and blacks are 4.5 percent to 5.6 percent and 15.8 percent to 19.4 percent, respectively). Most of the increases in the low income of Chinese families are due to the foreign-born (73 percent, which is similar to the Japanese

Table 6.4
Poverty Status of Asian-Americans, 1970–1980

Income less than poverty level

Ethnicity	1969		1979	
	persons	families	persons	families
Japanese	7.5	6.4	6.5	4.2
Chinese	13.3	10.3	13.5	10.5
Filipino	13.7	11.5	7.1	6.2
White	10.9	8.6	9.4	7.0
Black	35.0	29.8	29.9	26.5

Ratio of family income to poverty line

1969	Under .75	.75 to 1.49	1.50-1.99	2.00+
Japanese	4.5	7.1	7.1	81.3
Chinese	6.5	13.3	11.8	68.4
Filipino	7.5	16.2	13.6	62.7
White	5.5	11.4	10.6	72.5
Black	21.0	24.9	13.3	40.6

1979	Under .75	.75 to 1.49	1.50-1.99	2.00 +
Japanese	4.8	6.2	5.6	83.4
Chinese	9.6	13.3	9.3	67.8
Filipino	4.5	10.6	10.0	74.9
White	6.1	11.6	9.5	72.8
Black	21.5	23.0	12.3	43.2

Sources: 1970 U.S. Census, Subject Reports: Japanese, Chinese, and Filipinos in the U.S., Tables 9, 24, and 39; 1970 Detailed Characteristics: U.S. Summary, Table 259. 1980 U.S. Census, Subject Reports: General Social and Economic Characteristics: U.S. Summary, Tables 97, 129, and 165.

figures); contrast this with the Filipino low income, which is largely due to the native-born (60 percent—see Table 6.5).

Other indicators of deepening poverty do not support the contention that the Asian poor are becoming an underclass. Unemployment figures show that the unemployed Japanese have remained very stable over forty years, from 1940 to 1980, while Chinese and Filipino figures show a decline (see Table 6.6). The divorce rates have increased for all three groups over forty years, but the increase is not as great as the rise in the white divorce rate (Table 6.7). Finally, the

Figure 6.3
Changes Between and Within Group Scores, 1950–1980

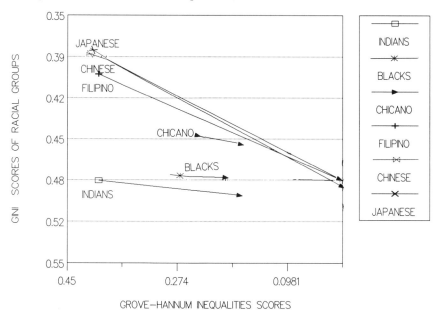

percentage of female-headed households of Asian-Americans has risen at approximately the same rate as their white counterparts, although the increase for Chinese-Americans is less than all other comparable groups (Table 6.8).

CONCLUSION

This chapter supports previous studies that have shown the progress of Asian-Americans since 1940. However, we have gone one step further and asked what kind of progress has been achieved. In comparison with other racial minorities in America, the process of overtaking the white majority has been skewed in favor of upper income Asians. The Asian poor clearly have not benefitted from the success of the middle to upper income Japanese, Chinese, and Filipinos.

On closer examination of the Asian poor, it is equally apparent that Chinese poverty has increased at a greater rate than Japanese or Filipino poverty. A substantial reason for this rise in the number of Chinese poor is the recent immigrants who start at the bottom. Other indicators such as unemployment rates and divorce rates do not suggest that Chinese poverty will result in a permanent underclass. Chinese immigrants often start out poor, but within one generation upward mobility takes place.

Table 6.5
Family Income of Asian-Americans, 1960–1980

Category 1	1959 (under $1,000)	1969 (under $2,000)	1979 (under $5,000) total	for.born	nat.born
Japanese	3.1	4.1	3.5	8.0	2.1
Chinese	3.3	5.1	7.6	8.8	3.3
Filipino	4.2	5.8	4.2	3.9	5.8
White	4.5	4.9	5.6	-	-
Black	15.8	14.7	19.4	-	-

2	($1,000-2,999)	($2,000-4,999)	($5,000-12,499)		
Japanese	8.1	8.4	11.3	19.6	8.6
Chinese	12.7	12.4	18.2	20.9	9.2
Filipino	16.4	13.9	15.8	15.4	17.7
White	14.1	13.0	19.4	-	-
Black	33.6	26.6	30.3	-	-

3	($3,000-4,999)	($5,000-8,999)	($12,500-19,999)		
Japanese	17.5	17.4	15.3	18.1	14.3
Chinese	21.5	23.2	17.7	18.7	14.4
Filipino	31.6	28.3	19.6	19.1	22.0
White	20.0	25.3	22.3	-	-
Black	25.2	29.0	20.9	-	-

4	($5,000-6,999)	($9,000-11,999)	($20,000-24,999)		
Japanese	23.1	17.1	13.5	14.0	13.3
Chinese	20.8	17.4	11.9	11.4	13.5
Filipino	22.8	18.1	13.9	13.7	15.2
White	23.9	19.5	15.0	-	-
Black	14.0	9.0	10.2	-	-

5	($7,000-9,999)	($12,000-14,999)	($25,000-34,999)		
Japanese	25.9	17.4	23.5	18.0	25.3
Chinese	20.2	13.5	19.4	18.0	24.2
Filipino	15.4	13.7	22.3	22.4	22.1
White	21.2	15.3	20.2	-	-
Black	8.0	12.9	11.8	-	-

6	($10,000-14,999)	($15,000-24,999)	($35,000-49,999)		
Japanese	16.0	28.3	20.9	13.1	23.6
Chinese	14.4	21.4	15.6	13.7	22.3
Filipino	7.6	16.1	15.7	16.4	12.7
White	11.2	17.0	11.4	-	-
Black	2.9	6.9	5.6	-	-

Sources: 1960 U.S. Census, Special Reports: Nonwhite Population, Tables 14, 16, 17, and 18; 1960 U.S. General Social and Economic Characteristics: U.S. Summary, Table 95; 1970 U.S. Census, Subject Reports: Japanese, Chinese, and Filipinos in the U.S., Tables 9, 24, and 39; 1970 Detailed Characteristics: U.S. Summary, Table 259. 1980 U.S. Census, Subject Reports: General Social and Economic Characteristics: U.S. Summary, Tables 97, 129, and 165.

Table 6.6
Unemployment Rate of Asian-Americans, 1940–1980

	1940	1950	1960	1970	1980
Japanese	3.3	4.3	2.8	2.5	3.1
Chinese	11.1	8.3	3.9	3.3	3.7
Filipino	9.9	9.2	7.2	4.8	4.8
White	14.2	4.5	4.7	4.1	5.8
Black	18.0	7.9	8.6	7.0	11.8

Sources: 1940 U.S. Census, Special Reports: Nonwhite Population, Tables 31, 37, and 43. 1950 U.S. Census, Special Reports: Tables 6, 10, 11, 12, and 13. 1960 U.S. Census, Special Reports: Tables 34, 35, and 36; General Social and Economic Characteristics, Table 82. 1970 U.S. Census, Subject Reports: Japanese, Chinese, and Filipinos in the U.S., Tables 6, 21, and 36; U.S. Summary, Table 215. 1980 U.S. Census, Subject Reports: Asian and Pacific Islander Population, Tables 23, 29, and 35; General Social and Economic Characteristics: U.S. Summary, Tables 86, 164.

Table 6.7
Divorce Rate of Asian-Americans, 1940–1980

	1940	1950 (widowed or divorced)	1960	1970	1980
Japanese	0.8	6.7	1.4	2.4	4.2
Chinese	0.4	5.7	1.5	1.5	2.4
Filipino	1.1	7.6	3.6	2.8	3.5
White	1.5	10.0	2.4	3.2	6.2

Sources: 1940 U.S. Census, Special Reports: Nonwhite Population, Tables 28, 34 and 40; General Characteristics: Table 15. 1950 U.S. Census, Special Reports: Tables 6, 11, 12, and 13. 1960 U.S. Census, Special Reports: Tables 11, 12, and 13; General Population Characteristics: Table 48. 1970 U.S. Census, Subject Reports: Japanese, Chinese, and Filipinos, Tables 5, 20, and 35; U.S. Summary, Table 203. 1980 U.S. Census, Subject Reports: Asian and Pacific Islander Population, Tables 22, 28, and 34; General Population Characteristics: U.S. Summary, Table 65.

NOTES

1. William Peterson, *Japanese Americans* (New York: Random House, 1971); and Harry Kitano and Stanley Sue, "The Model Minorities," *Journal of Social Issues* 29 (1973): 1–9.

2. Peterson, *Japanese Americans*; Francis Hsu, *The Challenge of the American Dream: The Chinese in the United States* (Belmont, CA: Wadsworth Publishing, 1971); William Caudill and George DeVos, "Achievement, Culture, and Personality: The Case of the Japanese-Americans," *American Anthropologist* 58 (1965): 1102–26; Audrey J. Swartz, "The Culturally Advantaged: A Study of Japanese-American Pupils," *Sociology and Social Research* 55 (1971): 341–53.

Table 6.8
Percentage of Female-Headed Households of Asian-Americans, 1940–1980

	1940	1950	1960	1970	1980
Japanese	6.3	–	6.7	10.3	11.9
Chinese	5.9	–	4.4	6.7	8.5
Filipino	1.5	–	3.8	8.6	11.8
White	7.3	–	9.8	12.5	11.2

Sources: 1940 U.S. Census, Special Reports: Nonwhite Population, Tables 29, 35, and 41. 1960
    U.S. Census, Special Reports: Nonwhite Population, Tables 11, 12, and 13; Detailed
    Characteristics: U.S. Summary, Table 181. 1970 U.S. Census, Subject Reports: Japanese,
    Chinese, and Filipinos, Tables 3, 18, and 33; U.S. Summary, Table 204. 1980 U.S.
    Census, Subject Reports: Asian and Pacific Islander Population, Tables 20, 26, and 32;
    General Population Characteristics: U.S. Summary, Table 66.

3. Peter S. Li, "Ethnic Business Among Chinese in the United States," *Journal of
Ethnic Studies* 4 (1977): 35–41; Samuel Miyamato, "An Immigrant Community in America," in *East Across the Pacific*, ed. Hilary Conroy and T. Scott Miyakawa (Santa Barbara,
CA: CUD Press, 1972); Ivan Light, *Ethnic Enterprises in America* (Berkeley, CA: University of California Press, 1972).

4. Charles Hirschman and Morrison Wong, "Trends in Socioeconomic Achievement
among Immigrant and Native-Born Asian-Americans, 1960–76," *Sociological Quarterly*
22 (1981): 495–513.

5. Arthur Hu, "Asian Americans: Model Minority or Double Minority?" *American
Journal* 15 (1989): 243–57.

6. Victor Nee and Brett de Bary Nee, *Longtime Californ': A Documentary Study of
an American Chinatown* (New York: Patheon, 1972).

7. Stanley Lieberson, "Rank-Sum Comparisons Between Groups," in *Sociological
Methodology*, ed. David Heisse (San Francisco: Jossey-Bass, 1976).

8. Hirschman and Wong, "Trends"; and Hirschman and Wong, "Socioeconomic
Gains of Asian-Americans, Blacks, and Hispanics: 1960–1976," *American Journal of
Sociology* 90 (1984): 584–607.

9. See Jack Gibbs, "Occupational Differentiation of Negroes and Whites in the United
States," *Social Forces* 44 (1965): 159–65. The formula for ASMD is:

$$ASMD = \frac{Xc - Yc}{2} (100)$$

where Xc is the standardized proportion of all members of the dominant group in the
occupation and Yc is the standardized proportion of all members of the nondominant
group in the occupation.

10. The formula for determining the occupational specialization index (OS) is the
following:

$$OS = \frac{Ncj/Nc}{Nij/Ni}$$

where Ncj is the number of individuals in ethnic group c employed in occupation j and Ni is the number of individuals employed in the labor force i.

11. D. John Grove and Robert Hannum, "On Measuring Intergroup Inequality," *Sociological Methods and Research* 15 (1986): 142–59. The inequality measure (I) is a ratio of means measure:

$$I = \sum [(P_i - Q_i) \times M_i]$$

The crossover measure (C) is composed of a distance-type measure and the ratio of means measure:

$$C = \frac{1}{2} \frac{\sum\limits_{i=1}^{k} |P_i - Q_i| M_i - \left| \sum\limits_{i=1}^{k} (P_i - Q_i) M_i \right|}{\sum\limits_{i=1}^{k} |P_i - Q_i| M_i}$$

where i = category of a ranked income distribution, P_i = cumulative proportion through category i of the first group, Q_i = cumulative proportion through category i of the second group, and M_i = midpoint of category.

Appendix: Data Tables

Table 6.A1
Educational Attainment of Asian-Americans, 1940–1980

	1940	1950	1960	1970	1980
PRIMARY					
(0-8 yrs)					
Japanese	54.0	26.4	26.0	19.0	8.9
Chinese	77.5	48.6	40.0	32.5	18.3
Filipino	70.8	54.6	48.8	31.9	15.6
White	57.2	44.5	34.2	26.6	16.6
Black	63.0	66.7	55.1	43.8	27.0
SECONDARY					
(9-12 yrs)					
Japanese	35.1	53.1	54.2	51.5	45.7
Chinese	14.7	28.3	33.5	30.9	31.9
Filipino	21.9	29.4	35.9	32.3	34.3
White	30.7	38.7	47.2	51.0	50.3
Black	26.5	25.4	38.2	45.9	43.5
HIGHER					
(13 yrs+)					
Japanese	9.0	17.0	19.8	29.5	45.4
Chinese	4.5	16.2	26.5	36.6	49.8
Filipino	5.4	9.2	15.3	34.9	50.1
White	10.8	14.0	18.6	22.3	33.1
Black	6.6	4.7	6.7	10.3	21.9

Sources: 1940 U.S. Census, Special Reports: Nonwhite Population by Race, Tables 30, 36, and 42; 1940 General Characteristics, Table 26. 1950 U.S. Census, Special Reports: Nonwhite Population by Race, Tables 10, 11, 12, and 13. 1960 U.S. Census, Special Reports: Nonwhite Population by Race, Tables 14, 21, 22, and 23. 1970 U.S. Census, Subject Reports: Japanese, Chinese, and Filipinos in the U.S., Tables 3, 18, and 33. 1980 U.S. Census, Subject Reports: Asian and Pacific Islander Population, Tables 22, 28, and 34.

Table 6.A2
Educational Attainment of Asian-Americans by Nativity, 1960–1980

	PRIMARY (0-8 yrs)		SECONDARY (9-12 yrs)		HIGHER (13 yrs +)	
	1960	1980	1960	1980	1960	1980
Japanese						
total	26.0	8.9	54.2	45.7	19.8	45.4
foreign born	45.1	11.9	40.7	46.3	14.2	41.8
native born	18.8	7.5	59.3	45.4	21.9	47.0
Chinese						
total	40.0	18.3	33.5	31.9	26.5	49.8
foreign born	53.2	22.7	22.0	30.3	24.8	46.9
native born	24.5	6.4	47.0	35.9	28.5	57.7
Filipino						
total	48.8	15.6	35.9	34.3	15.3	50.1
foreign born	58.0	17.5	24.3	27.6	17.7	54.9
native born	30.4	8.7	59.1	58.8	10.4	32.5

Sources: 1940 U.S. Census, Special Reports: Nonwhite Population by Race, Tables 30, 36, and 42; 1940 General Characteristics, Table 26. 1950 U.S. Census, Special Reports: Nonwhite Population by Race, Tables 10, 11, 12, and 13. 1960 U.S. Census, Special Reports: Nonwhite Population by Race, Tables 14, 21, 22, and 23. 1970 U.S. Census, Subject Reports: Japanese, Chinese, and Filipinos in the U.S., Tables 3, 18, and 33. 1980 U.S. Census, Subject Reports: Asian and Pacific Islander Population, Tables 22, 28, and 34.

Table 6.A3
Occupational Distribution of Asian-Americans, 1940–1980

Ethnicity	Professional /Technical	Administrative /Managerial	Farmer/Farm Managerial	Clerical /Sales	Craft Foremen	Operatives	Service	Labor	Not Represented
1940									
Percentage									
Japanese	0.030	0.114	0.147	0.113	0.020	0.730	0.149	0.347	0.007
Chinese	0.030	0.147	0.013	0.120	0.014	0.233	0.386	0.050	0.006
Filipino	0.009	0.012	0.017	0.013	0.008	0.042	0.316	0.580	0.003
White	0.085	0.086	0.110	0.199	0.116	0.193	0.091	0.109	0.001
Black	0.028	0.011	0.145	0.018	0.031	0.108	0.351	0.300	0.007
Average	0.036	0.074	0.086	0.093	0.031	0.261	0.259	0.277	
Proportion									
Japanese	0.833	1.541	1.709	1.215	0.645	2.797	0.575	1.253	
Chinese	0.833	1.986	0.151	1.290	0.452	0.893	1.490	0.181	
Filipino	0.250	0.161	0.198	0.140	0.258	0.161	1.220	2.094	
White	2.361	1.162	1.279	2.140	3.742	0.739	0.351	0.394	
Black	0.778	0.149	1.686	0.194	1.000	0.414	1.355	1.083	
1950									
Percentage									
Japanese	0.067	0.070	0.110	0.152	0.054	0.131	0.150	0.254	0.013
Chinese	0.071	0.198	0.012	0.160	0.136	0.063	0.314	0.031	0.015
Filipino	0.023	0.017	0.053	0.045	0.041	0.103	0.300	0.363	0.054
White	0.080	0.116	0.073	0.207	0.137	0.206	0.085	0.094	-
Black	0.033	0.018	0.093	0.047	0.053	0.188	0.305	0.250	0.013
Average	0.055	0.084	0.068	0.122	0.064	0.138	0.231	0.198	
Proportion									
Japanese	1.218	0.833	1.618	1.246	0.844	0.949	0.649	1.283	
Chinese	1.291	2.357	0.176	1.311	2.125	0.457	1.359	0.157	
Filipino	0.418	0.202	0.779	0.369	0.641	0.746	1.299	1.833	
White	1.455	1.381	1.074	1.697	2.141	1.493	0.279	0.475	
Black	0.600	0.214	1.368	0.385	0.828	1.362	1.320	1.263	
1960									
Percentage									
Japanese	0.136	0.074	0.076	0.219	0.124	0.129	0.112	0.089	0.040
Chinese	0.179	0.127	0.006	0.204	0.052	0.150	0.198	0.017	0.065
Filipino	0.094	0.018	0.019	0.097	0.083	0.159	0.202	0.259	0.069
White	0.121	0.117	0.043	0.227	0.138	0.179	0.099	0.074	-
Black	0.047	0.014	0.028	0.073	0.061	0.196	0.319	0.180	0.082
Average	0.115	0.070	0.034	0.164	0.092	0.163	0.186	0.124	

Table 6.A3 (continued)

Ethnicity	Professional /Technical	Administrative /Managerial	Farmer/Farm Managerial	Clerical /Sales	Craft Foremen	Operatives	Service	Labor	Not Represented
1960									
Proportion									
Japanese	1.183	1.057	2.235	1.335	1.348	0.791	0.602	0.718	
Chinese	1.557	1.814	0.177	1.244	0.565	0.920	1.065	0.137	
Filipino	0.817	0.257	0.559	0.591	0.902	0.975	1.086	2.089	
White	1.052	1.671	1.265	1.384	1.500	1.098	0.532	0.597	
Black	0.409	0.200	0.824	0.445	0.663	1.202	1.715	1.452	
1970									
Percentage									
Japanese	0.181	0.095	0.029	0.262	0.142	0.106	0.105	0.078	
Chinese	0.246	0.102	0.005	0.337	0.069	0.077	0.132	0.033	
Filipino	0.235	0.025	0.005	0.200	0.082	0.129	0.199	0.125	
White	0.148	0.114	0.024	0.247	0.135	0.170	0.107	0.056	
Black	0.083	0.023	0.006	0.160	0.090	0.237	0.283	0.117	
Average	0.179	0.072	0.014	0.241	0.104	0.144	0.165	0.082	
Proportion									
Japanese	1.011	1.319	2.071	1.087	1.365	0.736	0.636	0.951	
Chinese	1.374	1.417	0.357	1.398	0.633	0.535	0.800	0.402	
Filipino	1.313	0.347	0.357	0.830	0.788	0.896	1.206	1.524	
White	0.827	1.583	1.714	1.025	1.298	1.181	0.648	0.683	
Black	0.464	0.319	0.429	0.664	0.865	1.646	1.715	1.427	
1980									
Percentage									
Japanese	0.200	0.128	0.014	0.299	0.100	0.068	0.128	0.062	
Chinese	0.260	0.129	0.001	0.237	0.056	0.109	0.185	0.022	
Filipino	0.233	0.077	0.002	0.273	0.083	0.105	0.165	0.061	
White	0.161	0.113	0.015	0.282	0.134	0.127	0.114	0.051	
Black	0.115	0.025	0.003	0.225	0.090	0.195	0.231	0.086	
Average	0.194	0.100	0.007	0.263	0.093	0.121	0.165	0.056	
Proportion									
Japanese	1.031	1.280	2.000	1.137	1.075	0.562	0.776	1.107	
Chinese	1.340	1.290	0.143	0.901	0.602	0.901	1.121	0.393	
Filipino	1.201	0.770	0.286	1.038	0.892	0.868	1.000	1.089	
White	0.830	1.130	2.143	1.072	1.441	1.050	0.691	0.911	
Black	0.593	0.520	0.429	0.856	0.968	1.612	1.400	1.536	

Sources: 1940 U.S. Census, Special Reports: Nonwhite Population by Race, Tables 32, 38, and 44. 1950 U.S. Census, Special Reports: Nonwhite Population by Race, Tables 10, 11, 12, and 13. 1960 U.S. Census, Special Reports: Nonwhite Population by Race, Tables 34, 35, and 36. 1970 U.S. Census, Subject Reports: Japanese, Chinese, and Filipinos in the U.S., Tables 7, 22, and 37. 1980 U.S. Census, Subject Reports: Asian and Pacific Islander Population, Tables 21, 27, and 33.

Table 6.A4
Personal Income of Asian-Americans, 1950–1980

	1949	1959	1969 (male)	1979
MEDIAN				
Japanese	$ 1,839	$ 3,205	$ 7,574	$10,287
Chinese	$ 1,799	$ 3,021	$ 5,223	$ 8,133
Filipino	$ 1,689	$ 2,776	$ 5,019	$ 9,406
White	$ 2,053	$ 7,538	$ 8,549	$ 8,464
MEAN				
Japanese	-	-	$ 8,183	$13,104
Chinese	-	-	$ 6,877	$11,738
Filipino	-	-	$ 5,710	$11,468
White	-	-	$11,445	$11,718

Sources: 1950 U.S. Census, Special Reports: Nonwhite Population, Tables 10, 11, 12, and 13. 1960 U.S. Census, Special Reports: Nonwhite Population, Tables 39, 40, 41, 43, 44, and 45. 1970 U.S. Census, Subject Reports: Japanese, Chinese, and Filipinos in the U.S., Tables 6, 21, and 36. 1980 U.S. Census, Subject Reports: Asian and Pacific Islander Population, Tables 23, 29, and 35; General Social and Economic Characteristics: U.S. Summary, Table 95.

Table 6.A5
Personal Income of Asian-Americans by Nativity, 1960–1980

	1959		1979	
	total	for. born	total	for. born
MEDIAN INCOME				
Japanese	$ 3,205	$ 1,779	$10,287	$ 7,944
Chinese	$ 3,021	$ 2,711	$ 8,133	$ 7,528
Filipino	$ 2,776	$ 2,896	$ 9,406	$ 9,710
MEDIAN INCOME				
FOR MALES				
Japanese	$ 4,304	$ 2,505	$15,026	$14,142
Chinese	$ 3,471	$ 3,018	$10,797	$ 9,874
Filipino	$ 3,053	$ 3,053	$10,749	$10,853
MEAN INCOME				
Japanese	-	-	$13,104	$11,994
Chinese	-	-	$11,738	$11,245
Filipino	-	-	$11,468	$11,910

Sources: 1950 U.S. Census, Special Reports: Nonwhite Population, Tables 10, 11, 12, and 13. 1960 U.S. Census, Special Reports: Nonwhite Population, Tables 39, 40, 41, 43, 44, and 45. 1970 U.S. Census, Subject Reports: Japanese, Chinese, and Filipinos in the U.S., Tables 6, 21, and 36. 1980 U.S. Census, Subject Reports: Asian and Pacific Islander Population, Tables 23, 29, and 35; General Social and Economic Characteristics: U.S. Summary, Table 95.

CHAPTER 7

Native American Unemployment: Statistical Games and Coverups

GEORGE E. TINKER AND LORING BUSH

Unemployment is a tragedy for any American citizen old enough to work, but this tragedy is compounded for Native Americans by (1) a dramatic difference between Indian and non-Indian unemployment figures reported for any particular locale in the United States, and (2) what appears to be a severe undercount of Native American unemployment rates reported by federal and state government agencies. In part, this chapter tries to find some explanation of the discrepancy between these government statistics and the figures reported unofficially by many tribes themselves. These undercounts mask the reality of Native American unemployment rates that are apparently, in some cases, almost twenty times higher than what is reported by government agencies. Furthermore, such undercounts result in less funding for government programs that attempt to alleviate these high rates of unemployment. Most important, the undercounts point to the continuation of the corporate and institutional racism entrenched in a system that prevents Native Americans from improving their situation and procuring the resources necessary to ensure their well-being, both as individuals and as culturally discrete communities of people.

The chronic nature of Native American unemployment is well known in Indian circles. Although the reports referred to here were published in various years, it is precisely the chronic problem of Native American unemployment that allows us to validly compare these figures. Despite chronological gaps in the reporting of rates, it seems a virtual certainty that the high rate of unemployment has remained relatively constant. While overall unemployment statistics in the United States are relatively volatile, depending on general and/or local economic factors, Native American unemployment statistics have been relatively static and at an extraordinarily high level for an extended period of time. In this chapter, both published and unpublished reports are compared and used for a survey of three states with high populations of Native Americans and high rates of Native American unemployment.

NATIVE AMERICAN UNEMPLOYMENT STATISTICS

Definitions

Before beginning our analysis, the issue of the definitions used for determining members of the labor force and calculating unemployment rates must be addressed. Indeed, the fact that different government agencies use different definitions for unemployment has particular implications for unemployed Native Americans. These implications are addressed after surveying the data. But even before terms such as labor force and unemployment are defined, it must be noted that there is confusion over the definition of *Indian* or *Native American* on the part of government agencies. The Bureau of Indian Affairs (BIA), for instance, bases its Native American statistics on persons

who are members of Indian tribes, or who are one-fourth degree or more blood quantum descendants of a member of any Indian tribe, band, nation, rancheria, colony, pueblo, or community, including Alaska Native Villages or regional village corporations defined in or established pursuant to the Alaska Native Claims Settlement Act.[1]

On the other hand, the U.S. Department of Labor (DOL) defines Native Americans as those who classified themselves as such on 1980 census forms.

The DOL uses what is called the Local Area Unemployment Statistics (LAUS) methodology to measure unemployment. The data for this methodology are derived from a Current Population Survey (CPS), which is performed by the Bureau of the Census under a contract with the DOL. The CPS combines monthly surveys of approximately 60,000 households nationwide with unemployment claims activity to provide a statistical reflection of what is actually happening in the labor market.[2]

Characteristic data, such as race and age, are collected with the CPS.[3] However, the data by race are collected only for white, black, and Hispanic populations and exclude Native Americans. Thus, DOL does not track unemployment statistics for Native Americans. Some state labor divisions, particularly in areas with high Native American populations, do calculate Native American unemployment. These states use a census methodology of "sharing out" CPS figures by making future labor force projections for racial/ethnic groups based on proportions from the most recent national census data. It must be noted that individuals are not actually counted in this census methodology of sharing out data among racial/ethnic groups. Rather, a cumulative figure derived from the CPS is proportionally divided among racial/ethnic groups, including Native Americans, based on the racial/ethnic proportions from 1980 census information. It seems that assignment of numbers to categories that are over a decade old would result in arbitrary conclusions about the reality of Native American unemployment.

The DOL defines the *civilian labor force* as "All persons, 16 years of age and over, who are not in institutions nor in the Armed Forces and are either 'employed' or 'unemployed.' "[4]

DOL defines *those not in the labor force* as "Persons, 16 years old and over, who are not employed and not seeking employment or are unable or unavailable to work regardless of the reason, such as homemakers, students, retirees, disabled persons, or institutionalized persons."[5]

The *unemployed*, according to DOL, are

Individuals, 16 years of age and older, who are not working, but are looking for work and are available to work. Looking for work requires specific efforts such as sending resumes or canvassing employers. Discouraged workers (those who have given up looking for work because they feel there are no jobs available) are not counted as unemployed.[6]

Clearly implied, but never baldly stated in state labor reports, is that in addition to not counting as unemployed, *discouraged workers* are not included as part of the labor force in DOL unemployment statistics. According to Richard Pottinger, one reason for this exclusion of discouraged workers from the state labor force counts is that the LAUS methodology is structured with a "logical contradiction" between being trained and unemployed. In the LAUS methodology, it is assumed that those who have training and are unemployed will secure work again within the time limit set by DOL (four weeks). Pottinger explains DOL actions toward those who do not fall within the parameters established by the Department:

If these unemployed stop actively looking for jobs, through disillusionment or despair in confrontation with a lack of opportunity, they are actually dropped from the statistical tabulation of the "labor force"! Irrespective of the actual availability of jobs, they are no longer considered part of the labor force and are therefore no longer statistically "unemployed."[7]

This exclusion of discouraged workers from the parameters of DOL's official labor force definition has particular implications for Native Americans. The experience of the Native American work force consists primarily of isolation from job opportunities. Hence, a great many unemployed Native Americans do not have access to employers whom they can canvass for employment. As a result, we would argue that most unemployed Native Americans fall under DOL's definition of discouraged workers and are consequently dropped from calculations of Native American unemployment.

In addition to its methodological oversight of discouraged workers, DOL masks Native American unemployment statistics by calculating overall unemployment rates with figures for all races. When very low unemployment rates for whites are figured in with very high unemployment rates for racial/ethnic groups, and especially the high rates for Native Americans, the overall figure becomes diluted to the point where Native American rates are calculated out of the picture.

It would be expected that the Bureau of Indian Affairs (BIA) would account for this oversight. In its biannual *Indian Service Population and Labor Force Estimates*,[8] the BIA gives an indication that Native American unemployment statistics are consistently higher than figures for the rest of the population. A breakdown of BIA methodology does reveal the percentage of the labor force who are discouraged workers, and the BIA publishes statistics that account for Native American discouraged workers. In order to understand more fully the distinction of the BIA and DOL reports, it is necessary to look at the entire BIA unemployment statistic methodology.

According to its *Population and Labor Force Estimates*, local BIA agencies gather data from the tribes themselves—actual house-to-house surveys conducted by tribal programs and contracts, school and employment records, tribal election statistics, tribal membership rolls maintained by the tribes, and BIA program services records.[9] According to the report,

Accuracy of information varies due to size of geographic areas covered, isolation of many communities, and differing levels of cooperation among respondents. In the majority of cases, data is *estimated* and is not representative of an actual count. Data is reported as collected. In those areas where no new data was obtained, or the local agency regarded the collected information as invalid, 1986 statistics were used, as reported in the 1987 publication of this report.[10]

BIA methodology is distinct from DOL methodology by using raw data derived from sources closely in contact with actual Native American communities. By using only 1980 census proportions and Current Population Surveys that generally overlook Native American communities,[11] state labor divisions that make racial/ethnic distinctions estimate Native American unemployment based on data far removed from the Native American reality. Therefore, we would expect official BIA unemployment figures to be more accurate.

The BIA methodology must be analyzed carefully in order to understand how the unemployment figures reported by the agency fit into the discussion of Native American unemployment. The BIA approach to Indian unemployment is based on the correct assumption that the concept of a "labor force," as it is understood by the DOL, is not appropriate for rural areas such as Indian reservations. Many Native Americans who reside on the reservations are engaged in seasonal or subsistence labor. They are not engaging in behaviors that would include them in DOL labor force and unemployment statistics, such as filing unemployment claims and looking for work.

The BIA accounts for this important issue in its general concept of how Indian unemployment should be reported. The BIA publishes two sets of unemployment figures. One set of figures represents the potential labor force, which includes those seeking work as well as discouraged workers. The latter, however, are weeded out in a further calculation, and a second set of numbers is derived. These figures are published in the last column of the BIA report,[12] but the report does retain the higher figure that reflects the percent of discouraged workers. This higher figure is used by the Indian community, government representatives, and other community advocates because it is more consistent and includes discouraged workers.

Although a discouraged worker figure can be derived using BIA methodology, what must be noted is that, just as with DOL figures, the BIA official results ultimately mask the reality of Native American unemployment. In order to assess accurately the social well-being of American Indians, our statistics must somehow account for those too discouraged to look for work. The BIA differs from the DOL in that the BIA only counts Native Americans, so its official unemployment rate comes somewhat closer to the reality of Native American unemployment than does the DOL. But this provides only minimally greater accuracy that does not yet reflect the true magnitude of Indian unemployment.

Data Comparisons

The 1985 "First Friday Report," *American Indian Unemployment: Confronting a Distressing Reality*,[13] contrasts BIA unemployment figures for Native Americans and overall DOL unemployment figures. The "First Friday Report" uses BIA figures but not those officially reported as Indian unemployment. It uses statistics tucked away in the BIA report that do indeed include discouraged workers. By contrasting these figures with the figures derived from DOL methodology, the "First Friday Report" publicly articulates for the first time the severity of Native American unemployment and the nature of the undercounts in official government reporting.

The problem is best illustrated with actual data. According to the 1980 census, Arizona had the third highest population of Native Americans in the United States.[14] The "First Friday Report" contrasts BIA Native American unemployment rates for Arizona with DOL figures for that state. While DOL reported overall unemployment in the state to be 11.2 percent in 1985, BIA reported Indian unemployment in the state at 41 percent.[15] Using BIA estimates, the "First Friday Report" puts Navajo unemployment as high as 75 percent.[16]

The Navajo Nation is the most populated reservation in the United States, with a population of 94,451 in its Arizona sector in 1989 (the tribe also has some land holdings in Utah and extensive holdings in New Mexico). Of these residents, 88,739 (93.8 percent) are Native Americans, which is certainly to be expected on tribal lands.[17] Further, Native Americans comprise 88 percent of the labor force on Navajo lands in Arizona.[18] The overall 1989 Navajo reservation unemployment rate, which includes all races,[19] is reported by the Arizona Labor Market Information (ALMI) report as 17.8 percent.[20] A 1985 study of Navajo unemployment, however, estimates a reservation ratio of about 1 job for every 100 people.[21] As illustrated later, many of the scarce jobs on reservations are being filled by non-Indians. Given this information, the ALMI 1989 report records a surprisingly low Native American unemployment rate of 19.8 percent on the Navajo reservation.[22] This is in stark contrast to the 75 percent estimate of the "First Friday Report." Because Native American unemployment has been a chronic problem, it is appropriate to assume that their community's unemployment rate has not fluctuated by 55 percent over a 4-year period. This discrepancy demands some explanation.

The ALMI report does break down statistics with reference to racial/ethnic heritage, and the statistics reported are consistent with the already noted general tendency of a much higher unemployment figure for Native Americans than for the general population and other racial/ethnic groups. In 1985, there were between 6,000 and 7,000 jobs held by non-Navajos on the reservation.[23] Of the 188 Hispanics who were in the reservation work force, none were unemployed. Of the 2,396 whites in that particular labor force, 2.2 percent were unemployed.[24]

The discrepancy between Indian and non-Indian unemployment on the Navajo reservation and indeed on every reservation has its explanation in differences in Indian and non-Indian inculturation and in psychological factors related to the self-image of the people as aggressive, independent, and "in control" or as conquered and dependent. Non-Indians on a reservation typically are agriculturalists who lease Indian lands, small business traders who have the capital or access to the capital to run successful businesses targeting Indian people as their primary market, and management-level specialists brought in by the federal government or corporate business structures to provide administrative or technical expertise that the Indians are assumed unable to provide. Hence non-Indian unemployment figures are always characteristically low in any reservation context. Figures 7.1 and 7.2 graph these rates, as reported by ALMI, for the Arizona Navajo reservation.

Another perspective on the Arizona Indian unemployment situation is provided by the ALMI report, where statistics are given for what is classified as the Tribal Service Delivery Area (TSDA), including all reservations except the Navajo. In that area, Native Americans constitute 77 percent of the total population and 70 percent of the work force. ALMI sets the Native American unemployment rate at 22.4 percent, and the overall unemployment rate at 18.6 percent.[25] Figures 7.3 and 7.4 illustrate these statistics.

One of the reservations in this TSDA is the Tohono O'otom reservation, the fifth largest reservation in the United States with a population of 6,772.[26] At least half of Pima County is Tohono O'otom reservation land. ALMI reports unemployment statistics for Pima County but excludes the reservation. By their measurement, the December 1989 overall county unemployment rate was 5.8 percent. Native Americans who live in Pima County but off the reservation make

Figure 7.1
Population and Labor Force, Navajo Nation (ALMI), 1989

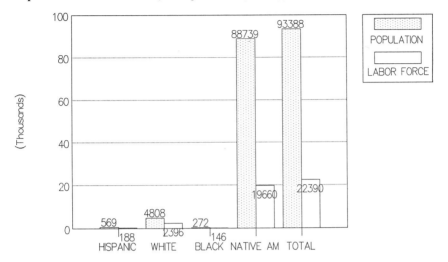

Figure 7.2
**Unemployment Rates, Navajo Nation, ALMI 1989 and "First Friday Report,"
1985**

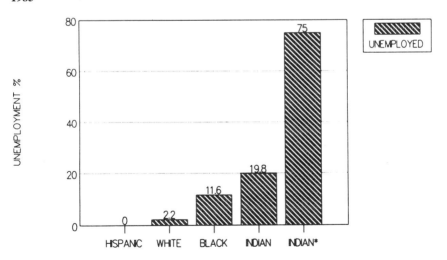

Figure 7.3
Population and Labor Force, TSDA (ex Navajo Nation) (ALMI), 1989

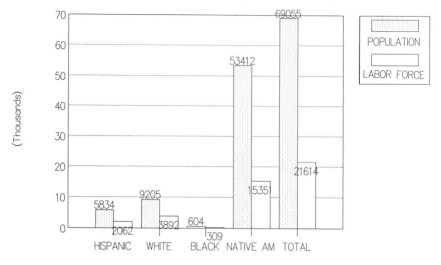

Figure 7.4
Unemployment Rates, TSDA (ex Navajo Nation) (ALMI), 1989

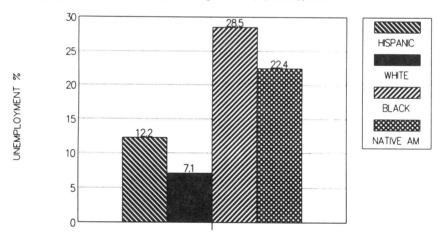

up less than 1 percent of the labor force but suffer a 13.4 percent unemployment rate according to ALMI statistics, that is, a rate 2.31 times the overall rate.[27] According to the "First Friday Report," in 1985 the Tohono O'otom reservation suffered a 30 percent unemployment rate.[28]

The metropolitan area of Phoenix provides further evidence for consistently

Figure 7.5
Population and Labor Force, Phoenix (ALMI), 1989

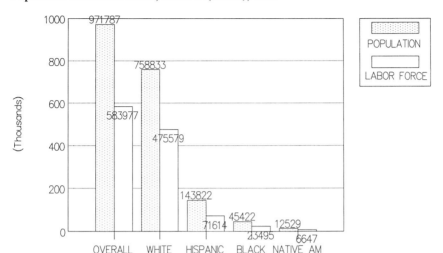

high rates of unemployment for Native Americans, again the highest rate for all ethnic groups in the region. Native Americans account for 1.1 percent of the Phoenix labor force and according to ALMI statistics, suffer a 12.5 percent unemployment rate.[29] The Phoenix Indian Center, however, estimates a much higher unemployment figure of 25 percent[30] for Native Americans in the Phoenix work force.[31]

The ALMI figures for other ethnic groups in the Phoenix area are somewhat lower than the official statistics for Native Americans and significantly lower for the white population of Phoenix. The overall unemployment rate was put at 5.8 percent, Hispanics at 9.3 percent, and African-Americans at 11 percent. By contrast, white unemployment was put at 4.9 percent, leaving the Native American official statistic more than two and a half times higher than that for the white population.[32] Figures 7.5 and 7.6 illustrate these statistical relationships.

The wider area of Maricopa County (less the reservations and Phoenix) follows the same pattern, as we see in Figures 7.7 and 7.8. Here the ALMI report states that 12.9 percent of the Native American labor force is unemployed, while the overall unemployment rate is 5.3 percent.[33] The Salt River Pima reservation is within Maricopa County but is not specifically counted in those ALMI statistics. The tribe itself estimates an unemployment statistic of 35 percent.[34]

Data Analysis

Now that we have considered statistics from several Native American communities, we can place this data in the context of the definition problems discussed

Figure 7.6
Unemployment Rates, Phoenix (ALMI and Phoenix Indian Center), 1989

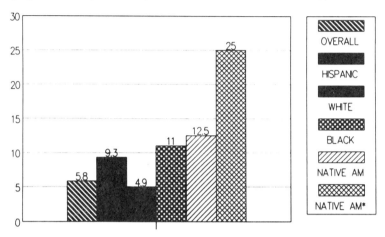

Figure 7.7
Population, Maricopa County, Ex Reservation and Phoenix (ALMI), 1989

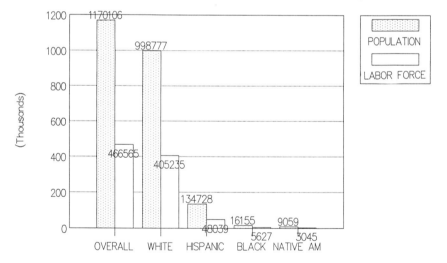

earlier, particularly in terms of discouraged workers. There is a not so subtle
lacuna here, immediately apparent to anyone who knows the context of the

Figure 7.8
**Unemployment Rates, Maricopa County, ALMI and Job Training and
Partnership Administration (JTPA) (Salt River), 1989**

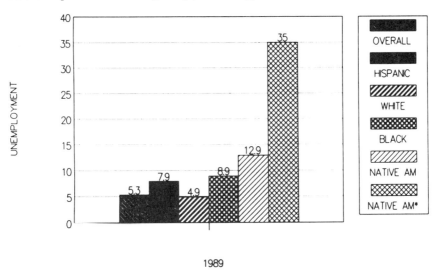

Native American world: The employment situation of the Indian people is so dismal that large numbers of people on nearly every reservation have indeed simply given up looking for work.

The issue is, however, complex. Government unemployment figures are reported by detached government agencies that are not immediately informed of unemployment realities as are agencies more on the "front lines" of the unemployment problem. Thus, government figures are at variance with the figures reported by these front-line agencies and organizations. There is also an analytical problem because the DOL calculates unemployment differently than the BIA. Tribal organizations and the BIA count only the Indian unemployed, so their unemployment statistics are correspondingly higher but are still an undercount. Although these are important points, they do not fully explain the issues that result in the masking of Native American unemployment.

The complexities at the heart of conflicting statistics and government undercounts of Native American unemployment are issues of the psychology of Indian versus white, historical factors, and structures of power in this country. The complexities involve decisions that were made by the federal government, such as the 1887 Dawes Severalty Act, the 1934 Indian Reorganization Act, the disastrous relocation policy initiated by the Eisenhower administration, and a multiplicity of other federal government attempts to "solve" the Indian "problem."

One important factor that has not been considered among these complexities is the perspective of the Indian people themselves. What do Native Americans see as the root of these problems, particularly concerning issues of unemployment?

Karen Thorne, Job Training and Partnership Administration (JTPA) director of the Phoenix Indian Center, and Charlee Hoyt, of the Pascua Yaqui Tribal Job Training and Placement Program, point to some of the major reasons that Native Americans not only have high rates of unemployment but also why they are discouraged workers and thus uncounted in the DOL methodology.[35] Thorne states that the high level of migration between the reservation and the urban area of Phoenix is a major factor in analyzing Native American unemployment. According to Thorne, Native Americans come to Phoenix because the job opportunities seem relatively better, yet most do not find jobs. As a result, many return to the reservation, to what is at least a marginally better support system, in part because of the continuing role of kinship systems and extended family and the comfort provided by cultural placement in some continuing traditional structure. This forces families to make difficult choices because the urban areas afford more employment opportunities. Families become separated so that one member can work in the city while the others stay on the reservation. Hoyt concurs on this point. She states that apart from the unavailability of jobs on the reservation, transportation problems invariably pose another major obstacle to Native American unemployment.

Both Thorne and Hoyt refer to cultural differences as another important barrier to full Indian employment. Thorne states that on the reservation, the pace of life is not as fast as in the urban centers. Punctuality and new technology are difficult for more traditional people. Furthermore, tribal cultures tend to teach cooperation rather than individual competition. By rising above the rest, an individual violates the culture.

Again, Hoyt offers a similar view. She gives the example of job interview techniques to illustrate the divergent cultural values of Native Americans and the dominant white culture. According to Hoyt, the Pascua Yaqui people are not as aggressive as those in the white culture, and thus they do not extol their virtues or talk about their talents during employment interviews. They do not maintain direct eye contact when they are speaking. These actions are often taken by majority culture employers as signs of passivity or lack of accomplishment on the part of Native Americans. Therefore, people such as Thorne and Hoyt, from job training programs, educate potential Native American employees in interview techniques and "front-run" through contact with personnel officers to answer cultural questions that they may have. Because of the realities in training Native Americans to function in a labor market driven by the majority culture, Thorne says that Native Americans must wear multiple hats. She notes that this causes difficulties in adjusting.

Table 7.1
1989 State DOL Unemployment Rates (all races) versus 1980 State Demographer Rates (Native Americans)

County	1989 State DOL Unemployment Rate (All Races)	1980 Demographer Unemployment Rate (Native Americans)
Anoka	3.2	7.0
Dakota	3.2	8.1
Hennepin	2.5	21.1
Ramsey	2.8	16.8
Washington	3.4	9.9

The issues raised by these two women are, for the most part, common concerns among members of the Native American community as they address their unemployment crisis. These issues must be kept in mind as we turn to a sample of unemployment statistics for Minnesota.

The Native American community of Minnesota resides largely on reservations that are much more distant from major metropolitan centers than in the case' of reservations in Arizona. The Minnesota urban centers are found in Minneapolis and St. Paul, where the "First Friday Report" indicates a 1985 unemployment rate of 49 percent.[36] Because of the chronic nature of Native American unemployment rates, it is assumed that this statistic remains roughly the same today.

As was the case in Arizona, the unemployment figures derived from DOL methodology that pertain directly to the Native American community are misleading because they show, with few exceptions, single-digit unemployment rates in areas where much higher unemployment rates can be expected due to the higher numbers of Native Americans in those particular populations. For the counties that intersect the Minneapolis/St. Paul area, however, the December 1989 state unemployment figures do not reflect the large numbers of unemployed Native Americans in the area. Table 7.1 illustrates this by comparing 1980 figures from the Minnesota State Planning Agency: Office of State Demographer[37] with reported December 1989 state unemployment figures for selected counties.[38] The Office of State Demographer does report statistics explicitly for Native American unemployment, but these statistics are predicated on DOL methodologies in census statistics.

These comparisons become more striking as we analyze counties that completely correspond with or partially intercept three Indian reservations at least ninety miles from the major metropolitan centers of Minneapolis and St. Paul. Table 7.2 illustrates these discrepancies with statistics from the December 1989 state unemployment report for all races and statistics from the 1980 State Demographer for Native Americans both in the selected county but living off the reservation as well as for those living on the reservations that are located within

Table 7.2
1989 State DOL Unemployment Rates (all races) versus 1980 State Demographer Rates (Native Americans) by County or Reservation

County	Reservation	1989 State DOL Unemployment Rate (All Races)	1980 Demographer Unemployment Rate (Native Americans)
Mahnomen		7.0	27.4
Becker		7.2	23.2
Clearwater		13.1	21.4
	White Earth	----	25.9
Clearwater		13.1	21.4
Beltrami		4.3	22.1
Lake/Woods		2.5	----
	Red Lake	----	24.6
St. Louis		4.3	22.4
Carlton		5.3	27.1
	Fond du Lac	----	38.0

those same counties.[39] The Minnesota Department of Labor does not keep unemployment statistics for Indian reservations.

The Minnesota State Demographer provides more evidence for the chronic nature of Native American unemployment with the following commentary, which accompanies the figures quoted in the tables.

Unemployment among Indians in the civilian labor force increased from 14.7 percent in 1970 to 20.6 percent in 1980 (statewide). In both years, the unemployment rate of American Indians was 3.5 times higher than the overall state rate. In 1980, unemployment was highest on Indian reservations where one out of every four American Indians was unemployed.[40]

It is appropriate to assume that these 1980 figures have remained relatively constant. In fact, on the basis of the trend toward steadily increased unemployment established statistically between 1970 and 1980, one could argue that Native American unemployment in Minnesota would have more likely increased.

South Dakota provides an especially good sample for comparing DOL unemployment rate methodology results with figures that are more truly representative of Native American unemployment. Several points highlight the significance of the data from South Dakota: the remoteness, poverty, and lack of job opportunity on the reservations in that state; and the request for a variance in DOL methodologies from a coalition directly concerned with Native American unemployment in North and South Dakota. This request is discussed after charting the comparisons of reservation unemployment statistics from the "First Friday Report" and the state labor agencies in South and North Dakota. Table

Table 7.3
1989 State DOL Unemployment Rates (all races) versus 1985 First Friday
Unemployment Rates (Native Americans)

County	Reservation	1989 State DOL Unemployment Rate (All Races)	1985 First Friday Unemployment Rate (Native Americans)
Jackson		3.2	----
Shannon		4.5	----
	Pine Ridge	----	87.0
Todd		5.5	----
	Rosebud	----	86.0
Dewey		5.8	----
Zieback		3.2	----
	Cheyenne River	----	55.0
Lyman		2.2	----
Hughes		3.6	----
	Lower Brule	----	50.0
Corson		2.8	----
Sioux		10.3	----
	Standing Rock	----	79.0

7.3 illustrates the large discrepancies between unemployment rates reported by both sources.[41] In addition to these statistics, the "First Friday Report" cited 5.9 percent as the statewide rate given by the Bureau of Labor Statistics while placing Native American unemployment across the state at 64 percent.[42] The South Dakota Department of Labor reports a statewide unemployment rate of 3.7 percent for December 1989.[43]

Pine Ridge reservation in South Dakota provides another example of the inaccurate reporting of Native American unemployment statistics that results when DOL methodologies are used to calculate unemployment rates in counties that intersect or are completely comprised of Indian reservations. Jackson County and Shannon County, South Dakota, together constitute the whole of Pine Ridge reservation—one of the poorest reservations in the country.

In Table 7.3, note that the "First Friday Report" gives an 87 percent rate of unemployment for Pine Ridge. The 1980 census reports that of the 11,868 residents counted, 61.8 percent were in the labor force.[44] The BIA estimates that 78 percent of the Pine Ridge work force was unemployed as of late 1989.[45] The South Dakota Labor Market Information Center reports, however, that in December 1989 Jackson County had an overall 3.2 percent unemployment rate, and Shannon County had an overall 4.5 percent unemployment rate.[46] Furthermore, Bennett County has many off-reservation Native American residents who undoubtedly face the same barriers to employment as do those who live in the surrounding Pine Ridge and Rosebud reservations, and yet the South Dakota Labor Market Information Center reports only 2.4 percent unemployment for that county.[47]

With statistics as sharply contradictory as these, it is appropriate to question the validity of the Department of Labor LAUS methodology of counting the unemployed as it applies to Native Americans. In October of 1988, this challenge was taken up jointly by Job Service North Dakota, the South Dakota Department of Labor, and the Standing Rock Sioux Tribe, whose reservation straddles both North and South Dakota. In response to "longstanding and substantial controversy" over the unemployment rates for counties containing Indian reservations,[48] these three parties collaborated to contract with the Bureau of the Census for a special census of the Standing Rock reservation. As noted in Table 7.3, Standing Rock has a very high unemployment rate as reported by the "First Friday Report." According to the Standing Rock study, the collaboration among these three entities to conduct a special census amounts to a governmental recognition of flaws in counting unemployed Native Americans. The study states, "There is concern that the official unemployment rates are not adequately reflecting the worsening economic situation nor the human capital available on Indian reservations, and are in turn impeding job development."[49]

In conducting the special census, the Standing Rock study located what was believed to be the major factor, overlooked in standard LAUS methodology, which could account for the consistent undercount and might provide a corrective to reflect more accurately Native American unemployment.

Employment opportunities are closely related to the availability of federal and tribal funds and to the starting and ending of programs administered by the federal and tribal governments. People enter the labor market as employment opportunities expand. For many workers on reservations, however, it is not possible to work long enough or earn enough wage credits to qualify for unemployment insurance and be counted in the claims data.

The results of the special census indicate that the major difference between the estimates derived from the LAUS methodology and those shown by the special census occur in the area of labor force entrants and reentrants. . . . [T]his makes perfect sense for a geographic area where the timing of work search is determined by news of job openings for short-term tribal or federal government programs or other short-term, seasonal work.[50]

Table 7.4 summarizes the major statistical findings of the study. In comparing these figures with the respective state labor department figures for Corson and Sioux counties, we can see that the Standing Rock study numbers are significantly higher.

Figures 7.9 and 7.10 graph our analysis of the breakdowns of the Standing Rock study statistics. Our purpose in representing the statistics in this way is to illustrate that although the Standing Rock study produces figures that are a more accurate reflection of Native American unemployment on the reservation, the new methodology has apparently been ignored. The DOL methodology was still used for the December 1989 report and consequently showed very low 1989

Table 7.4
Standing Rock Special Census Highlights

Population

	Stndg Rock			Sioux Cty.			Cor. Cty.	
Total	Ind.	Other	Total	Ind.	Other	Total	Ind.	Other
8,019	4,799	3,220	3,817	2,833	984	4,202	1,966	2,236

Labor Force Participation

	Civilian Non-Institutional Population (16 and older)	Labor Force	Participation Rate
Total Reserv.	4,688	2,624	56.0%
Indian	2,402	1,136	47.3
Non-Indian	2,286	1,488	65.1

Joblessness

		Official Unemployment Rate	Alternative Measure of Econ. hardship Joblessness Including "Discouraged"	Alternative Measure of Econ. hardship Joblessness Including "Discouraged" and "Under-employed"
Total Reserv.		14.1%	20.3%	24.4%
Indian		28.7	38.6	43.0
Non-Indian		3.0	4.3	8.2

Source: South Dakota Department of Labor, Press Release, Pierre, S.D., May 8, 1989, p. 4.

unemployment rates for the counties that constitute Standing Rock reservation. It should be acknowledged that the methodology variance was granted only in October 1989,[51] and there may be a significant delay before the results in state unemployment reports can be seen. However, if Corson County is taken as an example, the Labor Market Information Center reports an unemployment rate of 2.8 percent for December 1989. Figure 7.10 shows that this statistic, according to the Standing Rock study, represents only a fraction of the unemployed population in Corson County. Since the vast majority of unemployed in Corson County are Native Americans, the statistic functions to conceal Indian unemployment. Even if the variance does begin to rectify these severe undercounts on Standing Rock reservation in the future, it must be noted that Standing Rock is the *only* reservation in the country that has been granted this variance.[52] It is

Figure 7.9
Population and Labor Force, Standing Rock Special Study, October 1988

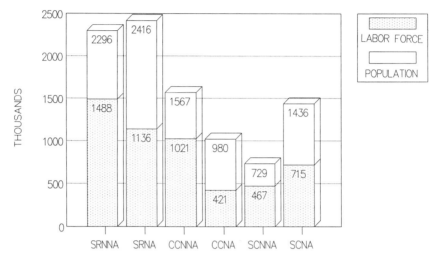

SRNNA: Standing Rock Non-Native American
SRNA: Standing Rock Native American
CCNNA: Corson County Non-Native American
CCNA: Corson County Native American
SCNNA: Sioux County Non-Native American
SCNA: Sioux County Native American

not at all certain that such a methodology variance will be implemented for any other reservation in the United States.

If the Standing Rock study methodology is implemented for other reservations, there is still the problem of unemployment undercounts of Native Americans in urban centers. They face many of the same difficulties as the Indians on the reservations, and we have shown that they also suffer high unemployment rates. We can expect that the undercount problem will continue.

Figures 7.9 and 7.10 illustrate another point that was considered when looking at the statistics from the Navajo Nation. In Standing Rock, as on the Navajo reservation, the white sector of the work force has the lowest rate of unemployment, while the Native American sector of the work force has the highest rate. This fact begins to make explicit the complex economic, political, and social issues that have resulted in not only the high rates of Indian unemployment but also the subsequent oversight of this information in DOL methodologies.

Figure 7.10
Unemployment Rates, Standing Rock Special Study, October 1988

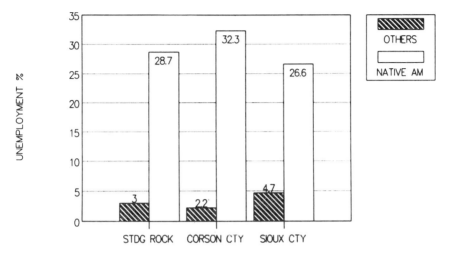

POLICY IMPLICATIONS

One must begin by asking which reality does current government policy reflect, and which reality must future policy address?[53] What becomes clear in sorting through the data on Native American unemployment is that the differing methodologies being used to measure unemployment of Native Americans seem to diverge on the definition of who is unemployed. This results in officially masking the magnitude of Indian unemployment and must eventually generate some conflict over public policy. The Department of Labor has made certain assumptions about how people respond to unemployment and then developed its methodology to quantify unemployment rates accordingly. The policymakers involved have not taken discrete cultural or sociological factors into account as to how Native Americans might respond to unemployment, as well as employment. As a result, Native Americans are not only excluded from DOL definitions but are excluded as well from employment opportunities and unemployment benefits. These policy oversights have been a consistent obstacle for Native Americans as they have tried to gain access to essential resources through employment. The obstacle was not placed arbitrarily, however, but has a history behind it that makes its presence predictable.

The history of this obstacle to full employment goes back to decisions made by the federal government to "solve" the Indian "problem." These attempts at resolution included the 1887 Dawes Severalty Act, the 1934 Indian Reorganization Act, and the relocation policies initiated by the Eisenhower administration.[54] These policies resulted in severe restrictions on what Amartya Sen has called the "entitlements" available to Indian people.[55] Entitlements, as he defines them,[56] are the resources people can command in society, using the rights or opportunities available to them through law, treaty, and policy so that they are able to satisfy their basic human needs. Because of misguided U.S. government policies that have unsuccessfully addressed the Indian "problem," and also because of the treaties with Indian people that have been broken, Native Americans have been denied participation in the economy and instead have had to present themselves variously as white-styled governments, impoverished people, underdeveloped areas, and enterprise zones to the U.S. government in order to gain access to the resources they need to survive.[57] Thus, Indian communities that suffer alarmingly high unemployment rates must add "unemployable" to the list of things they must "be" to the U.S. government and the dominant American society in order to procure necessary resources.

There are two contending arguments explaining the high unemployment rates of Indian people that must be examined in order to illustrate more fully our own argument. The first argument is articulated by Richard Pottinger, who presents evidence that reservations and urban Indian programs are caught in a vicious cycle of "selling" their poverty to the government in order to participate in what Pottinger calls a "grants economy."[58] He uses results from his study of the Navajo reservation to illustrate that the administration of these grants programs becomes, in many cases, the largest employer of Indians on reservations and in urban Indian centers.[59] The benefits do not go to the Indian community, however. The community remains stuck in this cycle of selling their misfortune to the government in order to work for the government. Part of the sales pitch becomes the high unemployment rates. According to Pottinger, this situation ignores the potential of what he states is actually a well-trained, highly qualified Navajo work force because so many people on the reservation have had an opportunity to live in an urban environment.[60] He attributes high Navajo unemployment rates to the public perception of an untrained and unskilled Navajo labor force, thus making "the reservation unattractive to the private sector, who fear the problems of having to utilize the 'hard core unemployed.' "[61]

Pottinger does not look for the underlying causes that generate high Navajo unemployment. He rearticulates his previous argument that the Navajo work force is in fact well trained and highly qualified and that high Navajo unemployment rates reflect a "misuse of talent."[62] Pottinger thus implies that private development on the Navajo reservation will draw upon the qualified work force available there and that this will lower the Navajo unemployment rates. He does address the benefit reaped by white investors and merchants from the "grants economy" and the extent to which this adds to the suffering of Indian people.

Yet in spite of lack of evidence he continues to support the argument that private sector development of the reservations—the capital for which will come primarily from white pockets—will alleviate the high levels of unemployment in Indian communities. The reason Pottinger's scenario will not work is an issue that he never addresses: the corporate racism toward Native Americans is entrenched in a system that prevents Indians from improving their situation.

Another argument is presented by Gary C. Anders, a Cherokee economist. Anders carries Pottinger's argument about the "grants economy" as a barrier to full Indian employment a step further by saying that the economic suffering of Indian people (which would include high unemployment rates) is caused by a dependency on the U.S. government. Anders argues that the contemporary result of colonialism has been the establishment of a "structure of dependency through the formation of *comprador* Indian elites, and these groups now condition the development alternatives open to the tribes."[63] Government grants are brokered through these "white Indians" (Indians who have been co-opted by white socioeconomic institutions), and while administrative jobs are created, the benefits of their employment go outside of the community. These "white Indians" take over tribal resources and transform tribal economies into economies "oriented toward using Indian poverty as a means of securing lucrative government anti-poverty grants that eventually wind up in the hands of the local white contractors, merchants, and businessmen."[64]

Here Anders begins to make explicit the issue of racism as it applies to the issue of Indian underdevelopment, including in the area of Indian employment. According to Anders, these *compradores*, or "white indians," "perpetuate . . . underdevelopment by using the tribe's resources to promote the interests of the dominant white economy at the expense of the tribe."[65] Anders refers directly to the racism that drives this system when he states that " . . . this stratification is intensified by racial discrimination against Indians and the fact that all the important political and economic decision-making institutions in the area are controlled by non-Indians, and therefore tend to reflect the interests of the dominant white economy."[66]

Anders points to the issues that are the basis of our explanation of high Indian unemployment rates. The problem must be tackled from two directions. First, Indian unemployment must be addressed from within the Indian community. High Indian unemployment rates cannot be adequately explained with Pottinger's argument regarding the "grants economy" that perpetuates high Indian unemployment. Anders expands this idea with a discussion of Indian *compradores* who participate in the oppression of the majority of Indian people.

Anders comes closer to what is likely to be a better explanation for high Indian unemployment rates when he identifies the implicit anti-Indian racism in U.S. government structures. The control of key government agencies by non-Indian bureaucrats dealing with Indian issues results in government Indian policy created by non-Indians. The implicit racism that infects DOL policies and results in such a significant undercount in Indian unemployment is just one example of how so many of these policies directly or indirectly impact the social well-being of Native Americans.

CONCLUSION

Indeed, American social structures must recognize their culpability in the codependent relationship in which subtle racist institutional structures use statistical devices in order to conceal massive social deficiencies in Indian communities. The political reality moves even further in blaming racial/ethnic peoples themselves for any social dysfunctionalities in their communities without attempting to put those dysfunctionalities into a broader context of oppression and social or cultural dislocation. It is an example of the victim being blamed for his or her own victimization.

The explanation of the unemployment crisis for Native Americans is found within the larger issue of corporate and institutional racism. Private enterprise alone—even if it is initiated from Native American rather than white capital[67]—will not remove the obstacles to full Indian participation in the U.S. economy because a tribal economy will always, for the foreseeable future, be dependent on the national economy of the United States. It is at that level that institutional racism always functions implicitly and, often enough, naively to create new obstacles. If Native Americans were really welcomed into the political and economic life of the United States, they would demonstrate unemployment rates on par with that of the white population. There would be no "grants economy" to keep Indian communities dependent on the U.S. government. The future of Indian lands would be determined by the people who live on those lands.

That is not the reality today. The reality that determines public policy toward Native Americans may best be illustrated through the analogies used by two racial/ethnic individuals, one black and one Native American. The contrast between these two people—both based on similar images—explains how Native Americans perceive themselves as more excluded from mainstream American society than other racial/ethnic groups. When recently asked about white antagonism toward affirmative action, a black university student replied that the dominant culture of this society does not see affirmative action as racial/ethnic people see it.[68] For this black citizen, affirmative action represented another trip to the rich master's "big house"—which is now the White House—in order to find opportunity in American society. In other words, not much has changed since the days of slavery. Racism still drives the American government, even in its liberal policies of affirmative action.

In testimony at hearings on Pine Ridge reservation regarding the Guaranteed Job Opportunity Program, Sandra Frazier, chairwoman of the Employment Services Department of the Cheyenne River Sioux Tribe, illustrated the overall situation of Native Americans in contemporary American society. Frazier repeated a story told by Felix Cohen, an expert on Indian law. As a rich man enjoyed a plentiful banquet at a table groaning under the weight of food and drink, he looked out the window and saw an old woman, half starved and weeping. The rich man's heart was touched with pity. Because the old woman was breaking his heart, he told his servant to chase her away. The same characterizes the treatment of Native Americans by the U.S. government. Frazier used this story to illustrate that "Many things in Indian country are like nothing else in America."[69]

Unlike the perception of the black student, who at least felt he could go to the "big house" to address his grievances, Native Americans have been consistently "chased away" by the U.S. government and American society as a whole. While we could argue that blacks and other racial/ethnic peoples have been (grudgingly) invited to share a room in the "big house" through affirmative action, Native Americans remain uninvited, despite affirmative action provisions that include Indian communities. All racial/ethnic peoples know who still owns this "big house." They are reminded every time unemployment rates are published for their minority group. For Native Americans, there is a double insult because their unemployment rates surpass those of other racial/ethnic groups and yet remain masked by governmental jargon and methodology. Today, after more than two decades of civil rights reforms in this country, racial/ethnic peoples can only imagine no longer being shut out of the American "big house" or being relegated to the status of a guest in that house. For North American racial/ethnic peoples, and particularly for Native Americans, having their own house remains a distant hope.

NOTES

1. *Indian Service Population and Labor Force Estimates* (Washington, DC: Bureau of Indian Affairs, U.S. Department of the Interior, January 1989).

2. There is a serious problem with the CPS methodology that ultimately has a direct impact on the Job Training and Partnership Administration (JTPA) services provided to Native Americans. This methodology is not inclusive of current statistics as they actually exist in the community surveyed by the CPS. The CPS methodology determines that a certain amount of households will be surveyed, and the community is then divided into survey sectors that do not correspond to the ethnic "pockets" of the area. The statistics derived from this survey are not indicative of the actual ethnic composition of the population and, because of distrust in the community, do not report accurate statistics. Therefore, CPS reports do not reflect the actual need in the community. This results in JTPA program standards being based on faulty statistical profiles of the communities they are to serve.

A further problem is that CPS and Bureau of Labor Statistics (BLS) staff do not include data gathered by community centers from which JTPA programs are administered. This data would be an important component of the Current Population Survey because it provides a more accurate reflection of the ethnic community served by the community center. According to Arlen Rhoads, executive director of the JTPA at the Denver Indian Community Center, a methodology should be developed that includes a weight for these ethnic pockets of the community so that this more accurate data can be reflected in the statistics. Furthermore, census takers from the ethnic community surveyed would be able to collect more accurate data. Interviews, Denver, October 18, 1990, and May 15, 1991.

3. *News* (Washington, DC: U.S. Department of Labor, Bureau of Labor Statistics, October 5, 1990).

4. Arizona Labor Market Information (ALMI), *Annual Planning Information: 1989–1990* (Phoenix: Arizona Department of Economic Security, in cooperation with the U.S. Department of Labor, January 1989), p. 265.

5. Ibid., p. 266.

6. Ibid., p. 268.

7. Richard Pottinger, "Indian Reservation Labor Markets: A Navajo Assessment and Challenge," *American Indian Culture and Research Journal* 9, no. 3 (1989): 11.

8. *Indian Service Population and Labor Force Estimates* (Washington, DC: Bureau of Indian Affairs, Department of the Interior, January 1989).

9. Ibid., p. 2.

10. Ibid., emphasis ours.

11. *Standing Rock: A Labor Force Survey of an American Indian Reservation*, Job Service North Dakota, Michael V. Deisz, Executive Director, prepared by Research and Statistics, Tom Pederson, Chief, Tom Gallagher, Primary Researcher, Labor Market Information Unit, released for printing, March 1990. This report points out the problems with the CPS as it applies to characteristics and issues common to Native American communities. In sampling theory

relatively large samples are required for small populations in order to achieve an equal degree of accuracy. For communities, most countries, and for reservations, monthly samples of households to accurately estimate local unemployment rates would be expensive. In the federal statistical system, *what gets measured is what is most important.* Under these circumstances, locality and community by default have become defined as among the least relevant factors associated with labor market outcomes. . . . What is costly from the standpoint of survey research has, at the same time, become defined as unimportant. (pp. 1–2, emphasis ours)

12. According to Norm Deweever of the Indian and Native American Employment and Training Coalition, Washington, DC, the BIA figures derived after weeding out discouraged workers are suspect because they are based on unsubstantiated data. For example, the BIA *Indian Service Population and Labor Force Estimates* show an overall unemployment rate of 87 percent for Standing Rock reservation and report the same 87 percent rate after the calculation to weed out discouraged workers (Table 3, p. 2). This would mean that on Standing Rock reservation, there are no discouraged workers, and we can be reasonably sure that this is not the case on a reservation that is extremely isolated and lacking in job opportunities. Norm Deweever, interview, November 1990.

13. John Lillie, Taly Rutenberg, Sarah Shella, and Janice View, eds., "First Friday Report," *American Indian Unemployment: Confronting a Distressing Reality* (Washington, DC: Full Employment Action Council and the Lutheran Council U.S.A. Office for Governmental Affairs and the Rural Coalition et al., October 4, 1985).

14. Dwight L. Johnson, Edna L. Paisano, and Michael J. Levin, *We, the First Americans* (Washington, DC: U.S. Department of Commerce, Bureau of the Census, December 1988), p. 4.

15. Lillie, et al., "First Friday Report," p. 11.

16. Ibid., p. 5.

17. ALMI, *Annual Planning Information: 1989–1990*, p. 231.

18. Ibid., p. 235.

19. Throughout this chapter, the overall rate refers to those figures that include all races.

20. ALMI, *Annual Planning Information: 1989–1990*, p. 233.

21. Pottinger, "Indian Reservation Labor Markets," p. 13.

22. ALMI, *Annual Planning Information: 1989–1990*, p. 233.

23. Pottinger, "Indian Reservation Labor Markets," p. 12.

24. ALMI, *Annual Planning Information: 1989–1990*, p. 233.

25. Ibid., pp. 217–20.

26. Johnson, et al., *We, the First Americans*, p. 9.

27. ALMI, *Annual Planning Information: 1989–1990*, p. 162.

28. Lillie, et al., "First Friday Report," p. 5.

29. ALMI, *Annual Planning Information: 1989–1990*, p. 136.

30. The figure as of October 1990 is 22 to 23 percent. Karen Thorne, JTPA Director, Phoenix Indian Center, telephone interview, October 29, 1990.

31. Thorne, interview, November 1989.

32. ALMI, *Annual Planning Information: 1989–1990*, p. 136.

33. Ibid., p. 125.

34. Adeline Tracy, JTPA Program Director, Salt River Pima—Maricopa Tribe, Scottsdale, AZ, interview, November 1989.

35. Thorne, interviews; and Charlee Hoyt, Human Resources Director, Employment and Training, Pascua Yaqui Tribal Council, Tucson, AZ, interview, November 1989.

36. Lillie, et al., "First Friday Report," p. 14.

37. "Social and Economic Characteristics of Minnesota's American Indian Population: 1980," *Population Notes* (St. Paul: Minnesota State Planning Agency: Office of State Demographer, March 1986), p. 4.

38. Research and Statistics, Minnesota Department of Labor, phone communication, December 1989.

39. Ibid., and "Social and Economic Characteristics," p. 4.

40. "Social and Economic Characteristics," p. 3.

41. *South Dakota Labor Bulletin* (Aberdeen, SD: Labor Market Information Center, January 1990), pp. 4–5; Lillie, et al., "First Friday Report," p. 8; and North Dakota Job Service, personal communication, April 1990.

42. Lillie, et al., "First Friday Report," p. 8.

43. *South Dakota Labor Bulletin*, p. 4.

44. Johnson, et al., *We, the First Americans*, p. 25.

45. Dennis King, JTPA Director, Pine Ridge, SD, interview, November 1989.

46. *South Dakota Labor Bulletin*, pp. 4–5.

47. Ibid., p. 4.

48. *North Dakota's and South Dakota's Request for a Variance to the Bureau of Labor Statistics' Local Area Unemployment Statistics Methodology for Estimating Labor Force Data for the Standing Rock Reservation*, submitted by Job Service North Dakota and South Dakota Department of Labor, June 15, 1989, p. 1.

49. Ibid.

50. Ibid., p. 6.

51. Public Information, South Dakota Department of Labor, press release, October 2, 1989.

52. State of South Dakota, "Corson County Designated Labor Surplus Area; Will Benefit from New Job Training Program," press release, October 24, 1990. This press

release states that the counties of Corson (Standing Rock reservation), Buffalo (Crow Creek reservation), Dewey (Cheyenne River reservation), and Shannon (Pine Ridge reservation) have been designated by the U.S. Department of Labor as labor surplus areas due to high unemployment. The labor surplus area classification follows the variance that was granted in calculating unemployment rates. This designation allows for government procurement dollars to be directed "into areas where people are in the most economic need" (p. 2). The labor surplus area designation is effective through September 30, 1991.

53. Pottinger raises this question; see "Indian Reservation Labor Markets," p. 14.

54. See Vine Deloria, Jr. and Clifford M. Lytle, *American Indians, American Justice* (Austin: University of Texas Press, 1983); and Deloria and Lytle, *The Nations Within: The Past and Future of American Indian Self-Government* (New York: Pantheon Books, 1984).

55. Amartya Sen, "Development: Which Way Now?" *The Economic Journal* 93 (1983): 750.

56. Ibid., p. 754. This is not to be confused with Native American treaty entitlements.

57. Based upon ibid., and Pottinger, "Indian Reservation Labor Markets."

58. Pottinger, "Indian Reservation Labor Markets," p. 9.

59. Ibid., pp. 9–10. Pottinger acknowledges that his argument is not clear on the issue of blaming Indian people for this situation, and he states that this portrayal has been criticized for committing a "profound disservice" against the Indian community, as well as being "misleading, morally irresponsible, and patronizing" (p. 10). Pottinger then does not go on to clarify the issue, which he could have done by explicitly addressing issues of white racism toward Indian people that lies at the heart of the "grants economy."

Moreover, Pottinger adds to the characterization of Indians as "unemployable" the label of "unreliable" without accounting for cultural differences that are interpreted as "unreliability" and "incompetence" by white employers. See Thorne and Hoyt interview, pp. 10–12.

60. Pottinger contends that there is a highly trained and educated Navajo work force available for work on the reservation ("Indian Reservation Labor Markets," pp. 2, 4, 6). He states that much of this work force is comprised of Indians who successfully migrated to urban centers and, upon their return to the reservation, significantly complemented the work force because of their work experience. Recent information from the Navajo Reservation Department of Employment and Training (Gordon Nez, Program and Contract Compliance Officer, interview, August 31, 1990) is at odds with Pottinger's argument. According to Nez, the population surveyed by Pottinger is not typical of the Navajo work force. The most recent unemployment rate from the reservation is 51 percent, with the highest rate reported at the interior agency of Chinle, where unemployment is 74 percent.

61. Pottinger, "Indian Reservation Labor Markets," p. 14.

62. Ibid.

63. Gary C. Anders, "Theories of Underdevelopment and the American Indian," *Journal of Economic Issues* 14, no. 3 (September 1980): 693.

64. Ibid., p. 694.

65. Ibid.

66. Ibid.

67. Pottinger, "Indian Reservation Labor Markets," p. 1.

68. "Campus Racism," *All Things Considered*, National Public Radio #890412, 1989.

69. "Pine Ridge Reservation," *Congressional Record—Senate*, S8060, June 14, 1990.

The Politics of Language and the Mexican American: The English Only Movement and Bilingual Education _____

PRISCILLA FALCON AND
PATRICIA J. CAMPBELL

In 1985, the Council for Inter-American Security conducted a special study concerning the domestic policy of bilingual education in relation to the Mexican population in the United States.[1] The policy report, entitled *On Creating a Hispanic America: A Nation Within a Nation*? and written by Rusty Butler, defines why U.S. policymakers should pass the Twenty-seventh Amendment to the Constitution of the United States declaring English as the official language. Senator Steve Symms (R–Idaho) writes in the introduction to this report that "Bilingual education and the bilingual ballots have created an American Apartheid system and that is why I have sponsored legislation in the Senate calling for English as the United States' official language."[2] According to Butler the policy problem of bilingual education affects two domains: federal funding and domestic policy application.

On one level, federally funded programs of bilingual education have "promoted a distinct Hispanic identity, preserving the Spanish language and engendered a separatist mentality,"[3] which, he concludes, could be exploited by the "growing menace of Soviet bloc forces in Nicaragua and infecting Mexico."[4] Butler then proceeds to discredit passage of previous legislation supporting bilingual education. In particular, he writes, "most liberal idealists regard bilingual education as a sacred cow with no concern for [the] internal security of the United States. . . . Bilingual education was to be a form of atonement for the nations' sins against Hispanics and a means of easing America's guilt.'"[5] Butler continues this line of argument by pointing out that the problem with bilingual education is that it has perpetuated the "maintenance of heritage and language and an allegiance to their (Mexican) roots, diminishing a sense of Americanism.''[6] Butler continues his attack on bilingual education claiming that it has national security implications and that "bilingual education has ceased to be an educational question, but rather, it is a political issue."[7] In summary, Butler weaves together his analysis for challenging current U.S. policies that federally fund bilingual education: First, bilingual education, according to Butler, was an ill-conceived policy funded by the federal government with no concern for national security; second, bilingual education has diminished the sense of patriotism among the Mexican population toward the United States; and third, Butler raises the specter of the communist menace. The volatile combination of factors— federal monies, patriotism, and communism—form the unholy trinity of Butler's analysis that the current bilingual education policy is an inappropriate policy and a threat to national security. In an effort to correct all these mistakes, Butler calls for the passage of an English Only amendment to the Constitution of the United States.

Butler then proceeds to the domestic level, specifically focusing on the Mexican population of the southwest. He begins by outlining how the United States conquered the southwest, occupying California, New Mexico, Arizona, Utah, Nevada, Colorado, and Texas since the war of 1848. Butler correctly suggests that many Mexicans have bitterly resented U.S. violation of their national sovereignty.

Butler conveniently omits that, as a result of the war, the Mexican population of the southwest was relegated to the status of a colony within the borders drawn by the United States. The birth of internal colonialism can be traced directly to the military conquest and forceful incorporation of Mexico's northern territories and its inhabitants into the United States. Mexicans today are not colonized in the classic sense. Internal colonialism differs from the classic variety in that it entails not the subordination of a distant land but the acquisition of a contiguous territory.[8] Once that territory is acquired, the local elites are deposed from power and indigenous institutions are completely destroyed. Since the Mexican southwestern United States is a *de facto* colony, the process of colonization has generally gone undetected, and many would argue that while Mexicans were once militarily conquered, today they are a volunteer immigrant group.[9] To view Mexicans as an immigrant group is to miss the essence of internal colonialism. A person of Mexican ancestry living in the United States, whether a recent arrival or a native of the southwest, is subjected to the same conditions of internal colonialism. The conception that Mexicans are an immigrant group reflects the world view of the dominant society.[10] (The significance of this misperception in relation to bilingual education is discussed further below.) Such a concept ignores the fact that the border was established and imposed by the conquering nation. It is a political, militarily imposed border rather than a cultural border. Unlike European immigrants who entered the United States as individuals or families on a voluntary basis, internally colonized people are incorporated into the dominant society by force and as a total population. In addition, the dominant society seeks to exploit and degrade the culture of the internal colony, which experiences prejudice, persecution, subordination, and segregation in order that the dominant group may exercise power and control over the population of the internal colony.[11] The current English Only Movement (EOM), a phenomenon of the 1980s and the 1990s, is a continuation of the process of internal colonialism and the destruction of the language of the Mexican population.

In 1979, a Carnegie Corporation Report indicated that "Bilingual education was the preeminent civil rights issue within Hispanic communities."[12] According to the various studies of the U.S. Civil Rights Commission (1967–1975), bilingual education also surfaced as an issue of primary concern among Mexican community organizations. It was also indicated that the U.S. educational system negated the cultural heritage of the Mexican population, which created a negative impact leading to feelings of inferiority. The systematic destruction of a people's culture and heritage is a violation of basic human rights to language and cultural survival.

Butler claims that these two themes—the history of the United States' acquisition of the southwest and the Mexican demand for bilingual education—combined with the civil rights movement of the 1960s, which led to the formation of advocacy organizations throughout the southwest, are the basis for concerns of the national security of the United States. Butler quotes Dutch criminal psychologist Dick Mudler; "there is a danger that language situations could feed and guide terrorism in the United States."[13] This leads to the conclusion that those who support or actively call for bilingual education become suspect or targeted as terrorists or subversives.

Butler mixes into his equation the proximity of the border and the issue of immigration. He writes, "because of Mexico's proximity many commute on a regular basis, thus preserving a sense of identity and strengthening ties with the native language and culture."[14] Butler acknowledges that the Mexican population has a higher fertility rate than Anglos, and "this combined with the large number of illegal Hispanic immigrants, cemented by common linguistic-cultural ties, could spell trouble for the United States."[15]

In summary, Butler's perception is that the southwest was once a part of Mexico, and that has not been erased from the consciousness of the Mexican people on either side of the border; and the fertility rates and continued immigration lead to the rising demographics.

By the year 2000, the population of the southwest will be over 50 percent Mexican. Immigration has the effect of strengthening and reinvigorating cultural heritage. Mexicans, in general, view language preservation as a human right. The solution, as Butler views it, is the passage of a federal amendment to the Constitution that would thereby effectively curtail federal funding for bilingual education and identify those groups that call for bilingual education as potential threats to the national security of the United States. The focus of this chapter delves into the English Only Movement and attempts to answer the following questions: What groups are behind the movement? What is the basis for their wide support at the grassroots level? And what specific implications exist for bilingual education? Finally, the foregoing will be tied to the further marginalization and perpetuation of the Hispanic community as an increasingly significant part of the growing underclass in the United States.

U.S. ENGLISH AND ENGLISH FIRST

On the national level, the passage of the English Only amendment in California was a victory for the advocates of U.S. English and English First. It gave legislative form to a backlash against bilingualism and biculturalism. Between 1986 and 1989 similar proposals were considered by voters and legislators in thirty-nine states, which brought the total of official English amendment states to seventeen. These states include Arkansas, California, Georgia, Indiana, Mississippi, Tennessee, Nebraska, Illinois, Virginia, Kentucky, North Dakota, Arizona, Colorado, Florida, North Carolina, South Carolina, and Hawaii (which in 1978 adopted a constitutional amendment recognizing both English and native Hawaiian as official languages). The English Only lobby has succeeded in bringing bilingual education policy to the forefront of national debate, calling into question the pedagogical approach of bilingual education and also calling for a federal amendment to the U.S. Constitution that would make English the official language of the United States.

U.S. English was organized in 1983 as an offshoot of the Federation for American Immigration Reform (FAIR), a Washington, DC–based lobby that advocates tighter restrictions on immigration. Its founders were former Senator S. I. Hayakawa, the first sponsor of the English language amendment, and John Tanton, a Michigan ophthalmologist, environmentalist, and population control advocate.[16] Tanton served as president of Zero Population Growth before founding FAIR in the 1970s. U.S. English was born highlighting the "cultural impact" of immigration and calling for stricter immigration controls. By 1988, U.S. English outgrew FAIR, claiming a membership of 350,000.

The stated goal of U.S. English is a constitutional amendment designating English as the official language of the United States.[17] U.S. English is the most prominent of the national English Only organizations, formed to "defend the public interest in the growing debate on bilingualism and biculturalism."[18] The founding Board of Directors included Hayakawa, Tanton, Gerda Bikales, Leo Sorenson, and Stanley Diamond, and its Board of Advisors included Senator Joseph Corcoran, Clarence Barnhart, Walter Annenberg, Andre Emmerich, Walter Cronkite, Alistair Cooke, Saul Bellow, Arnold Schwarzenegger, and others. The 1988 budget of U.S. English was $7 million.[19] U.S. English has been involved in various legislative lobbying activities. These include efforts within Congress to (a) have English declared the official language of the United States; (b) oppose federal legislation for bilingual education and the Voting Rights Act; and (c) oppose FCC licensing application for Spanish-language broadcasts.

U.S. English is dedicated to working, organizing, and helping to finance state-by-state campaigns to make English the official language in a minimum of thirty-seven states in order to lay the groundwork for the passage of the federal amendment to the Constitution. According to a federal tax return, which the Internal Revenue Service makes available to the public in the case of nonprofit organizations, U.S. English was a project of U.S. Inc., a tax-exempt corporation that also channels large grants to FAIR, Americans for Border Control, and Californians for Population Control.

The California English Only campaign, which described itself as a local state group, was financed by U.S. English with between $800,000 and $900,000 for organizing and obtaining signatures to put the issue on the ballot.[20] The national office of U.S. English provided volunteers to the California campaign. In Colorado, U.S. English pumped over $100,000 into the Official English Only campaign, again to acquire enough signatures to put the issue on the ballot and to cover legal expenses. Petition circulators were paid $1 per signature by the national U.S. English office, which as a result of the opposition to the amendment was forced to open an office in Denver before the 1988 election.[21] In the Arizona campaign, U.S. English contributed $160,000 or 97 percent of the total financial support given to the Arizona proposition.[22]

Language politics was the major domestic policy emphasis of the late 1980s and will continue through the 1990s. Language politics is based on dismantling current bilingual education programs. This movement is nothing more than a sophisticated, well-funded racist attack on the Mexican population, which has been able to employ simplistic patriotism to move its policy agenda forward.

In conjunction with U.S. English, another national organization, English First, is also spearheading the national English Only Movement. English First claims a membership of 200,000 and an annual budget exceeding $2 million.[23] English First was created for the express purpose of making the English language amendment the Twenty-seventh Amendment to the U.S. Constitution. It is the only such organization that is registered to lobby Congress directly for action. According to Representative Jim Horn (R–Texas), the proposal for a Twenty-seventh Amendment has been introduced in Congress by Representative Norman Shumway of California, and a similar version was introduced in the Senate by Senator Symms. According to Representative Horn the ''Constitutional Amendment is a simple and direct solution to the dangerous spread of bilingualism in the United States society. Passage of a Constitutional Amendment will end the bilingual ballot and it will let states limit bilingual education without having the anti-English coalitions overturn them in courts.''[24] English First clearly views a federal amendment to the Constitution as the key point in its strategy because courts could not reverse this decision involving bilingual education cases. They cite in particular the *Lau v. Nichols* Supreme Court ruling of 1974 as opening the floodgates of bilingualism. English First proposes that the only way to counter these court decisions effectively is through a constitutional amendment.

Larry Pratt, a former state legislator from Virginia, is spearheading the national campaign of English First. The selling point of this project is the high cost to taxpayers of financial support for bilingual programs. An even more inflammatory claim made by English First has been the statement that "radical activists have been caught sneaking illegal aliens to the polls on election day and using bilingual ballots to cast fraudulent votes."[25]

FUNDING OF THE ENGLISH ONLY MOVEMENT

In 1987, U.S. English hired Linda Chavez, former staff director of the U.S. Commission on Civil Rights, as president, which they hoped would "clean up their image." Chavez lent a certain credibility to the U.S. English forces, dispelling charges that it was in fact a racist organization espousing a racist philosophy. The Linda Chavez–U.S. English relationship ended with her resignation in 1989. Events began with the publication of a memorandum by John Tanton, in which Chavez was described as repugnant and inexcusable, and Chavez felt that actions of chairman and founder of U.S. English, John Tanton, undermined her ability to defend the organization against the charge that it was anti-Hispanic. In the memo Tanton also reflected his bias against Hispanics and Catholics.[26] In the infamous memo, Tanton warned of a Mexican political takeover of the United States through immigration and high birthrates. In other words, to populate is to govern, and he posed the question "will the present majority peaceably hand over political power to a group that is simply more fertile?"[27] Tanton wrote in October 1986, "as whites see their power and control over their lives declining, will they simply go quietly into the night? Why don't non-Hispanic whites have a group identity as do Blacks, Jews, Hispanics?"[28] Tanton responded to his own questions in the following manner: "[N]on-Hispanic white identity must be protected. The Washington based U.S. English has this fall (1989) sponsored referendums in Florida, Arizona, and Colorado to make English the Official Language."[29] According to Tanton the United States is in a crisis. He wrote, "[I]s Apartheid in Southern California's future? The demographic picture in South Africa now is startlingly similar to what we'll see in California in 2030. . . . In South Africa, a white minority speaks one language . . . a non-white majority speaks a different language."[30]

There also occurred a disclosure that involved two large contributors to U.S. English and FAIR that had financed racist propaganda about immigrants and advocated policies of eugenicist sterilization. Chavez explained that she had been denied access to most of U.S. English's financial records.

The funding sources were Cordelia Scaife May, heiress to the Mellon fortune, and the Pioneer Fund, a little known foundation dedicated to racial betterment through eugenics. Scaife May has contributed at least $3.5 million to U.S. English, FAIR, and several other organizations since 1980. She also financed the Laurel Foundation, which in 1983 financed and distributed the *Camp of Saints*, a futuristic novel by French writer Jean Raspail, in which Third World immigrants destroy European civilization.[31] Chavez described the book as racist, xenophobic, and paranoid. She was disturbed to see U.S. English staff members reading it.[32]

The Pioneer Fund was created in 1937 by Harry Laughlin and H. F. Osbourne, eugenicists of the 1920s and 1930s, who supported Hitler.[33] Laughlin described the Fund's objectives as "practical population control by influencing those forces which govern immigration, the sterilization of degenerates and mate selection in favor of American racial strains and solid family stocks."[34] The Pioneer Fund's first project was to popularize "applied genetics in present day Germany," based on Hitler's program of forced sterilization of persons judged to be genetically inferior. John B. Trevor, an officer of the Pioneer Fund, testified in 1965 against repeal of racial preferences in the U.S. immigration law, warning that the change would produce a conglomeration of racial and ethnic elements and lead to a serious decline in culture.[35] In the 1970s, the Pioneer Fund financed the racist genetics research by William Shockley and Arthur Jensen, which purported that blacks have lower IQs than whites. Pioneer also funded the work of Roger Pearson, the author of *Eugenics and Race*, a book that promoted the Aryan superiority theories of Hans Gunther, a racial theorist who published *Racial Elements of European Civilization*. Gunther was a top member of the Third Reich and a racial theoretician, and he was also an associate of Pearson, chairperson of the World Anti-Communist League. Pearson began his career as a racial propagandist during his stay in India as a tea planter.[36] Pearson wrote in 1966, in *Eugenics and Race*, "if a nation with a more advanced, more specialized or in any way superior set of genes mingles with instead of exterminating an inferior tribe, it then commits racial suicide."[37]

Within this web of racial conspirators we find that a U.S. English consultant, Gary Imhoff, a profilic writer on behalf of U.S. English and FAIR, attempted to influence domestic policy. Imhoff coauthored with former Colorado Governor Richard Lamm the *Immigration Time Bomb*, which FAIR helped promote. It is reported that Lamm received money from Tanton to help found a think tank from which Lamm could continue his racist crusade.[38]

In summary, a constellation of right-wing forces was woven together linked by political ideology, propaganda, and funding sources in an effort to create a national campaign to make English the official language of the United States. The umbrella that shielded these groups for a time from public scrutiny was the simplistic patriotism of seeking to make English the official language of the United States; once the umbrella was lifted it was not difficult to identify the forces behind the campaign.

BILINGUAL EDUCATION

Bilingual education has been studied, analyzed, and reanalyzed for decades. Its need, use, methodology, and in fact its definition have been under attack since its conception. The following does not reanalyze this as such but instead discusses bilingual education and the human rights implications of the EOM's impact on language minority groups and more specifically the Hispanic community in the United States. This section addresses the psychosocial dimensions of this within a historical context.

Assimilation versus Pluralism

The debate over whether the United States is an assimilationist or a pluralist society is centuries old. Some argue that the United States is a "melting pot," whereby people of various nations settle in America and assimilate, that is, become an American in the total sense of the word.

The key to understanding modern America is the acculturation process. Acculturation is the "cultural change that results from continuous first-hand contact between two distinct cultural groups."[39] According to John Berry, a leading specialist in refugee and migrant studies, there are four dimensions or four paths for the acculturation process:

1. Assimilation: the relinquishing of one's own cultural identity and moving into the larger society.

2. Integration: some maintenance of the cultural identity of the group as well as becoming an integral part of the larger societal framework.

3. Separation: no substantial relations with the larger society accompanied by a maintenance of ethnic identity and traditions (this differs from segregation, which is forced by the dominant group, whereas separation is chosen).

4. Marginalization: the striking out against the larger society, loss of identity accompanied by feelings of alienation and acculturative stress, and the group's loss of psychological and cultural contact with traditional culture and larger society either by exclusion or withdrawal.

Therefore, according to Berry and others, assimilation is possible.[40]

However, others, including Peter W. Van Arsdale, argue that complete assimilation, while theoretically possible, is not in keeping with the migrant experience: Witness the celebrations of various ethnic holidays, rituals, and so on throughout the United States.[41] This is more in keeping with the pluralist argument, which suggests that U.S. society is more like a salad with each of its ingredients retaining a distinct identity. This contradicts the "melting pot" theory, which suggests a loss of identity for each group entering the society.

Another important aspect of Berry's work has been his studies comparing voluntary and involuntary migrants. From these studies he concludes that involuntary migrants display more indicators of acculturative stress than voluntary migrants. Acculturative stress is defined by Berry as "a generalized physiological and psychological state of the organism brought about by the experience of stressors in the environment and which requires some reduction (for normal functioning to occur) through a process of coping until some satisfactory adaption to the new situation is achieved."[42] Given Berry's work, the Hispanic experience should be seen as unique and therefore of only limited applicability to other immigrant groups.

As already noted, opponents of bilingual education and EOM supporters see bilingual education as antiassimilationist and separatist. Imhoff asserts that native language maintenance is divisive for American society. He claims Hispanic leaders urge language maintenance and the politicalization of bilingual education in order to maintain power. He also points to a distinction between the terms ''immigrant'' and ''minority group''; he suggests that Hispanics are immigrants and that Hispanic leaders are using the term ''minority group'' to politicize issues and thus maintain power.[43] The implication, which is in accordance with Berry's work, is that there is a significant difference between voluntary and involuntary groups. It becomes important here to refer to the more than 70,000 Mexicans who became Americans as a result of the War of 1848 and to the additional thousands of Puerto Ricans who, as a result of the War of 1898, also became Americans.[44] The promises of protection of culture and language have not been fulfilled. While these groups would not classify as refugees, they certainly would also not classify as voluntary migrants or immigrants. Thus, as already noted, we find a situation in which internal colonialism exists and where the target group did not volunteer to enter the acculturation process. Therefore, any comparison with the European immigrant that suggests that the same experiences have held for both groups is an incorrect premise from which incorrect theories such as the Council for Inter-American Security's Atzlan emerge. It is into this context that the debate over bilingual education emerges.

Historical Background

Bilingual education, contrary to popular belief, is not new. It emerged in the midwest in 1830 as a German-English program. The large numbers of German immigrants settling in the midwest provided the demand for this innovative teaching strategy.[45] The success of this program led to its wide usage throughout the area up until the turn of the century. World War I and the wave of ethnocentrism and the exclusionary mentality of the United States during the postwar period saw the near complete elimination of bilingual programs. German language instruction was even dropped from foreign language curricula in high schools and universities.[46] Retaining a native language came to be seen as antiassimilationist and separatist. The ''melting pot'' theory dominated popular thought in the United States. Therefore, those who resisted by maintaining their original language were seen as unpatriotic.

Richard Ruiz makes an interesting comparison between folk/ethnic languages and elite/foreign languages. Folk/ethnic languages are looked down upon by the dominant society, while it is prestigious to study and speak foreign languages.[47] Judith Lessow-Hurley also supports this distinction and goes further by suggesting that language minorities' retention of their language is undesirable, while dual language capability for the elite society is rewarded with praise.[48] The implication, then, for those language minority groups who retain their mother tongue is that they are refusing to assimilate and therefore do not really want to be here; thus, they should not receive the same benefits or privileges as the dominant society. Retention of a folk language is also used as an excuse to exclude and discriminate against minority groups. It is important to acknowledge that the United States has always been a multilingual society.[49]

For the purpose of this chapter, this point becomes important when comparing the European immigrant experience to that of the internally colonized involuntary Hispanic migrant. As already noted, this is not a fair comparison, but the contrast should be examined in order to understand the EOM's motivations.

Those against bilingual education argue that other immigrant groups came and learned the language with little or no assistance from the federal government. This becomes irrelevant in light of the foregoing, that is, the German-English bilingual programs and the vast differences between voluntary and involuntary migrants. The argument that "these people just do not want to learn English" is proven false if one simply looks at the extremely long waiting lists of people for English-as-a-second-language (ESL) classes across the country.

More specifically, bilingual education has come under attack for maintaining the student's language and culture and therefore not mainstreaming the student into American society. Thus, it perpetuates cultural differences and prevents the "melting pot" theory from becoming a reality. Before delving deeper into this issue, it is important to step back and explain how bilingual education reemerged after its demise in the first quarter of this century.

Bilingual education was "reborn" in the early 1960s in Miami, Florida. Language difficulties for the middle-class, well-educated Cuban migrants hindered their academic performance in American schools.[50] The bilingual program's success and popularity became well known. However, it was not until 1968 that the Bilingual Education Act was signed into law.

The new Title VII of the Elementary and Secondary Education Act (ESEA) authorized resources to support educational programs, to train teachers and aides, to develop and disseminate instructional materials and to encourage parental involvement. In spite of its name, the original Bilingual Education Act did not require schools to use a language other than English to receive funding.[51]

However, it was not until the 1970s with the famous *Lau v. Nichols* case that the courts became actively involved in what had been a legalistic debate. In 1974 the U.S. Supreme Court ruled in favor of several Chinese-speaking students in California that their right to a public education had been denied because they could not understand the lessons that were being taught in English. It did not, however, rule specifically in favor of bilingual education but instead put forth "that some form of effective education programming must be available to 'open the instruction' to language minority students."[52] It was the first in a long series of court decisions regarding bilingual education.[53] Today, according to James

Crawford, there are "thirty states [which] have statutes expressly permitting native-language instruction."[54]

Following upon the heels of this came the great bilingual debate. The questions asked were whether or not bilingual education was effective and what types of programs were most or least effective. Critics of bilingual education argued for the "sink or swim" method, also known as immersion. The idea was to completely immerse a student in an English environment where he or she would be forced to learn the language. Canada's immersion program was held as an appropriate example for the United States to emulate. Canada's program had an incredible success rate in making children bilingual.[55] However, proponents of this idea failed to take into account several things: (1) The program was voluntary; (2) it was the dominant language group and not the minority group that was targeted; (3) it offered a chance to acquire another language and not to lose the native language; and (4) the Canadian designers of the program made it clear that the program was designed for the Canadian situation, which was targeting the language majority population instead of what would be in the United States a language minority population.[56]

Other types of programs include Transitional Bilingual Education (TBE), which intends to wean the student off his or her native language and onto English in a few years. Others argue for maintenance of the native language along with the acquisition of English. Still others argue that both TBE and maintenance programs are less important than the amount of language proficiency the child enters school with. Here Anthony Sancho argues that social economic status is a better predictor of achievement than the presence of TBE or maintenance programs. He also notes that "the development and maintenance of two languages in the classroom increases the ability of bilingual children to perform logical and abstract operations such as those required in math."[57] The most widely used, and most widely researched, program is TBE. The evidence on both sides appears to be inconclusive as to which is the most effective program.[58]

However, one needs to keep in mind just what the researchers are trying to find out. Some link a successful bilingual program to lower dropout rates without taking into consideration the social economic status or other variables that play a role in dropout rates. Others view it in terms of unemployment, and still others see it in terms of proficiency in English alone. With various goals or outcomes in mind for research on the topic, it is not surprising that research has proven inconclusive.

CONCLUSION

While the EOM argues for a quick transitional bilingual program, it has also been instrumental in promoting the elimination of funds from bilingual programs. In light of the foregoing, it becomes apparent that what the EOM wants to portray as a simple issue, that is, should the United States have an official language, is much more complicated and carries with it a hidden agenda. Keeping in mind the psychosocial aspects of this argument, and particularly with respect to Berry's work, the EOM should be seen as yet another way to discriminate against the Hispanic community. This attempt to perpetuate the Hispanic position in the growing underclass of the United States only further marginalizes an increasingly large group of Americans, thus causing divisiveness rather than preventing it. As noted throughout this book, there are various ways in which the underclass is being perpetuated in the United States. Therefore, it is important to be aware of the subtle ways in which this is occurring. Language is simply another way of ensuring the dominant class's position in society.

NOTES

1. Rusty Butler, *On Creating a Hispanic America: A Nation Within a Nation?* report prepared for the Council for Inter-American Security (Washington, DC: Council for Inter-American Security, 1985). Rusty Butler is a businessman, columnist, and consultant for the National Council on Educational Research. He is a former university professor in Canada and a former U.S. immigration officer.

2. Ibid., p. 1.

3. Ibid., p. 2.

4. Ibid.

5. Ibid., p. 6.

6. Ibid., pp. 8–9.

7. Ibid., p. 10.

8. Alfredo Mirande, *The Chicano Experience: An Alternative Perspective* (Notre Dame, IN: University of Notre Dame Press, 1985); and Evangelina Enriquez and Alfredo Mirande, *La Chicana: The Mexican American Woman* (Chicago: University of Chicago Press, 1979), pp. 8–13.

9. Mirande, *The Chicano Experience*, chapter 1.

10. Ibid., pp. 1–17.

11. Ibid., pp. 18–47.

12. Rusty Butler, *On Creating a Hispanic America*, p. 7.

13. Ibid., p. 9.

14. Ibid.

15. Ibid., p. 13.

16. Edward Chen, "English-Only: Breeding Bigotry in the U.S.," *Resist Newsletter*, August-September 1988, pp. 3–6; and "U.S. English Started in 1983 in California," *Rocky Mountain News*, September 24, 1988, p. 37.

17. Juan Espinoza, "Pueblo Hispanics Suspicious of Poll," *The Chieftain* (Pueblo, CO), October 8, 1988, p. 1–B; Gail Diane Cox, "English Only: A Legal Polyglot," *National Law Journal*, October 26, 1987, p. 9; and *UP-Date* (U.S. English, Washington, DC) 5, no. 6 (November-December 1987): 6.

18. S. I. Hayakawa, *U.S. English Newsletter*, Washington, DC, undated.

19. Dick Kirschten, "Speaking English," *National Journal* 21, no. 24 (June 17, 1989): 1556–61; *UP-Date* 5, no. 6 (November-December 1987): 6; and "U.S. English Started," p. 37.

20. "Legal Team Gears Up for Proposition 63 Fight," *California United* 1, no. 1 (October 1987); Luis Torres, "Proposition 63—English Only in California, Past and

Future," paper presented at Colorado Coalition Against the English-Only Conference, May 28, 1988, Denver.

21. Tom McAvoy, "Romer Raps Outside Funds in Campaign for Official English," *The Chieftain*, September 27, 1988, p. 5A; "Official English Proponents File More Signatures," *The Chieftain*, October 5, 1988, p. 7A; and Sue Lindsay, "U.S. English Joins English Effort," *Rocky Mountain News*, September 24, 1988, p. 10.

22. James Crawford, *Bilingual Education: History, Politics, Theory and Practice* (Trenton, NJ: Crane Publishing, 1989); and *UP-Date* 6, no. 4 (July-August 1988).

23. Crawford, *Bilingual Education*, p. 66.

24. *UP-Date* 6, no. 4 (July-August 1988).

25. Torres, "Proposition 63—English Only."

26. Larry Lopez, "Pro-English Group Hit by Two Resignation Flaps," *The Chieftain*, October 5, 1988, p. 7A; Careth Ellingson and Cristina Garcia, "Only English Spoken Here," *Time*, December 5, 1988, p. 29; and "Cronkite Quits U.S. English," *Denver Post*, October 15, 1988, p. 1A.

27. Juan Espinoza, "Chicano Democratic Caucus Serious About Official English," *The Chieftain*, October 16, 1988, p. 1A; and Crawford, *Bilingual Education*, p. 57.

28. Lawrence Mosqueda, "English-Only Has Deep Roots in the Ultra-Right," *The Guardian* (New York), November 30, 1988, p. 6.

29. *UP-Date* 5, no. 6 (November-December 1987), p. 6.

30. Michael Novik, "U.S. English and English First: Tied to Racist, Fascist Right," *L.E.A.D.* (Los Angeles), n.d.

31. Peter Strescino, "U.S. English Chief Resigns Her Position," *The Chieftain*, October 18, 1988, p. 1A.

32. Crawford, *Bilingual Education*, p. 66.

33. Russ Bellant, *Old Nazis, the New Right and the Reagan Administration* (Cambridge, MA: Political Research Associates, 1988); and Barry Mehler, "Rightist on the Rights Panel," *The Nation*, May 7, 1988, p. 641.

34. Crawford, *Bilingual Education*, pp. 53–67.

35. Ibid.

36. Bellant, *Old Nazis*, pp. 51–54.

37. Ibid., p. 52; and Roger Pearson, *Eugenics and Race* (London: Clair Press, 1966), p. 26.

38. Crawford, *Bilingual Education*, p. 62.

39. John Berry, Vichol Kim, Thomas Minde, and Doris Mok, "Comparative Studies of Acculturative Stress," *International Migration Review* 21, no. 3 (Fall 1987): 491–492; and John Berry, "Refugee Acculturation and Adaption: An Introduction," *High Plains Applied Anthropologist*, in press.

40. Ibid.

41. Peter W. Van Arsdale, "Theoretical Foundations: Processes of Adjustment, Adaptation and Acculturation," seminar presented at the University of Denver, April 18, 1988.

42. Berry, "Refugee Acculturation"; and Berry et al., "Comparative Studies," p. 492.

43. Gary Imhoff, "The Position of U.S. English on Bilingual Education," *Annals of the American Academy of Political and Social Sciences* 508 (March 1990): 48–61.

44. Colmon Brez Stein, Jr., *Sink or Swim: The Politics of Bilingual Education* (New York: Praeger, 1986).

45. Richard Ruiz, "Bilingualism and Bilingual Education in the United States," in *International Handbook of Bilingualism and Bilingual Education*, ed. Christina Bratt Paulston (Westport, CT: Greenwood Press, 1988), pp. 539–58; and Joel Perlmann, "Historical Legacies 1840–1920," *Annals of the American Academy of Political and Social Sciences* 508 (March 1990): 27–37.

46. See Crawford, *Bilingual Education*; and Ruiz, "Bilingualism and Bilingual Education."

47. Ruiz, "Bilingualism and Bilingual Education."

48. Judith Lessow-Hurley, *The Foundations of Dual Language Instruction* (New York: Longman, 1990).

49. Arturo Madrid, "Official English: A False Policy Issue," *Annals of the American Academy of Political and Social Sciences* 508 (March 1990): 62–65.

50. See Stein, *Sink or Swim*; and Crawford, *Bilingual Education*.

51. Cited in Crawford, *Bilingual Education*, p. 32.

52. Joel Perlmann, Diane August, and Eugene Garcia, *Language Minority Education in the United States: Research, Policy and Practice* (Springfield, IL: Charles C. Thomas Publisher, 1988).

53. See Crawford, *Bilingual Education*; Ruiz, "Bilingualism and Bilingual Education"; and Perlmann, August, and Garcia, *Language Minority Education in the United States*, p. 60.

54. Crawford, *Bilingual Education*, p. 33.

55. Lessow-Hurley, *The Foundations*.

56. See Stein, *Sink or Swim*; Crawford, *Bilingual Education*; and Lessow-Hurley, *The Foundations*.

57. Anthony Sancho, "Bilingual Education: A Three-Year Investigation Comparing the Effects of Maintenance and Transitional Approaches on English Language Acquisition and Achievement on Young Bilingual Children," *Outstanding Dissertations in Bilingual Education: 1981* (Rosslyn, VA: Inter-American Research Association, 1981), pp. 141–51.

58. See Crawford, *Bilingual Education*; and Keith A. Baker and Adriana A. de Kanter, "Federal Policy and the Effectiveness of Bilingual Education," in *Bilingual Education: A Reappraisal of Federal Policy*, ed. Keith A. Baker and Adriana A. de Kanter (Lexington, MA: Lexington Books, D. C. Heath, 1982).

PART IV

Conclusions

CHAPTER 9

Discrimination, the Underclass, and State Policy: An Assessment

GEORGE W. SHEPHERD, JR. AND DAVID PENNA

This book does not answer as many questions as it raises. It was not intended to answer questions but is an attempt to:

1. raise issues that have been ignored in current debates on state policy, particularly the recognition of problems of the underclass;

2. document the relationship between state policy and structural discrimination relating to the maintenance of an underclass; and

3. suggest what directions modifications of state policy should take to confront the problems of a growing underclass.

This chapter assesses the project in each of these areas.

Before assessing the work of this study, one should note the perspective employed. Each contributor has started with his or her own conception of "underclass." This is fitting since the definition, existence, and causes of the underclass are already the focus of much debate. It is clear from the work collected here that the contributors reject the notion of underclass as a "culture of poverty" that stems from inappropriate cultural processes among groups of racial or ethnic subclasses.[1] Instead, the underclass is conceptualized as a segment of the poor unable to overcome their circumstances of poverty and growing violence. This study highlights the structural factors that are the key obstacles this group of poor must overcome. While the underclass is not entirely made up of racial and ethnic minorities, they do constitute a very significant portion of the underclass. Therefore, this study has emphasized the significance of race by focusing upon

racial discrimination—both personal (if subtle) and structural—as policy in rein-
forcing the disadvantages of the underclass.[2]

Racial factors are important for several reasons. Racial and ethnic minority
groups compose a growing proportion of the underclass; therefore, remedies,
even those that are proposed as nonracial,[3] are likely to be seen as benefitting
particular racial groups and threatening to lower-middle-class and dominant,
privileged whites. This, in part, explains the racist backlash against affirmative
action and integration noted by George W. Shepherd. Thus, this study finds that
race cannot be regarded as a secondary factor in policies related to the underclass.[4]
The contributions of Gregory Kellam Scott on affirmative action, David Penna
and Jose Blas Lorenzo on racist violence, and Priscilla Falcon and Patricia J.
Campbell on English Only all identify racial discrimination as primary.

The results of our study suggest that race is an important factor in attempting
to resolve the problems of the underclass. Race-neutral remedies are likely to
be inadequate in resolving the problems; at the same time, race-specific remedies
are likely to be politically unpopular as well as ineffective in assisting that portion
of the underclass that is white.

RECOGNITION

Neoconservatives often reject plans to assist the underclass on the ground that
such social engineering is ineffective. The poor are expected to rise up as earlier
generations of poor are perceived to have done: through hard work and participation in the dominant culture. This analysis ignores both historical and structural
dimensions of the underclass problem. Historically, it was much easier for the
poor to escape poverty in eras when industrial capitalism was expanding.[5] The
argument also mistakes the elimination of ''official'' discrimination for the elimination of structural discrimination (i.e., the persistence of economic, political,
and social structures that originally were based on overt discrimination, such as
housing and employment patterns) and the persistence of subtle private discrimination as noted by Penna and Lorenzo in the increasing pattern of racial violence.
The persistence of these latter factors means that inaction by the state results in
the perpetuation of past patterns of discrimination. In that sense, when the state
utilizes existing economic, political, and social structures, it is enforcing discrimination.

Racism should not only be considered social discrimination or prejudice.
Racism by individual employers is reflected in the opportunities offered to minority individuals. This racism need not be equivalent to race hatred; it can be
merely extreme ethnocentrism. For example, employers may view the culture
of Native Americans neutrally in a social sense but still not wish to hire Native
Americans because the employer perceives them, as a group, as unreliable. While
we have begun to change this perception through education, the larger problem

is what George E. Tinker and Loring Bush show as an enormous unemployment gap between Native Americans and others, especially whites.

This is related to a larger structural problem of discrimination. The dominant state economic policy focuses on creating a favorable climate for business. As part of this policy, labor costs are kept low, making it difficult for the underclass to gain fair employment opportunities or compensation, thus limiting opportunities for the underclass to achieve a decent standard of living or to accumulate capital. It is clear that relief of poverty requires active state efforts to end discrimination.

Several authors raise issues that have been overlooked in the underclass debate. Peter Weiss discusses the underclass and human rights from an international perspective. The problem of the underclass is not only an American problem but a global problem. The domination of the global political, social, and economic system by the United States has contributed to the establishment of the global underclass. This global underclass is not a small ethnic ''minority'' in any sense; it comprises the majority of the population of the world. Therefore, the implications of Weiss's work are twofold. First, the global underclass must have human rights if the claims of universality by advocates of human rights are to have any foundation. Indeed, how can human rights be universal if they are routinely denied to the majority of humans? Second, the solution to the underclass problem must be international or, in reality, transnational since the solution must involve a redistribution of resources in order to achieve social justice. Such a redistribution is likely to be difficult in a world where nation states stubbornly pursue their own narrow interests.

The work on immigration reform in the U.S. done by Debra Kreisberg Voss, Joy Sobrepeña, and Peter W. Van Arsdale suggests alternative policies. They find that U.S. immigration policy, as implemented, increased the chance for marginalization of immigrants, both legal and illegal. This necessarily contributes to the growth of the underclass in the United States. If it is also considered that dire economic, political, and social circumstances in the Third World tend to increase the pressure to migrate to the developed states, one can predict that increased marginalization of the Third World will lead to the continued growth of an underclass in the United States unless greater efforts are made to enhance the skills of the immigrant. It may be in the enlightened self-interest of nations such as the United States to at least begin a process that brings about the fulfillment of the rights of the global underclass, even if that process involves substantial redistribution of resources.

As other authors note, however, ignorance of underclass issues is not limited to U.S. foreign policy. As Tinker and Bush note, U.S. policy toward Native Americans not only has contributed to the establishment and maintenance of an underclass of Native Americans but also has effectively masked the problem through inefficient and ineffective means of gathering information on the problem. Again, such masking is not limited to the recognition of the problems of

Native Americans but also to inner-city residents and the homeless who were the focus of so much debate during the recent census. A state can most effectively exclude individuals and groups from participation in human rights by simply refusing to acknowledge that these individuals and groups exist.

All of these issues have been relatively ignored in the underclass debate and even more so in the debate on state policy in the Reagan-Bush era. Indeed, there are many issues that have been ignored by the study itself: the homeless, the plight of women-headed households, AIDS, and other important issues that are critical to the underclass. We can only hope that these issues will remain on future research agendas.

STATE POLICY AND THE UNDERCLASS

Most of the authors of this study have documented the relationship between state policy and the creation and maintenance of an underclass. Voss, Sobrepeña, and Van Arsdale demonstrate that this relationship can be either inherent in the policy itself or the unintentional result of inefficient implementation. Clearly, then, there is a relationship between state policy and the establishment and maintenance of an underclass; the underclass is not the result of genetic inferiority or the failure of initiative of any particular group of people but the result of additional hurdles erected by state policy, intentionally or unintentionally, that members of the underclass must overcome.

Not all authors are in agreement on some of these points. John Grove and Jiping Wu note that it is difficult to establish the current existence of an underclass among all groups of Asian immigrants. However, their study does have other implications. First, the statistics presented do indicate that, at least initially, economic and social progress is not shared among immigrants in a group or among different groups, despite the myth of the "model minority." Perhaps, indeed, this myth may have actually helped Asian immigrants to break out of the underclass by stereotyping them as successful, just as less favorable societal stereotypes of other ethnic groups prepare both group members and the majority population to expect the failure of members of those groups. Additionally, as Tinker and Bush illustrate, and Grove and Wu acknowledge, accurate census data on members of the underclass are difficult to obtain and are often skewed toward underrepresentation of the underclass. Finally, there also may be very different results regarding the economic and social status of different Asian immigrant groups such as the Vietnamese, Cambodians, Laotians, and Koreans. In any case, the Grove and Wu study lays the groundwork for more complete studies of the social movement of underclass minorities and raises an important question: What are the dynamics of the emergence of groups and individuals from the underclass? This has important implications for the formulation of state policy with regard to the underclass.

Penna and Lorenzo also demonstrate some linkages between state policy and the underclass. They suggest that even policies that are intended to benefit the underclass directly, such as laws against the expression of racial hatred, may have unintended detrimental effects on the underclass. They imply that attempting to benefit the underclass by piecemeal social legislation is likely to be both ineffective and dangerous, so long as structural conditions remain that effectively isolate the underclass from power and decision making. This implies that the underclass cannot be dealt with as mere victims but must actively participate in their own empowerment. This will involve substantial restructuring of political, social, and economic institutions. Indeed, even more effective implementation of existing laws requires modification of public perspectives on poverty and race.

The inequality in power structure and the resulting state policy is demonstrated by Falcon and Campbell in their discussion of the English Only Movement. In cultural spheres where the underclass is seen as a security threat, powerful political forces attempt to coopt the cultural life of the underclass but actually further marginalize the underclass from mainstream society. These proposed policies, such as the elimination of bilingual education, are supposedly justified as in the best interest of integrating the underclass into mainstream U.S. society. This raises important issues regarding the unitary and pluralist models of U.S. society as well as highlighting the importance of empowering the underclass to participate in the policy process while maintaining group identity. Multicultural education in the school systems, integration programs, job training, and bilingual education all need careful research for application to the needs of the underclass.

SUGGESTIONS

Most of the authors suggest changes in the formulation or implementation of policy to benefit the underclass. Most of these suggestions are very broad and involve process rather than policy; none of these suggestions claim to resolve the problems of the underclass alone. Instead, they propose an integrated, participatory approach to debate on the underclass problem.

In his discussion of the reorientation of the affirmative action debate, Scott suggests that the United States must recognize that the Civil War amendments were intended to resolve the political, economic and social disruption of society caused by centuries of enslavement of African-Americans. The promise of these amendments were never fulfilled, and the basic disruptions remain unaddressed. Therefore, one must approach civil rights jurisprudence not from a perspective where slavery is an ancient, unfortunate historical fact but rather a historical fact that has continuing social relevance in the servitude of the underclass. When contemporary civil rights jurisprudence is reoriented to provide economic and social equality, the necessary legal bases for addressing underclass issues can then be found in the Constitution.

As Scott demonstrates, even well-intentioned policies can be ineffective or, as Shepherd notes, be used to challenge the gains made by the underclass when they are controlled and implemented by a political structure that protects privileges. The Supreme Court of the late nineteenth century simply refused to implement the Civil War amendments as written. The Supreme Court of the late twentieth century refuses to recognize structural racial discrimination as a continuing problem as shown by its attacks on affirmative action and integration.

The results of this study suggest, first, that we must be honest about facts. We cannot dispel the reality of the underclass through clever definitions of unemployment and poverty. We must face this reality when making policy, even if this means that academic assumptions valid in one culture must be discarded when analyzing another.

The need to recognize diversity as not only a reality but an ideal also suggests that attacks against bilingualism and the affirmative action backlash are counterproductive. If real progress is to be made, these attacks must be confronted since the basis of these reactions is the interest of a small percentage of dominant whites who do not represent the majority. This is particularly true if the needs of the underclass are objectively presented to the American public who, according to polls, support programs of rectification.

Programs of poverty reduction, as suggested by Shepherd, need to be implemented. These programs will have to take into account two realities: (1) the cultures of groups comprising the underclass, and (2) the reality of discrimination, both individual and structural. These programs should offer members of the underclass an opportunity to participate in "dominant" culture without having to sacrifice their own heritage, as suggested by Falcon and Campbell.

Therefore, what must be changed is process and not merely policy. The underclass should not be merely helped but permitted to help themselves. This can only be accomplished through comprehensive reform of the American social and political fabric. The goal should not be the mainstreaming of the underclass but the strengthening of diversification in American society. The underclass must be permitted not merely to "participate" in American society but empowered to change it.

The American or global society does not have to exist with an underclass. Greater justice for all can evolve with regard to the basic principles of inclusion, participation, social justice, and human rights.

NOTES

1. See the excellent discussion in Leslie Inniss and Joe R. Feagin, "The Black 'Underclass' Ideology in Race Relations Analysis," *Social Justice* 16, no. 4 (Winter 1989): 13–34.

2. See William J. Wilson, *The Declining Significance of Race: Blacks and Changing American Institutions*, 2d ed. (Chicago: University of Chicago Press, 1980). Wilson does not regard race as secondary but places it in the context of economic variables.

3. See William J. Wilson, *The Truly Disadvantaged: The Inner City, the Underclass and Public Policy* (Chicago: University of Chicago Press, 1987), pp. 140–64.

4. See Gerald Bennett, "Racial Inequality and the Poor: A Critique of W. J. Wilson's *The Truly Disadvantaged*," *Social Justice* 16, no. 4 (Winter 1989): 202–7. See p. 203 for criticism of Wilson's underemphasis of race.

5. Inniss and Feagin, "The Black 'Underclass' Ideology," p. 27.

Selected Bibliography

THE UNDERCLASS: GENERAL

Auletta, Ken. *The Underclass*. New York: Random House, 1982.

Cottingham, Clement. *Race, Poverty and the Urban Underclass*. Lexington, MA: Lexington Books, 1982.

Delgado, Richard. "Zero-Based Racial Politics: An Evaluation of Three Best-Case Arguments on Behalf of the Non-White Underclass." *Georgetown Law Journal* 78, no. 6 (August 1990): 1929.

Dewart, Janet, ed. *The State of Black America, 1990*. New York: National Urban League, 1990.

Glasgow, Douglas G. *The Black Underclass: Poverty, Unemployment and Entrapment of Ghetto Youth*. San Francisco: Jossey-Bass Publishers, 1980.

Graham, Hugh Davis. *The Civil Rights Era: Origins and Development of National Policy, 1960–1972*. New York: Oxford University Press, 1990.

Hagedorn, John M. *People and Folks: Gangs, Crime and the Underclass in a Rust-Belt City*. Chicago: Lakeview Press, 1988.

Hammonds, Andre D. "The Black Underclass: Conflicting Perspectives." *Western Journal of Black Studies* 13, no. 4 (Winter 1990): 217.

Harding, Vincent. *Hope and History: Why We Must Share the Story of the Movement*. Maryknoll, NY: Orbis, 1990.

Harris, Fred R., and Roger W. Wilkins, eds. *Quiet Riots: Race and Poverty in the United States*. New York: Pantheon, 1988.

Innis, Leslie, and Joe R. Feagin. "The Black 'Underclass' in Race Relations Analysis." *Social Justice* 16, no. 4 (Winter 1989): 13–34.

Katz, Michael B. *The Undeserving Poor: From the War on Poverty to the War on Welfare*. New York: Pantheon, 1989.

Massey, Douglas S. "American Apartheid: Segregation and the Making of the Underclass." *American Journal of Sociology* 96, no. 2 (September 1990): 329.

Mincy, R. B., I. V. Sawhill, and D. A. Wolf. "The Underclass: Definition and Measurement." *Science* 248, no. 4954 (April 27, 1990): 450–453.

Moore, Joan. "Is There a Hispanic Underclass?" *Social Science Quarterly* 70, no. 2 (June 1989): 265.

Morris, Michael. "From the Culture of Poverty to the Underclass: An Analysis of a Shift in Public Language." *American Sociologist* 20, no. 2 (Summer 1989): 123.

Morris, Michael, and John B. Williamson. *Poverty and Public Policy: An Analysis of Federal Intervention Efforts*. Westport, CT: Greenwood Press, 1986.

Nathan, Richard P. "Institutional Change and the Challenge of the Underclass." *Annals of the American Academy of Political and Social Sciences* 501 (January 1989): 170.

Palley, Howard A., and Dana A. Robinson. "Black-on-Black Crime: Poverty, Marginality and the Underclass Debate from a Global Perspective." *Social Development Issues* 12, no. 3 (Spring 1990): 52.

Rex, John. *The Ghetto and the Underclass: Essays on Race and Social Policy*. Brookfield, VT: Aveburg, 1988.

Symposium. "What's Wrong with Integration?" *Sojourners* (August/September 1990): 4–30.

Tienda, Marta. "Puerto Ricans and the Underclass Debate." *Annals of the American Academy of Political and Social Sciences* 501 (January 1989): 105.

Walters, Ronald. "White Racial Nationalism in the United States." *Without Prejudice* 1, no. 1 (Fall 1987): 7–29.

Wilson, William J. "The Underclass: Issues, Perspectives, and Public Policy." *Annals of the American Academy of Political and Social Sciences* 501 (January 1989): 182.

———. *The Truly Disadvantaged: The Inner City, the Underclass and Public Policy*. Chicago: University of Chicago Press, 1987.

———. *The Declining Significance of Race: Blacks and Changing American Institutions*, 2d ed. Chicago: University of Chicago Press, 1980.

———. *Power, Racism and Privilege: Race Relations in Theoretical and Sociohistorical Perspective*. New York: Macmillan, 1973.

THE LAW AND THE UNDERCLASS

Bell, Derrick. "Xerces and the Affirmative Action Mystique." *George Washington Law Review* 57, no. 6 (August 1989): 1595.

———. *And We Are Not Saved: The Elusive Quest for Racial Justice*. New York: Basic Books, 1987.

Cruse, Harold. *Plural but Equal*. New York: William Morrow, 1987.

Delgado, Richard. "Words that Wound: A Tort Action for Racial Insults, Epithets and Name-Calling." *Harvard Civil Rights and Civil Liberties Review* 17 (1982): 133.

France, Steve. "Hate Goes to College." *ABA Journal* 76 (July 1990): 44.

Hodulik, Patricia B. "Prohibiting Discriminatory Harassment by Regulating Student Speech: A Balancing of First Amendment and University Interests." *Journal of College and University Law* 16, no. 4 (1990): 573.

Kalven, Harry. *A Worthy Tradition: Freedom of Speech in America*. New York: Harper and Row, 1988.

Lively, Donald E. "The Supreme Court and Affirmative Action: Whose Classification Is Suspect?" *Hastings Constitutional Law Quarterly* 17, no. 3 (Spring 1990): 483.

Matsuda, M. "Public Response to Racist Speech: Considering the Victim's Story." *Michigan Law Review* 87, no. 8 (1989): 2320.

Richardson, Dean M. "Racism: A Tort of Outrage." *Oregon Law Review* 61 (1982): 267–83.

Rosenfeld, Michael. "Decoding *Richmond*: Affirmative Action and the Elusive Meaning of Constitutional Equality." *Michigan Law Review* 87, no. 7 (June 1989): 1729.

Selig, Joel L. "Affirmative Action in Employment after *Croson* and *Martin*: The Legacy Remains Intact." *Temple Law Review* 63, no. 1 (Spring 1990): 1.

Sher, George. "Ancient Wrongs and Modern Rights." *Philosophy and Public Affairs* 10, no. 1 (Winter 1981): 3.

Smolla, Rodney A. "Rethinking First Amendment Assumptions About Racist and Sexist Speech." *Washington and Lee Law Review* 47 (1990): 171.

Sullivan, Kathleen M. "*City of Richmond v. J. A. Croson Co.*: The Backlash Against Affirmative Action." *Tulane Law Review* 64, no. 4 (June 1990): 1609.

IMMIGRATION AND THE UNDERCLASS

Bach, Robert L. "Immigration: Issues of Ethnicity, Class and Public Policy in the United States." *Annals of the American Academy of Political and Social Sciences* 485 (May 1986): 139–52.

Bessette, Diane M. "Getting Left Behind: The Impact of the 1986 Immigration Reform and Control Act Amnesty Program on Single Women with Children." *Hastings International and Comparative Law Review* 13 (Winter 1990): 287–304.

Borjas, George J. *Friends or Strangers: The Impact of Immigrants on the U.S. Economy*. New York: Basic Books, 1990.

Chiswick, Barry R. *Illegal Aliens: Their Employment and Employers*. Kalamazoo, MI: W. E. Upjohn Institute, 1988.

Harwood, Edwin. *In Liberty's Shadow: Illegal Aliens and Immigration Law Enforcement*. Stanford, CA: Hoover Institute, 1986.

Hong, Nathaniel. "The Origin of American Legislation to Exclude and Deport Aliens for Their Political Beliefs, and Its Initial Review by Courts." *Journal of Ethnic Studies* 18, no. 2 (Summer 1990): 1–36.

Jensen, Leif. *The New Immigration: Implications for Poverty and Public Assistance Utilization*. Westport, CT: Greenwood Press, 1989.

Merino, Catherine L. "Compromising Immigration Reform: The Creation of a Vulnerable Subclass." *Yale Law Journal* 98 (1988): 409–26.

Morales, Julio. *Puerto Rican Poverty and Migration: We Just Had to Try Elsewhere*. New York: Praeger, 1986.

Nanda, Ved P., ed. *Refugee Law and Policy: International and U.S. Responses*. Westport, CT: Greenwood Press, 1989.

Porebin, Mark P., and Eric D. Poole. "South Korean Immigrants and Crime: A Case Study." *Journal of Ethnic Studies* 17, no. 3 (Fall 1989): 47–80.

Reischaur, Robert D. "Immigration and the Underclass." *Annals of the Academy of Political and Social Sciences* 501 (January 1989): 120.

Sassen, Saskia. "America's Immigration 'Problem.' " *World Policy Journal* 6, no. 4 (1990): 811–32.

Select Commission on Immigration and Refugee Policy. *U.S. Immigration Policy and the National Interest.* Final Report and Recommendations of the Select Commission on Immigration and Refugee Policy to the Congress and the President of the United States, March 1, 1981.

Stojny, Andrew M., and Lisa K. Channoff. "IRCA's Antidiscrimination Provision: A Three Year Perspective." *Immigration Journal* 13, no. 1 (January 1, 1990): 5–8.

Wattenberg, Ben J., and Karl Zinmeister. "The Case for More Immigration." *Commentary* (April 1990): 19–25.

LANGUAGE, EDUCATION, AND THE UNDERCLASS

Adler, Sol. *Poverty Children and Their Language: Implications for Teaching and Treating.* New York: Grune and Stratton, 1979.

Cavazos, Lauro F. "Reflections on the Politics of Bilingual Education." *Journal of Law and Politics* 6, no. 3 (Spring 1990): 573.

Cox, Gail Diane. "English Only: A Legal Polyglot." *National Law Journal*, October 26, 1987, p. 1.

Crawford, James. *Bilingual Education: History, Politics, Theory and Practice.* Trenton, NJ: Crane Publishing, 1989.

Imhoff, Gary. "The Position of U.S. English on Bilingual Education." *Annals of the American Academy of Political and Social Sciences* 508 (March 1990): 48–61.

Kirschten, Dick. "Speaking English." *National Journal* 21, no. 24 (June 17, 1989): 1556–61.

Kleven, Thomas. "Cultural Bias and the Issue of Bilingual Education." *Social Policy* 19, no. 1 (Summer 1988): 9.

Lankshear, Colin. "Reading and Righting Wrongs: Literacy and the Underclass." *Language and Education* 3, no. 3 (1989): 167.

Madrid, Arturo. "Official English: A False Policy Issue." *Annals of the American Academy of Political and Social Sciences* 508 (March 1990): 62–65.

Ruiz, Richard. "Bilingualism and Bilingual Education in the United States. In "International Handbook of Bilingualism and Bilingual Education, edited by Christina Bratt Paulston, 539–58. Westport, CT: Greenwood Press, 1988.

Stein, Colmon Brez, Jr. *Sink or Swim: The Politics of Bilingual Education.* New York: Praeger, 1986.

NATIVE AMERICANS

Anders, Gary C. "Theories of Underdevelopment and the American Indian." *Journal of Economic Issues* 14, no. 3 (September 1980): 693.

Churchill, Ward, ed. *The State of Indigenous America.* Boston: South End Press, 1990.

Churchill, Ward, and Jim Vander Wall. *Agents of Repression: The FBI's Secret Wars Against the Black Panther Party and the American Indian Movement.* Boston: South End Press, 1988.

Forbes, Jack D. "Undercounting Native Americans: The 1980 Census and the Manipulation of Racial Identity in the United States." *Wicazo sa Review* 6, no. 1 (Spring 1990): 2.

Makofsky, Abraham. "The Experience of Native Americans at a Black College: Indian Students at Hampton Institute, 1878–1923." *Journal of Ethnic Studies* 17, no. 3 (Fall 1989): 31–46.

Pottinger, Richard. "Indian Reservation Labor Markets: A Navajo Assessment and Challenge." *American Indian Culture and Research Journal* 9, no. 3 (1989): 11.

Symposium. "Indigenous Peoples." *Global Justice* 1, no. 3 (October/November 1990): 3.

Index

About the Editors and Contributors _____

GEORGE W. SHEPHERD, JR. is professor of International and African Studies at the University of Denver Graduate School of International Studies and director of the Center on Rights Development. Formerly, Shepherd was the director of the Center on International Race Relations and has authored and edited books and articles on human rights and African politics, including *Emerging Human Rights* (with Mark Anikpo) (1990), *The Trampled Grass* (1987), *Human Rights and Third World Development* (with Ved P. Nanda) (1985), and *Anti-Apartheid* (1978).

DAVID PENNA is adjunct professor of Political Science and director of publications at the Center on Rights Development at the University of Denver Graduate School of International Studies. He received his J.D. from the University of Denver College of Law. He has contributed articles to *Global Justice*, *African Rights Monitor*, and *Africa Today*.

LORING BUSH is a graduate student at the University of Denver Graduate School of International Studies, specializing in human rights.

PATRICIA J. CAMPBELL is a Ph.D. candidate at the University of Denver Graduate School of International Studies, specializing in refugee and migrant issues.

PRISCILLA FALCON is assistant professor of Political Science at Adams State College in Alamosa, Colorado.

JOHN GROVE is associate professor of International Relations at the University of Denver and the director of the Undergraduate Program in International Studies. He specializes in comparative politics and race and ethnic relations. Grove was the editor of *Global Inequality: Political and Socio-Economic Perspectives* (1978).

JOSE BLAS LORENZO is a candidate for Ph.D. and J.D. at the University of Denver Graduate School of International Studies and the College of Law, specializing in human rights and international law.

GREGORY KELLAM SCOTT is an associate professor of Law at the University of Denver and director of the Stuart-James Research Center. He received a B.S. and Ed.M. from Rutgers University and a J.D. from Indiana University.

JOY SOBREPEÑA is a Ph.D. candidate at the University of Denver Graduate School of International Studies, specializing in human rights. She is the editor of the periodical *Global Justice*.

GEORGE E. TINKER is professor of Theology at the Iliff School of Theology and associate pastor of the Living Waters Native American Lutheran Episcopal Church in Denver, Colorado. Tinker specializes in crosscultural issues in theology. He has served as president of the Native American Theological Association.

PETER W. VAN ARSDALE is a refugee and immigrant specialist for the Colorado Division of Mental Health and is adjunct assistant professor at the University of Denver Graduate School of International Studies. He specializes in applied crosscultural research and immigrant and refugee issues.

DEBRA KREISBERG VOSS is a Ph.D. candidate at the University of Denver Graduate School of International Studies. She has published chapters and articles on refugee issues and was formerly a program associate with the Colorado Mental Health Refugee Assistance Program.

PETER WEISS is a partner in the law firm Weiss, Dawis, Fross, Zelnick and Lehrman and the vice president of the Center for Constitutional Rights. He was one of the founders of the American Committee on Africa.

JIPING WU is from the People's Republic of China and is a graduate student at the School of Advanced International Studies at Johns Hopkins University.